CHELSEA HOUSE PUBLISHERS
Modern Critical Views

Further titles in preparation.

Modern Critical Views

WILLA CATHER

Modern Critical Views

WILLA CATHER

Edited with an introduction by

Harold Bloom

Sterling Professor of the Humanities
Yale University

1985
CHELSEA HOUSE PUBLISHERS
New York

PROJECT EDITORS: Emily Bestler, James Uebbing
ASSOCIATE EDITOR: Julia Myer
EDITORIAL COORDINATOR: Karyn Gullen Browne
EDITORIAL STAFF: Laura Ludwig, Linda Grossman, Peter Childers
DESIGN: Susan Lusk

Cover illustration by Ken Mitchell

Printed and bound in the United States of America

10 9 8 7 6 5 4 3 2

Library of Congress Cataloging in Publication Data

Willa Cather.
    (Modern critical views)
    Bibliography: p.
    Includes index.
    1. Cather, Willa, 1873–1947—Criticism and interpreta-
tion—Addresses, essays, lectures.   I. Bloom, Harold.
II. Series.
PS3505.A87Z938   1985   813'.52   85–6669
ISBN 0-87754-623-1

Chelsea House Publishers
95 Madison Avenue, New York, NY 10016
345 Whitney Avenue, New Haven, CT 06511
5068B West Chester Pike, Edgemont, PA 19028

Contents

Editor's Note

This volume gathers together a representation of the best literary criticism that has been devoted to Willa Cather over the last half-century. The essays included are presented here in the order of their publication, beginning with Lionel Trilling's judicial analysis of her limitations, in the perspective of the year 1937. Alfred Kazin's account of Cather's achievement as elegist is followed by two very different interpretations of *The Professor's House* by E. K. Brown and by David Daiches. Morton Zabel keenly sets forth the temporal stance of Cather's best work, an emphasis developed further in the reading of *My Ántonia* by James E. Miller, Jr.

Something of the same sense of the past is explored in John H. Randall III's interpretation of *Sapphira and the Slave Girl*. A full conspectus of Cather by the distinguished general critic of fiction Dorothy Van Ghent prepares for two further readings of *My Ántonia* by Terence Martin and by Blanche H. Gelfant. Donald Sutherland's critical appreciation of Cather's achievement is matched by Eudora Welty's tribute to her fellow novelist. The focus shifts to Cather's two other largest achievements, with John Murphy's perspectivizing of *Death Comes For the Archbishop* and John Hollander's subtle introduction to her truest masterpiece, *A Lost Lady*. The volume concludes with Marilyn Arnold's recent study of what may be Cather's two finest short stories.

Introduction

I

Willa Cather, though now somewhat neglected, has few rivals among the American novelists of this century. Critics and readers frequently regard her as belonging to an earlier time, though she died in 1947. Her best novels were published in the years 1918–31, so that truly she was a novelist of the 1920's, an older contemporary and peer of Hemingway and of Scott Fitzgerald. Unlike them, she did not excel at the short story, though there are some memorable exceptions scattered through her four volumes of tales. Her strength is her novels and particularly, in my judgment, *My Ántonia* (1918), *A Lost Lady* (1923) and *The Professor's House* (1925); fictions worthy of a disciple of Flaubert and Henry James. Equally beautiful and achieved, but rather less central, are the subsequent historical novels, the very popular *Death Comes for the Archbishop* (1927) and *Shadows on the Rock* (1931). Her second novel, *O Pioneers!* (1913), is only just short of the eminence of this grand sequence. Six permanent novels is a remarkable number for a modern American writer; I can think only of Faulkner as Cather's match in this respect, since he wrote six truly enduring novels, all published during his great decade, 1929–39.

Cather's remoteness from the fictive universe of Fitzgerald, Hemingway and Faulkner is palpable, though all of them shared her nostalgia for an older America. She appears, at first, to have no aesthetic affinities with her younger contemporaries. We associate her instead with Sarah Orne Jewett, about whom she wrote a loving essay, or even with Edith Wharton, whom she scarcely resembles. Cather's mode of engaging with the psychic realities of post-World War I America is more oblique than Fitzgerald's or Hemingway's, but it is just as apposite a representation of the era's malaise. The short novel *A Lost Lady* (1923) is not out of its aesthetic context when we read it in the company of *The Waste Land, The Comedian as the Letter C, The Sun Also Rises, The Great Gatsby* and *An American Tragedy*. Subtler and gentler than any of these, *A Lost Lady* elegizes just as profoundly a lost radiance or harmony, a defeat of a peculiarly American dream of innocence, grace, hope.

II

Henry James, Cather's guide both as critic and novelist, died in England early in 1916. The year before, replying to H. G. Wells after being satirized by him, James wrote a famous credo: "Art *makes* life, makes interest, makes importance." This is Cather's faith also. One hears the voice of James when, in her essay "On the Art of Fiction," she writes: "Any first-rate novel or story must have in it the strength of a dozen fairly good stories that have been sacrificed to it." Those sacrifices of possibility upon the altar of form were the ritual acts of Cather's quite Paterian religion of art, too easily misread as a growing religiosity by many critics commenting upon *Death Comes for the Archbishop.* Herself a belated Aesthete, Cather emulated a familiar pattern of being attracted by the aura and not the substance of Roman Catholicism. New Mexico, and not Rome, is her place of the spirit, a spirit of the archaic and not of the supernatural.

Cather's social attitudes were altogether archaic. She shared a kind of Populist anti-Semitism with many American writers of her own generation and the next: Sherwood Anderson, Theodore Dreiser, Ezra Pound, Thomas Wolfe, even Hemingway and Fitzgerald. Her own version of anti-Semitism is curiously marked by her related aversion to heterosexuality. She had lost her first companion, Isabelle McClung, to a Jewish violinist, Jan Hambourg, and the Jewish figures in her fiction clearly represent the aggressivity of male sexuality. *The Professor's House* is marred by the gratuitous identification of the commercial exploitation of Cather's beloved West with Marcellus, the Professor's Jewish son-in-law. Doubtless, Cather's most unfortunate piece of writing was her notorious essay in 1914, "Potash and Perlmutter," in which she lamented, mock-heroically, that New York City was becoming too Jewish. Perhaps she was learning the lesson of the master again, since she is repeating, in a lighter tone, the complaint of Henry James in *The American Scene* (1907). She repeated her own distaste for "Jewish critics," tainted as they were by Freud, in the essay on Sarah Orne Jewett written quite late in her career, provoking Lionel Trilling to the just accusation that she had become a mere defender of gentility, mystically concerned with pots and pans.

This dark side of Cather, though hardly a value in itself, would not much matter except that it seeped into her fiction as a systemic resentment of her own era. Nietzsche, analyzing resentment, might be writing of Cather. Freud, analyzing the relation between paranoia and homosexuality, might be writing of her also. I am wary of being reductive in such observations, and someone perpetually mugged by Feminist critics as "the Patriarchal critic" is too battered to desire any further polemic. Cather, in my judgment, is aesthetically strongest and most persuasive in her loving depiction of her heroines and of Ántonia and the lost lady Mrs. Forrester in particular. She resembles Thomas Hardy in absolutely nothing, except in the remarkable ability to seduce the reader into joining the novelist at falling in love with the heroine. I am haunted by memories of having fallen in love with Marty South in *The Woodlanders*, and with Ántonia and Mrs. Forrester when I was a boy of fifteen. Rereading *My Ántonia* and *A Lost Lady* now at fifty-four, I find that the love renews itself. I doubt that I am falling again into what my late and honored teacher William K. Wimsatt named as the Affective Fallacy, since love for a woman made up out of words is necessarily a cognitive affair.

 Cather's strength at representation gives us Jim Burden and Niel Herbert as her clear surrogates, unrealized perhaps as figures of sexual life, but forcefully conveyed as figures of capable imagination, capable above all of apprehending and transmitting the extraordinary actuality and visionary intensity of Ántonia and Mrs. Forrester. Like her masters, James and Pater, Cather had made her supposed deficiency into her strength, fulfilling the overt program of Emersonian self-reliance. But nothing is got for nothing, Emerson also indicated, and Cather, again like James and Pater, suffered the reverse side of the law of Compensation. The flaws, aesthetic and human, are there, even in *My Ántonia*, *A Lost Lady* and *The Professor's House*, but they scarcely diminish the beauty and dignity of three profound studies of American nostalgias.

III

Cather is hardly the only vital American novelist to have misread creatively the spirit of his or her own work. Her essential imaginative knowledge was of loss, which she interpreted temporally, though her loss was aboriginal, in the Romantic mode of Wordsworth, Emerson and all their varied descendants. The glory that had passed away belonged not to the pioneers but to her own transparent eyeball, her own original relation to the universe. Rhetorically, she manifests this knowledge, which frequently is at odds with her overt thematicism. Here is Jim Burden's first shared moment with Ántonia, when they both were little children:

> We sat down and made a nest in the long red grass. Yulka curled up like a baby rabbit and played with a grasshopper. Ántonia pointed up to the sky and questioned me with her glance. I gave her the word, but she was not satisfied and pointed to my eyes. I told her, and she repeated the

word, making it sound like "ice." She pointed up to the sky, then to my eyes, then back to the sky, with movements so quick and impulsive that she distracted me, and I had no idea what she wanted. She got up on her knees and wrung her hands. She pointed to her own eyes and shook her head, then to mine and to the sky, nodding violently.

"Oh," I exclaimed, "blue; blue sky."

She clapped her hands and murmured, "Blue sky, blue eyes," as if it amused her. While we snuggled down there out of the wind, she learned a score of words. She was quick, and very eager. We were so deep in the grass that we could see nothing but the blue sky over us and the gold tree in front of us. It was wonderfully pleasant. After Ántonia had said the new words over and over, she wanted to give me a little chased silver ring she wore on her middle finger. When she coaxed and insisted, I repulsed her quite sternly. I didn't want her ring, and I felt there was something reckless and extravagant about her wishing to give it away to a boy she had never seen before. No wonder Krajiek got the better of these people, if this was how they behaved.

One imagines that Turgenev would have admired this, and it would not be out of place inserted in his *A Sportman's Sketchbook*. Its naturalistic simplicity is deceptive. Wallace Stevens, in a letter of 1940, observed of Cather: "you may think she is more or less formless. Nevertheless, we have nothing better than she is. She takes so much pains to conceal her sophistication that it is easy to miss her quality." The quality here is partly manifested by an exuberance of trope and a precision of diction, both in the service of a fresh American myth of origin. Nesting and curling up in an embowered world of baby rabbits and grasshoppers, the children are at home in a universe of "blue sky, blue eyes." Heaven and earth come together, where vision confronts only the gold of trees. Ántonia, offering the fullness of a symbolic union to him, is rebuffed partly by the boy's shyness, and partly by Cather's own proleptic fear that the reckless generosity of the pioneer is doomed to exploitation. Yet the passage's deepest intimation is that Jim, though falling in love with Ántonia, is constrained by an inner recalcitrance, which the reader is free to interpret in several ways, none of which need exclude the others.

This is Cather in the springtide of her imagination. In her vision's early fall, we find ourselves regarding her lost lady Mrs. Forrester and we are comforted, as the boy Niel Herbert is, "in the quick recognition of her eyes, in the living quality of her voice itself." The book's splendor is that, like Mrs. Forrester's laughter, "it often told you a great deal that was both too direct and too elusive for words." As John Hollander shrewdly notes, Mrs. Forrester does not become a lost lady in any social or moral sense, but imaginatively she is transformed into Niel's "long-lost lady." Lost or refound, she is "his" always, even as Ántonia always remains Jim Burden's "my Ántonia." In her ability to suggest a love that is permanent, life-enhancing, and in no way possessive, Cather touches the farthest limit of her own strength as a novelist. If one could choose a single passage from all her work, it would be the Paterian epiphany or privileged moment in which Mrs. Forrester's image returned to Niel as "a bright, impersonal memory." Pater ought to have lived to have read this marvelous instance of the art he had celebrated and helped to stimulate in Cather:

> Her eyes, when they laughed for a moment into one's own, seemed to provide a wild delight that he had not found in life. "I know where it is," they seemed to say, "I could show you!" He would like to call up the shade of the young Mrs. Forrester, as the witch of Endor called up Samuel's, and challenge it, demand the secret of that ardour; ask her whether she had really found some ever-blooming, ever-burning, ever-piercing joy, or whether it was all fine play-acting. Probably she had found no more than another; but she had always the power of suggesting things much lovelier than herself, as the perfume of a single flower may call up the whole sweetness of spring.

It is the perfection of Cather's difficult art, when that art was most balanced and paced, and Mrs. Forrester here is the emblem of that perfection. Cather's fiction, at its frequent best, also suggests things much lovelier than itself. The reader, demanding the secret of Cather's ardour, learns not to challenge what may be remarkably fine play-acting, since Cather's feigning sometimes does persuade him that really she had found some perpetual joy.

LIONEL TRILLING

Willa Cather

In 1922 Willa Cather wrote an essay called "The Novel Démeublé" in which she pleaded for a movement to throw the "furniture" out of the novel—to get rid, that is, of all the social fact that Balzac and other realists had felt to be so necessary for the understanding of modern character. "Are the banking system and the Stock Exchange worth being written about at all?" Miss Cather asked, and she replied that they were not. Among the things which had no "proper place in imaginative art"—because they cluttered the scene and prevented the free play of the emotions—Miss Cather spoke of the factory and the whole realm of "physical sensation." Obviously, this essay was the rationale of a method which Miss Cather had partly anticipated in her early novels and which she fully developed a decade later in *Shadows on the Rock*. And it is no less obvious that this technical method is not merely a literary manner but the expression of a point of view toward which Miss Cather had always been moving—with results that, to many of her readers, can only indicate the subtle failure of her admirable talent.

If we say that Miss Cather has gone down to defeat before the actualities of American life, we put her in such interesting company that the indictment is no very terrible one. For a history of American literature must be, in Whitman's phrase, a series of "vivas for those who have failed." In our literature there are perhaps fewer completely satisfying books and certainly fewer integrated careers than there are interesting canons of work and significant life stories. Something in American life seems to prevent the perfection of success while it produces a fascinating

From *Speaking of Literature and Society.* Copyright © 1980 by Diana Trilling and James Trilling. Harcourt Brace Jovanovich, 1980.

kind of search or struggle, usually unavailing, which we may observe again and again in the collected works and in the biographies of our writers.

In this recurrent but heroic defeat, the life of the American writer parallels the life of the American pioneer. The historian of frontier literature, Professor Hazard, has pointed out that Cooper's very first presentation of Deerslayer, the type of all pioneers, shows him a nearly broken old man threatened with jail for shooting a deer, a pitiful figure overwhelmed by the tides of commerce and speculation. In short, to a keen observer, the pioneer's defeat was apparent even in 1823. The subsequent decades that opened fresh frontiers did not change the out-come of the struggle. Ahead of the pioneer there are always the fields of new promise, with him are the years of heartbreaking effort, behind him are the men who profit by his toil and his hope. Miss Cather's whole body of work is the attempt to accommodate and assimilate her perception of the pioneer's failure. Reared on a Nebraska farm, she saw the personal and cultural defeat at first hand. Her forebears had marched westward to the new horizons; her own work is a march back toward the spiritual East—toward all that is the antithesis of the pioneer's individualism and innova-tion, toward authority and permanence, toward Rome itself.

II

The pioneer, as seen by a sophisticated intelligence like Miss Cather's, stands in double jeopardy: he faces both the danger of failure and the danger of success. "A pioneer . . . should be able to enjoy the idea of things more than the things themselves," Miss Cather says; disaster comes when an idea becomes an actuality. From O Pioneers! to The Professor's House, Miss Cather's novels portray the results of the pioneer's defeat, both in the thwarted pettiness to which he is condemned by his material failures and in the callous insensitivity produced by his material success. "The world is little, people are little, human life is little," says Thea Kronborg's derelict music teacher in The Song of the Lark. "There is only one big thing—desire." When there is no longer the opportunity for effective desire, the pioneer is doomed. But already in Miss Cather's Nebraska youth the opportunities for effective desire had largely been removed: the frontier had been closed.

A Lost Lady, Miss Cather's most explicit treatment of the passing of the old order, is the central work of her career. Far from being the delicate minor book it is often called, it is probably her most muscular story, for it derives power from the grandeur of its theme. Miss Cather shares the American belief in the tonic moral quality of the pioneer's life; with the passing of the frontier she conceives that a great source of fortitude has been lost. Depending on a very exact manipulation of symbols, the point of *A Lost Lady* (reminiscent of Henry James's *The Sacred Fount*) is that the delicacy and charm of Marian Forrester spring not from herself, but from the moral strength of her pioneer husband. Heavy, slow, not intelligent, Forrester is one of those men who, in his own words, "dreamed the railroads across the mountains." He shares the knightly virtues which Miss Cather unquestioningly ascribes to the early settlers; "impractical to the point of magnificence," he is one of those who could "conquer but not hold." He is defeated by the men of the new money interests who "never risked anything"—and the perdition of the lost lady proceeds in the degree that she withdraws from her husband in favor of one of the sordid new men, until she finds her final degradation in the arms of an upstart vulgarian.

But though the best of the pioneer ideal is defeated by alien forces, the ideal itself, Miss Cather sees, is really an insufficient one. In her first considerable novel, *O Pioneers!*, she already wrote in an elegiac mood and with the sense that the old ideal was not enough. Alexandra Bergson, with her warm simplicity, her resourcefulness and shrewd courage, is the essence of the pioneering virtues, but she is distinguished above her neighbors because she feels that, if she is to work at all, she must believe that the world is wider than her cornfields. Her pride is not that she has triumphed over the soil, but that she has made her youngest brother, "a personality apart from the soil." The pioneer, having reached his goal at the horizons of the earth, must look to the horizons of the spirit.

The disappearance of the old frontier left Miss Cather with a heritage of the virtues in which she had been bred, but with the necessity of finding a new object for them. Looking for the new frontier, she found it in the mind. From the world of failure which she portrayed so savagely in "A Wagner Matinée" and "The Sculptor's Funeral," and from the world of fat prosperity of *One of Ours*, she could flee to the world of art; for in art one may desire illimitably. And if, conceivably, one may fail—Miss Cather's artists never do—it is still only as an artist that one may be the eternal pioneer, concerned always with "the idea of things." Thea Kronborg, of the breed of Alexandra Bergson, turns all the old energy, bogged down in mediocrity, toward music. Miss Cather rhapsodizes for her: "O eagle of eagles! Endeavor, achievement, desire, glorious striving of human art."

But art is not the only, or a sufficient, salvation from the débâcle of pioneer culture. For some vestige of the old striving after new worlds which cannot be gratified seems to spread a poison through the American soul, making it thin and unsubstantial, unable to find peace and solidity. A foreigner says to Claude Wheeler of *One of Ours*, "You Americans are always looking for something outside yourselves to warm you up, and it is no way to do. In old countries, where not very much can happen to us, we know that, and we learn to make the most of things." And with the artists, Miss Cather puts those gentle spirits who have learned to make the most of things—Neighbor Rosicky, Augusta and, preëminently, My Ántonia. Momentarily betrayed by the later developments of the frontier, Ántonia at last fulfills herself in child-bearing and a busy household, expressing her "relish for life, not overdelicate but invigorating."

Indeed, "making the most of things" becomes even more important to Miss Cather than the eternal striving of art. For, she implies, in our civilization even the best ideals are bound to corruption. *The Professor's House* is the novel in which she brings the failure of the pioneer spirit into the wider field of American life. Lame as it is, it epitomizes as well as any novel of our time the disgust with life which so many sensitive Americans feel, which makes them dream of their preadolescent integration and innocent community with nature, speculate on the "release from effort" and the "eternal solitude" of death, and eventually reconcile themselves to a life "without delight." Three stories of betrayal are interwoven in this novel: the success of Professor St. Peter's history of the Spanish explorers, which tears him away from the frontier of his uncomfortable and ugly old study to set him up in an elegant but stifling new home; the sale to a foreign collector of the dead Tom Outland's Indian relics, which had made his spiritual heritage; and the commercialization of Outland's scientific discovery with its subsequent corruption of the Professor's charming family. With all of life contaminated by the rotting of admirable desires, only Augusta, the unquesting and unquestioning German Catholic seamstress, stands secure and sound.

Not the pioneering philosophy alone, but the whole poetic romanticism of the nineteenth century had been suffused with the belief that the struggle rather than the prize was admirable, that a man's reach should exceed his grasp, or what's a heaven for? Having seen the insufficiency of this philosophy Miss Cather must find another in which the goal shall be more than the search. She finds it, expectably enough, in religion. The Catholicism to which she turns is a Catholicism of culture, not of doctrine. The ideal of unremitting search, it may be said, is essentially a Protestant notion; Catholic thought tends to repudiate the ineffable and to seek the sharply defined. The quest for Moby Dick, that dangerous beast, is Protestant; the Catholic tradition selects what it can make immediate and tangible in symbol, and Miss Cather turns to the way of life that

WILLA CATHER • 11

"makes the most of things," to the old settled cultures. She attaches a mystical significance to the ritual of the ordered life, to the niceties of cookery, to the supernal virtues of *things* themselves—sherry, or lettuce, or "these coppers, big and little, these brooms and clouts and brushes," which are the tools for making life itself. And with a religious ideal one may safely be a pioneer. The two priests of *Death Comes for the Archbishop* are pioneers; they happen to be successful in their enterprise, but they could not have been frustrated, Miss Cather implies, because the worth of their goal is indisputable.

From the first of her novels the Church had occupied a special and gracious place in Willa Cather's mind. She now thinks with increasing eloquence of its permanence and certainty and of "the universal human yearning for something permanent, enduring, without shadow of change." The Rock becomes her often repeated symbol: "the rock, when one comes to think of it, was the utmost expression of human need." For the Church seems to offer the possibility of satisfying that appealing definition of human happiness which Miss Cather had made as far back as *My Ántonia*—"to be dissolved in something complete and great . . . to become a part of something entire, whether it is sun and air, goodness and knowledge."

It is toward that dissolvement that Miss Cather is always striving. She achieves it with the "sun and air"—and perhaps few modern writers have been so successful with landscape. She can find it in goodness and in society—but only if they have the feudal constriction of the old Quebec of *Shadows on the Rock*. Nothing in modern life, no possibility, no hope, offers it to her. She conceives, as she says in the prefatory note to her volume of essays, *Not Under Forty*, that the world "broke in two in 1922 or thereabouts," and she numbers herself among the "backward," unaware that even so self-conscious and defiant a rejection of her own time must make her talent increasingly irrelevant and tangential—for any time.

III

"The early pioneer was an individualist and a seeker after the undiscovered," says F. J. Turner, "but he did not understand the richness and complexity of life as a whole." Though Miss Cather in all her work has recognized this lack of understanding of complexity and wholeness, and has attempted to transcend it, she ends, ironically enough, in a fancier but no less restricted provincialism than the one she sought to escape. For the "spirituality" of Miss Cather's latest books consists chiefly of an irritated exclusion of those elements of modern life with which she will not cope. The particular affirmation of the verities which Miss Cather makes requires that the "furniture" be thrown out, that the social and political facts be disregarded; the spiritual life cannot support the intrusion of all the facts the mind can supply. The unspeakable Joseph Joubert, the extreme type of the academic verity-seeker, says in one of his *pensées:* " 'I'm hungry, I'm cold, help me!' Here is material for a good deed but not for a good work of art." Miss Cather, too, is irked by the intrusion of "physical sensations" in the novel. And one remembers Joubert's hatred of energy—he believed that it hindered the good life and scorned Balzac for his superabundant endowment of it—and one sees what is so irksome in Miss Cather's conception of ordered living: it is her implied praise of devitalization. She can recognize the energy of assiduous duty but not the energy of mind and emotion. Her order is not the channeling of insurgent human forces but their absence.

We use the word "escape" too lightly, no doubt; when we think how each generation must create its own past for the purposes of its own present, we must realize that the return to a past way of thought or of life may be the relevant criticism of the present. The only question, then, is the ends such criticism serves. Henry Adams's turn to the twelfth century was the attempt to answer the complex questions of the *Education* and to discover a better direction of energy; Eugene O'Neill's movement toward Catholic theology, crude as it may seem, has the profound interest of an energetic response to confusion. But Miss Cather's turn to the ideals of a vanished time is the weary response to weariness, to that devitalization of spirit which she so brilliantly describes in the story of Professor St. Peter. It is a weariness which comes not merely from defeat but from an exacerbated sense of personal isolation and from the narrowing of all life to the individual's sensitivities, with the resulting loss of the objectivity that can draw strength from seeking the causes of things. But it is exactly Miss Cather's point that the Lucretian *rerum natura* means little; an admirer of Virgil, she is content with the *lacrimae rerum,* the tears for things.

Miss Cather's later books are pervaded by the air of a brooding ancient wisdom, but if we examine her mystical concern with pots and pans, it does not seem much more than an oblique defense of gentility or very far from the gaudy domesticity of bourgeois accumulation glorified in the *Woman's Home Companion.* And with it goes a culture-snobbery and even a caste-snobbery. The Willa Cather of the older days shared the old racial democracy of the West. It is strange to find the Willa Cather of the present talking about "the adopted American," the young man of German, Jewish or Scandinavian descent who can never appreciate Sarah Orne Jewett and for whom American English can never be more than a means of communicating ideas: "It is surface speech: he clicks the words out as a bank clerk clicks out silver when you ask for change. For him the language has no emotional roots." This is indeed the gentility of Katherine Fullerton Gerould, and in large part the result, one suspects, of what Parrington calls "the inferiority complex of the frontier mind before the old and established."

Yet the place to look for the whole implications of a writer's philosophy is in the esthetic of his work. *Lucy Gayheart* shows to the full effect of Miss Cather's point of view. It has always been a personal failure of her talent that prevented her from involving her people in truly dramatic relations with each other. (Her women, for example, always stand in the mother or daughter relation to men; they are never truly lovers.) But at least once upon a time her people were involved in a dramatic relation with themselves or with their environments, whereas now *Lucy Gayheart* has not even this involvement. Environment does not exist, fate springs from nothing save chance; the characters are unattached to anything save their dreams. The novel has been *démeublé* indeed; but life without its furniture is strangely bare.

ALFRED KAZIN

Elegy: Willa Cather

"It's memory: the memory that goes with the vocation."
— WILLA CATHER on Sarah Orne Jewett

The "new freedom" after the war was not a movement; it was a succession of opportunities for writers who were themselves often in open conflict. To the "middle generation" of writers like Mencken, Anderson, Lewis, Cabell, and Hergesheimer, Willa Cather and Ellen Glasgow, it meant long-delayed triumphs after years of preparation or neglect. To the younger writers who began to come up immediately after the war, like Fitzgerald, Cummings, Hemingway, and Dos Passos, men who felt themselves part of a tougher and disillusioned generation, writing was to seem as much a rejection of what the "middle generation" already represented as it was a testament to their experiences in the war. Layer on layer, emancipation by emanicipation, the pattern of a modern American literature took shape out of that simultaneous emergence of so many different educations, talents, and aspirations; and nothing so illuminated the richness and variety of that literature as the fact that everything suddenly seemed to come together in the post-war scene. At the very moment that Fitzgerald was writing his tales of "the flapper age," and Cummings, Hemingway, and Dos Passos were writing their bitterly scornful antiwar novels, Anderson and Lewis were leading " the revolt from the village." At the very moment that the younger writers were going to school to Gertrude Stein in Paris and working away at a new American style, two richly gifted women of an older generation,

Willa Cather and Ellen Glasgow, had finally achieved recognition, and were just beginning to publish their best works. Ellen Glasgow had published her first novel in 1897, when most of the lost-generation novelists were one year old; and there were whole worlds, as it seemed, between *The Sun Also Rises* and *A Lost Lady,* or between *The Great Gatsby* and *The Romantic Comedians.* Yet it was the famous liberation of the twenties that brought them together, and at the time they even seemed to express a common postwar spirit of revolt and—especially with Ellen Glasgow—of satire.

Like the younger writers, both Willa Cather and Ellen Glasgow had a brilliant sense of style and an instinct for craftsmanship. But their feeling for style demanded none of the formal declarations and laborious experiments that Hemingway and Dos Passos brought to theirs. Like so many women in modern American writing from Emily Dickinson to Katherine Anne Porter, they had a certain dignity of craft from the first, a felicity all their own. In a period so marked by devotional estheticism in writing, and one when it was easy to slip into the ornamental fancywork of men like Cabell and Hergesheimer, Willa Cather and Ellen Glasgow stood out as examples of serious craftsmanship; and it is strange how easy it has always been to forget how much more brilliant a stylist Ellen Glasgow is than most of the younger writers, and how much more deeply imaginative an artist Willa Cather proved than Hemingway.

Yet their craftsmanship had no gestures, no tricks, and—this is less true of Ellen Glasgow—no glitter. They were good, almost too serenely good; it was always so easy to put them into their placid niches. Yet if they seemed to be off on their own, it was largely because the experience that became the substance of their books now seemed distant and the hold of the past on them so magnetic. Willa Cather soon became a conscious traditionalist, as Ellen Glasgow satirized traditionalism; but what isolated them both was the fact that they brought the resources of the modern novel in America—and frequently not a little of the bitterness of the postwar spirit—to the persistent exploration and evocation of the past. Unlike so many of their postwar contemporaries, they used modernism as a tool; they did not make it their substance. Sharing in the self-consciousness and freedom of the new literature, their minds persistently ranged below and beyond it. Yet unlike writers like Irving Babbitt and Paul Elmer More, who went directly against the current of the new literature, they were wholly a part of it. Indeed, they testified by their very presence, as writers so diverse as F. Scott Fitzgerald and Anderson, Mencken and Van Wyck Brooks, Hemingway and Cabell, had already testified, to the variety and freedom of the new American literature.

II

Willa Cather and Nebraska grew up together. Born in Virginia, she was taken at eight to a country moving in the first great floodtide of Western migration in the eighties. Within a single decade half a million people— Yankee settlers, sod-house pioneers out of the Lincoln country, Danes, Norwegians, Germans, Bohemians, Poles—pulled up stakes or emigrated from the farms of northern and eastern Europe to settle on the plains of a region that had been "a state before there were people in it." Nebraska was the first of the great settlements beyond the Mississippi after the Civil War, and the pace of its settlement and the polyglot character of its people were such that they seemed to mark a whole new society in flower. The successive stages of economic and social development were leaped quickly, but not too quickly; as late as 1885 the state was mostly raw prairie, and for the children of the first pioneers history began with the railroad age roaring in from the East. Nebraska was a society in itself, a bristling new society, proud of its progress and of values and a morality consciously its own. The prairie aristocracy that was to play as triumphant and even didactic a role in Willa Cather's novels as the colonial aristocracy had played in Edith Wharton's may have been composed out of the welter of emigration; but it was a founding class, and Willa Cather never forgot it.

Her enduring values were the values of this society, but they were not merely pioneer and agrarian values. There was a touch of Europe in Nebraska everywhere during her girlhood, and much of her distinctive literary culture was to be drawn from it. The early population numbered so many Europeans among it that as a young girl she would spend Sundays listening to sermons in French, Norwegian, and Danish. There was a Prague in Nebraska as well as in Bohemia. Europe had given many brilliant and restless young men to the West. Amiel wrote letters to a nephew who died among the Nebraska farmers; Knut Hamsun worked on a farm just across the state line in South Dakota; a cousin of Camille Saint-Saëns lived near by in Kansas. One could walk along the streets of a county seat like Wilber and not hear a word of English all day long. It was in this world, with its accumulation of many cultures, a world full of memories of Grieg and Liszt, of neighbors who taught her Latin and two grandmothers at home with whom she read the English classics, that Willa Cather learned to appreciate Henry James and at the same time to see in the pioneer society of the West a culture and distinction of its own. Her first two years there, she wrote later, were the most important to her as a writer.

All through her youth the West was moving perpetually onward, but it seemed anything but rootless to her; it suggested a distinctive sense of permanence in the midst of change, a prairie culture that imparted to her education a tender vividness. Unconsciously, perhaps, the immigrants came to symbolize a tradition, and that tradition anchored her and gave her an almost religious belief in its sanctity. Growing up in a period of violent disruption and social change, she was thus brought up at the same time to a native and homely traditionalism. Later she was to elegize it, as all contemporary America was to elegize the tradition of pioneer energy and virtue and hardihood; but only because it gave her mind an abiding image of order and—what so few have associated with the pioneer tradition—of humanism. Her love for the West grew from a simple affection for her own kind into a reverence for the qualities they represented; from a patriotism of things and place-names into a patriotism of ideas. What she loved in the pioneer tradition was human qualities rather than institutions—the qualities of Antonia Shimerda and Thea Kronberg, Alexandra Bergson and Godfrey St. Peter—but as those qualities seemed to disappear from the national life she began to think of them as something more than personal traits; they became the principles which she was to oppose to contemporary dissolution.

Willa Cather's traditionalism was thus anything but the arbitrary or patronizing opposition to contemporary ways which Irving Babbitt personified. It was a candid and philosophical nostalgia, a conviction and a standard possible only to a writer whose remembrance of the world of her childhood and the people in it was so overwhelming that everything after it seemed drab and more than a little cheap. Her distinction was not merely one of cultivation and sensibility; it was a kind of spiritual clarity possible only to those who suffer their loneliness as an act of the imagination and the will. It was as if the pervasive and incommunicable sense of loss felt by a whole modern American generation had suddenly become a theme rather than a passing emotion, a disassociation which one had to suffer as well as report. The others were lost in the new materialism, satirized or bewailed it; she seceded, as only a very rare and exquisite integrity could secede with dignity. Later, as it seemed, she became merely sentimental, and her direct criticism of contemporary types and manners was often petulant and intolerant. But the very intensity of her nostalgia had from the first led her beyond nostalgia; it had given her the conviction that the values of the world she had lost were the primary values, and everything else merely their degradation.

It was this conflict, a conflict that went beyond classes and could be represented only as a struggle between grandeur and meanness, the two poles of her world, that became the great theme of her novels. She did not celebrate the pioneer as such; she sought his image in all creative spirits—explorers and artists, lovers and saints, who seemed to live by a purity of aspiration, an integrity or passion or skill, that represented everything that had gone out of life or had to fight a losing battle for survival in it. "O Eagle of Eagles!" she apostrophized in *The Song of the Lark*. "Endeavor, desire, glorious striving of human art!" The world of her first important novels—*O Pioneers! The Song of The Lark, My Ántonia*— was unique in its serenity and happiness. Its secret was the individual discovery of power, the joy of fulfilling oneself in the satisfaction of an appointed destiny. The material Alexandra Bergson and Thea Kronberg worked with was like the naked prairies Jim Burden saw in *My Ántonia* on the night ride to his grandparents farm. "There was nothing but land: not a country at all, but the material out of which countries are made." It was always the same material and always the same creative greatness impressed upon it. Ántonia was a peasant and Thea a singer, but both felt the same need of a great and positive achievement; Alexandra was a farmer, but her feeling for the land was like Thea's feeling for music. The tenacious ownership of the land, the endless search of its possibilities, became the very poetry of her character; the need to assert oneself proudly had become a triumphant acceptance of life.

Yet even as Willa Cather's pale first novel, *Alexander's Bridge*, had been a legend of creative desire and its inevitable frustration, so in these novels the ideal of greatness had been subtly transformed into a lesson of endurance, Even in *My Ántonia*, the earliest and purest of her elegies, the significance of achievement had become only a rigid determination to see one's life through. The exultation was there, but it was already a little sad. Her heroines were all pioneers, pioneers on the land and pioneers of the spirit, but something small, cantankerous, and bitter had stolen in. The pioneer quality had thinned, as the pioneer zest had vanished. Ántonia might go on, as Thea might flee to the adobe deserts and cliff cities of the Southwest for refuge, but the new race of pioneers consisted of thousands of farm women suffering alone in their kitchens, living in a strange world amidst familiar scenes, wearing their lives out with endless chores and fears.

> On starlight nights I used to pace up and down those long, cold streets, scowling at the little, sleeping porches on either side, with their storm-windows and covered back porches. They were flimsy shelters, most of them poorly built of light wood, with spindle porch-posts horribly mutilated by the turning-lathe. Yet for all their frailness, how much jealousy and envy and unhappiness some of them managed to contain!

The life that went on in them seemed to me made up of evasions and negations; shifts to save cooking, to save washing and cleaning, devices to propitiate the tongue of gossip.

By 1920, the stories in *Youth and the Bright Medusa* hinted at a growing petulance, and in stories like "A Wagner Matinée" and "The Sculptor's Funeral" there was nothing to indicate that Willa Cather thought any better of small-town life than Zona Gale or Sinclair Lewis. Yet by their bitterness, so much more graphic than the dreary tonelessness of *Miss Lulu Bett*, these stories revealed how sharp her disillusionment had been, and when she developed the theme of small-town boorishness in *One of Ours* into the proverbial story of the sensitive young man, she could only repeat herself lamely. She was writing about an enemy—the oppressively narrow village world—which seemed only one of the many enemies of the creative spirit, but she did not have Zona Gale's inverted sentimentality, or anything like the spirit of Lewis's folksy and fundamentally affectionate satire. *One of Ours* was a temporary position for an artist whose need for an austere ideal was so compelling. Claude Wheeler was only the Midwest *révolté*; her authentic heroes were something more than sensitive young men who "could not see the use of working for money when money brought nothing one wanted. Mrs. Ehrlich said it brought security. Sometimes he thought that this security was what was the matter with everybody: that only perfect safety was required to kill all the best qualities in people and develop the mean ones." The farmer's wife in "A Wagner Matinée" had felt something deeper when, after her few moments of exultation at the concert, she turned and cried: " 'I don't want to go, Clark. I don't want to go!' Outside the concert hall lay the black pond with the cattle-tracked bluffs; the tall, unpainted house with weather-curled boards, naked as a tower; the crook-backed ash seedlings where the dish-clothes hung to dry; the gaunt moulting turkeys picking up refuse about the kitchen door."

The climax in Willa Cather's career came with two short novels she published between 1923 and 1925, *A Lost Lady* and *The Professor's House*. They were parables of the decline and fall of the great tradition, her own great tradition; and they were both so serenely and artfully written that they suggested that she could at last commemorate it quietly and even a little ironically. The primary values had gone, if not the bitterness she felt at their going; but where she had once written with a naïvely surging affection, or a rankling irritation, she now possessed a cultivated irony, a consummate poise, that could express regret without rancor or the sense of irretrievable loss without anguish. She had, in a sense, finally resigned herself to the physical and moral destruction of her ideal in the modern world, but only because she was soon to turn her back on that world entirely in novels like *Death Comes for the Archbishop* and *Shadows on the Rock*. In the person of a Captain Forrester dreaming railroads across the prairies, of a Godfrey St. Peter welding his whole spirit into a magnificent history of the Spanish explorers in America, she recaptured the enduring qualities she loved in terms of the world she had at last been forced to accept. These were the last of her pioneers, the last of her great failures; and the story she was now to tell was how they, like all their line, would go down in defeat before commerce and family ties and human pettiness.

Only once in *A Lost Lady* did her submerged bitterness break through, in her portrait of Ivy Peters, the perfect bourgeois:

> Now all this vast territory they had won was to be at the mercy of men like Ivy Peters, who had never dared anything, never risked anything. They would drink up the mirage, dispel the morning freshness, root out the great brooding spirit of freedom, the generous, easy life of the great landholders. The space, the colour, the princely carelessness of the pioneer they would destroy and cut up into profitable bits, as the match factory splinters the primeval forest. All the way from Missouri to the mountains this generation of shrewd young men, trained to petty economies by hard times, would do exactly what Ivy Peters had done.

The theme was corruption, as it was to be the theme of *The Professor's House*. It was as explicit as Marian Forrester's dependence on her husband's frontier strength and integrity, as brutal as Ivy Peters's acquisition of Marion Forrester herself. And at the very moment that Willa Cather recognized that corruption in all its social implications, gave its name and source, she resigned herself to it. It had been her distinction from the first to lament what others had never missed; she now became frankly the elegist of the defeated, the Amiel of the novel. The conflict between grandeur and meanness, ardor and greed, was more than ever before the great interest of her mind; but where she had once propounded that conflict, she now saw nothing but failure in it and submitted her art almost rejoicingly to the subtle exploration of failure. In any other novelist this would have made for sickliness and preciosity; now that she was no longer afraid of failure as a spiritual fact, or restive under it, her work gained a new strength and an almost radiant craftsmanship.

The significance of this new phase in Willa Cather's work is best seen in *The Professor's House*, which has been the most persistently underrated of her novels. Actually it is one of those imperfect and ambitious works whose very imperfections illuminate the quality of an imagination. The story of Godfrey St. Peter is at once the barest and the most elaborately symbolic version of the story of heroic failure she told over and over again, the keenest in insight and the most hauntingly suggestive. The violence with which she broke the book in half to tell the long and discursive narrative of Tom Outland's boyhood in the Southwest was a technical mistake that has damned the book, but the work as a whole is the most brilliant statement of her endeavor as an artist. For St. Peter is at once the archetype of all her characters and the embodiment of her own beliefs. He is not merely the scholar as artist, the son of pioneer parents who has carried the pioneer passion into the world of art and thought; he is what Willa Cather herself has always been or hoped to be—a pioneer in mind, a Catholic by instinct, French by inclination, a spiritual aristocrat with democratic manners.

The tragedy of St. Peter, though it seems nothing more than a domestic tragedy, is thus the most signal and illuminating of all Willa Cather's tragedies. The enemy she saw in Ivy Peters—the new trading, grasping class—has here stolen into St. Peter's home; it is reflected in the vulgar ambition of his wife and eldest daughter, the lucrative commercial use his son-in-law has made of the invention Tom Outland had developed in scholarly research, the genteel but acquisitive people around him. St. Peter's own passion, so pure and subtle a pioneer passion, had been for the life of the mind. In the long and exhaustive research for his great history, in the writing of it in the attic of his old house, he had known something of the physical exultation that had gone into the explorations he described. As a young man in France, studying for his doctorate, he had looked up from a skiff in the Mediterranean and seen the design of his lifework reflected in the ranges of the Sierra Nevada, "unfolded in the air above him." Now, after twenty years of toil, that history was finished; the money he had won for it had gone into the making of a new and pretentious house. The great creative phase of his life was over. To hold onto the last symbol of his endeavor, St. Peter determined to retain his old house against the shocked protests of his family. It was a pathetic symbol, but he needed some last refuge in a world wearing him out by slow attrition.

In this light the long middle section of the novel, describing Tom Outland's boyhood in the desert, is not a curious interlude in the novel; it becomes the parable of St. Peter's own longing for that remote world of the Southwest which he had described so triumphantly in his book. Willa Cather, too, was moving toward the South, as all her books do: always toward the more primitive in nature and the more traditional in belief. Tom Outland's desert life was thus the ultimate symbol of a forgotten freedom and harmony that could be realized only by a frank and even more romantic submission to the past, to the Catholic order and doctrine, and the deserts of California and New Mexico in which the two priests of *Death Comes for the Archbishop* lived with such quiet and radiant perfection. Her characters no longer had to submit to failure; they lived in a charming and almost antediluvian world of their own. They had withdrawn, as Willa Cather now withdrew; and if her world became increasingly recollective and abstract, it was because she had fought a losing battle that no one of her spirit could hope to win. It was a long way from the Catholic Bohemian farmers of Nebraska to the eighteen-century Catholicism of the Southwest, but she had made her choice, and she accepted it with an almost haughty serenity. When she came to write "The Novel *Démeublé*," her essay on fiction, she defined her rejection of modern industrial culture explicitly, and asked for a pure novel that would throw the "social furniture" out of fiction. Even a social novelist like Balzac, she now insisted, wrote about subjects unworthy of him; for the modern social novelists she had only a very gracious and superior contempt. "Are the banking system and the Stock Exchange worth being written about at all?" she asked. She thought not, and itemized the "social furniture" that had to be thrown out of the novel, among them the factory and a whole realm of "physical sensation." It was but a step from the colonial New Mexico of *Death Comes for the Archbishop* to old Quebec in *Shadows on the Rock* and the lavender and old lace of *Lucy Gayheart*. Her secession was complete.

E.K. BROWN

"The Professor's House"

Willa Cather's fiction unlike Virginia Woolf's preserves most of the conventional elements; but in her writing there is a steadily growing concern with what is too subtle or too large to be wholly fixed in a story, or in people, or even in setting, a concern with what calls for the hovering of suggestion rather than for bold and outright statement. Even in her early novels, in *O Pioneers!*, *My Ántonia*, *The Song of the Lark*, there was something neither story nor persons nor places, something felt by those who feel it at all as a large background of emotion. As she grew older the large background of emotion claimed more and more of her attention; and by its demands the structure of her novels underwent very interesting and beautiful change. The change is apparent in *The Professor's House*, although the triumphant use of the new structure is in the subsequent *Death Comes for the Archbishop*, which she wisely judged her finest book. In *The Professor's House*, there is energetic narrative, there are memorable people, and there is a strong and yet delicate realization of setting. You may read the book for any of these, or for all three, but you will not be reading the novel that Willa Cather wrote unless you find something else. There is an astonishing comment on *The Professor's House* in Alexander Porterfield's essay on Willa Cather, the most considered English estimate of her novels. Mr. Porterfield says: "Briefly, it is the story of a scholarly professor at a Middle Western university, passing through the critical uneasy period between middle and old age—at least it should be taken as a study of such, otherwise its meaning is difficult to perceive exactly." Well, its meaning is difficult to perceive exactly, but I am startled to find a critic shutting the door on his

From *Rhythm in the Novel*. Copyright © 1950 by University of Toronto Press.

perception that there is more in a book than he can quite apprehend, and shaking himself, and deciding that his apprehension is the measure of the novelist's meaning.

The Professor's House has been a perplexity to most critics. For my part I believe that it is by scrutinizing the author's approach to houses that we may best discover the extraordinary relation between the three parts into which, like To the Lighthouse, it is explicitly divided.

At the outset Willa Cather presents Professor Godfrey St. Peter living between two houses. There is the expensive conventional new house that he has built because his wife wanted it, and into which he has moved with reluctance, with a positive distaste that greatly surprises him; and there is the old rented frame house, ugly, inconvenient, run down, in which he has lived for thirty years—for the whole of his adult life, the whole of his career, the whole of his marriage. He finds that he can write, and think, only in its attic study, encumbered with the forms on which a dressmaker has fitted clothes for his wife and daughters ever since he was a young husband. It is oil-lit, and stove-heated; it has almost every disadvantage a room can have; but it has been the house of his mind and spirit. It is very easy to mark the two houses as symbols, of no mysterious depth. Nor do they acquire in the first part of the novel any depth beyond the practice of a Sinclair Lewis or a James Farrell.

The obviously startling element in the structure of The Professor's House is its second part, a long story inserted after the fashion of Cervantes or Smollett. The length, vitality, and power of the intercalated tale are startling, and not only at a first reading. The substance in this middle part of the novel is the crucial episode in the life of Tom Outland. Once and once only in the thirty years of his teaching, St. Peter had encountered a mind and personality of the first order, a student from whom he learned, and whose impress is strong upon the many-volumed history of Spanish exploration in America which brought St. Peter his fame, gave him his full mental and personal growth, and as a by-product provided the new house, built with literary prize money. When the novel opens Tom Outland is dead, killed, like one of the Ramsay sons, in the First World War.

The central event in Tom Outland's life was the discovery of a Cliff Dweller village in a New Mexican canyon. That discovery gave a new dimension to American life for Outland and later for St. Peter. Here was beauty, the beauty of pure and noble design, unspoiled by clutter or ornament, undistracted by cosiness, uncontradicted by the ugliness of machinery and industry. An expert to whom Tom showed some of the pottery was struck by its likeness to the decorative art of early Crete, and in this suggestion there is nothing fantastic. The effect Willa Cather produces in her account of the Cliff Dwellers is very near Keats's evocation of the Greek town in the "Ode on a Grecian Urn." The houses of the Cliff Dwellers are never overtly contrasted with those in the Middle Western university town where the first and third parts of the novel are laid; and in the modern town the emphasis falls upon individual buildings, in the ancient village, significantly, on the architectural as on the social unity of the whole.

There is a light but telling stroke which is worth a pause—it will suggest how firmly the novel has been stitched together. Between his discovery of the village in the canyon and his death a few years later Tom made physics his principal study; he devised and patented a bulkheaded vacuum which after his death became the nucleus of a great improvement in aircraft. He had willed everything to his fiancée, one of the professor's daughters, but with not a particle of the professor in her make-up. With some of the immense fortune the invention brought her, she and her husband, a born front-office man, built a country house and called it "Outland." Now the professor's new house is a wrong house, but only by its acceptance of prevailing convention. The memorial to Tom Outland is much more deeply a wrong house. Although it stands on a high site it holds no reminiscence of the village in the canyon—it is a Norwegian manor set down in the sultry Middle West, without a vestige of American feeling. We are spared a sight of its interior; but we are told of what is to furnish it—the loot of the antique shops of Europe imported by way of a Spanish American port in a scheme to evade customs duties.

This is the worst of all houses in the novel, but there are many modern houses, none of them with any affinity with the village of the Cliff Dwellers. With the kind of past it represents the busy ugly insensitive present seems to have no conceivable bond.

But in the third and final part the bond is suddenly revealed. The first and second parts of the book which have seemed so boldly unrelated are brought into a profound unity. It is in this third part of the novel that the large background of emotion, which demands rhythmic expression if we are to respond to it as it deserves, becomes predominant. In the first part it was plain that the professor did not wish to live in his new house, and did not wish to enter into the sere phase of his life correlative with it. At the beginning of the third part it becomes plain that he cannot indefinitely continue to make the old attic study the theatre of his life, that he cannot go on prolonging or attempting to prolong his prime, the phase of his life correlative with that. The personality of his mature years—the personality that had expressed itself powerfully and in the main happily in his teaching, his scholarship, his love for his wife, his domesticity—is now quickly receding, and nothing new is flowing in. What begins to dominate St. Peter is something akin to the Cliff Dwellers, something primitive which had ruled him long ago when he was a boy on a pioneer farm in the rough Solomon valley in north-western Kansas. To this primitive being not many things were real; the food, love, and society which make up so much of the splendour in life for Virginia Woolf do not seem to have counted for very much; what counted was nature, and nature seen as a web of life, and finally of death.

The essential passage, the binding passage, is in terms of houses, and I do not know of any interpreter who has made use of it:

> The Professor really didn't see what he was going to do about the matter of domicile. He couldn't make himself believe that he was ever going to live in the new house again. He didn't belong there. He remembered some lines of a translation from the Norse he used to read long ago in one of his mother's few books, a little two-volume Ticknor and Fields edition of Longfellow, in blue and gold, that used to lie on the parlour table:
>
> > For thee a house was built
> > Ere thou wast born;
> > For thee a mould was made
> > Ere thou of woman camest.
>
> Lying on his old couch he could almost believe himself in that house already. The sagging springs were like the sham upholstery that is put in coffins. Just the equivocal American way of dealing with serious facts, he reflected. Why pretend that it is possible to soften that last hard bed?
>
> He could remember a time when the loneliness of death had terrified him, when the idea of it was insupportable. He used to feel that if his wife could but lie in the same coffin with him, his body would not be so insensible that the nearness of hers would not give it comfort. But now he thought of eternal solitude with gratefulness; as a release from every obligation, from every form of effort. It was the Truth.

All that had seemed a hanging back from the future—the clinging to the old attic study, the absorption in Tom Outland and in the civilization of the Cliff Dwellers, the revival of interest in the occupations of his childhood and its pleasures—was something very unlike what it had seemed. It was profound, unconscious preparation for death, for the last house of the professor.

Again, I believe, the great chords are sounding. Willa Cather had begun on the surface, with a record of mediocrities, of the airless prosaic world of a small college town—how airless, how prosaic only those who have lived in one can know. The mediocrities do not have everything their own way: against them is Professor St. Peter, and he is not quite alone. He is not confined to the here and the now: he has on him the mark of Mediterranean civilization—he almost looks like a Latin—and the mark of the Spanish explorers. Still, the professor and those who are more or less of his stripe are not dominant in his first book; they appear to belong to a minority weak in force as well as in numbers, and close to extinction. Then in the second book Willa Cather inverted the roles. The mediocrities are few and weak; and against them is the revelation of life as the Cliff Dwellers' village records and suggests it. More boldly, more simply than Virginia Woolf she sings the splendour of life.

The surprise for the reader who really reads the novel is not the startling intercalated story: it is the strange short third part. The common quality between life in the Middle Western college town and life in the Cliff Dwellers' village is that both kinds of life end in death. That is something for which neither the first nor the second part of the novel had prepared us. Dominated by the feeling that both kinds of life end in death, we know how to measure them, the ancient and the contemporary. What aspect of dignity, of beauty, would the ruins of the college town possess for Macaulay's New Zealander if he were to pause on this continent on his way to sketch the ruins of St. Paul's? Great chords are sounding, and as they sound they alter radically the impression we had before we approached the end of the novel. I do not wish to press a musical analogy here, . . . but perhaps it may be said that in *To the Lighthouse* the arrangement of the themes and their interweaving are conventional according to sonata form, but that the arrangement and interweaving in *The Professor's House*, with the shock, the revelation in the final part, are highly and stirringly experimental.

DAVID DAICHES

The Claims of History

The expansiveness of such novels as
O Pioneers! and *My Ántonia* gradually gives away, in Miss Cather's work,
to more concentrated novels of more limited scope. *A Lost Lady*, though it
still has something of the western background, is focused throughout on a
single character. In *The Professor's House*, which followed in 1925, the
scope is similarly restricted. The novel is essentially the study of a middle-
aged professor wrestling with his own sensitivities on the one hand and his
family responsibilities on the other, but, interwoven with the professor's
story and acting as a catalyst in projecting that story, is the story of Tom
Outland, the brilliant, unconventional student who had been killed in the
early days of the first World War. In both Tom Outland and the professor
Miss Cather is exploring certain phases of sensibility, aspects of character
which in some degree and at some time are bound to come in conflict
with the demands of the conventional world.

We can trace the growth of this interest in the earlier novels. To
some extent, it is present in *Alexander's Bridge*, but it gives way in the
pioneering novels to sturdier themes, emerging there only in incidental
characters, until we see it again more fully revealed in Claude of *One of
Ours*. *The Professor's House* is Miss Cather's first full-length treatment of a
theme which has become so important in the twentieth-century novel,
the first of her novels which links her, however tenuously, to what might
be called the modern novel of sensibility so successfully practiced in
England by Virginia Woolf and still very much alive. Not that there is any
real resemblance between Miss Cather and Mrs. Woolf in attitude or
technique—their art had very different foundations; but the exploration of

From *Willa Cather: A Critical Introduction*. Copyright © 1951 by Cornell University. Cornell
University Press, 1951.

individual sensitivity, so central in Virginia Woolf's fiction, does come to be one of Willa Cather's main interests at this stage in her career.

Willa Cather seems to have had a *mystique* about professors: we can see something of it in the picture of Gaston Cleric, the "brilliant and inspiring young scholar" in the third book of *My Ántonia*, and in the brief but enthusiastic account of the history professor in *One of Ours* for whom Claude wrote a thesis on Jeanne d'Arc. *The Professor's House* has for its hero Professor Godfrey St. Peter, author of *Spanish Adventurers in North America*, intelligent, sensitive, unconventional, and, at the time the book opens, recently the recipient of an Oxford prize for history. The prize has enabled the professor, on his wife's suggestion, to build a fine new house. He does not, however, share his wife's enthusiasm for the new house, preferring the shabby attic of the old house to the glories that await him in the new. In that study his great work was written, and it is associated with all that he considers most worthwhile in his own life. The book opens with his reluctant move from the old house to the new and his decision to continue renting the old house so that he can continue to use his beloved study.

At this crisis in his life—for we first see him at the dangerous period of middle age when restlessness and an undefined dissatisfaction begin to haunt him—he feels himself more and more removed from the normal world of bright and polite social behavior, and although there is no breach with his wife it is made clear that his increasing lack of interest in the world in which she moves is drawing him apart from her. His series of volumes on the Spaniards in North America (which on publication were looked upon with suspicion by conventional academic historians, but which have eventually won him fame among a limited number of initiates who understand what he was doing) evidence an interest in the adventurous side of history and are also bound up with his interest in Tom Outland. Outland had descended on the professor many years before as a young man with an unconventional New Mexico background. His full story is told in Book Two of the novel, where we learn that he had been orphaned in infancy and had worked as a railroad callboy in Pardee, New Mexico, and then, with his friend Rodney Blake, as a cowboy for a big New Mexico cattle company. It was while riding the range that he and Rodney had discovered, on the top of a long unexplored mesa, "a little city of stone," the perfectly preserved home of long-vanished pueblo Indians. He had fallen in love with this town in the cliffs and with Rodney Blake had explored it passionately and lovingly. He had spent some time in Washington trying to get officials of the Smithsonian Institution interested in excavating it, but without success. On his return from

Washington he found that Blake, despairing of Washington interest and misunderstanding the nature of Outland's interest, had sold the pottery in which Cliff City (as they called it) abounded for a handsome sum to a German entrepreneur. Outland's fury at finding what his friend had done (though it had been done with the best of intentions and the money had been deposited in the bank in Outland's name) led to the separation of the friends, and Outland eventually turned up at the professor's university seeking an education. He had already received some education, including a good grounding in Latin, from a Catholic priest who had been interested in him.

In the first part of the novel, however, all we know of Tom Outland is that he had appeared from the unknown, had been befriended by the professor and his family, and had turned out a brilliant physicist. He had invented the Outland vacuum, which "revolutionized aviation." On the outbreak of the first World War he had quixotically gone off to Europe to enlist in the French Foreign Legion. There he was killed before he was thirty years old and, having before his departure become engaged to the professor's elder daughter Rosamond, left her in his will everything that he owned. It was later realized that the Outland vacuum, if properly exploited, would make a fortune, and the flamboyant and able Louie Marsellus, himself an electrical engineer, who fell in love with Rosamond and married her, investigated the commercial possibilities of the patent which now belonged to his wife and made a great financial success of it.

The professor's younger daughter, Kathleen, more sensitive and much less rich than Rosamond, is married to Scott McGregor, a young journalist who manages to earn a moderate income by writing, among other things, a daily "prose poem" for the popular press. Being a sensitive and ambitious young man, he is disgusted with his way of earning a living and ashamed at his own facility in turning out such stuff. His brother-in-law Louie Marsellus, assured, generous, and completely the extrovert, inevitably arouses Scott's hostility, while Kathleen resents her elder sister's wealth and arrogant bearing, a resentment reciprocated by Rosamond who feels that her sister and brother-in-law privately mock her own and her husband's social pretensions.

The professor is not unaware of the tension that exists between his two daughters. His own favorite is Kathleen, while his wife seems to take a greater interest in the flashier Rosamond and her smooth and charming husband, who adores his mother-in-law and plays up to her on every possible occasion. All are haunted by the memory of Tom Outland, whose names flits like a disturbing ghost through their conversation. Marsellus is building a pretentious country house and announces his decision to call it "Outland," in recognition of Tom's achievement and to show that he is aware of the source of his fortune. This decision, applauded by Rosamond and by Mrs. St. Peter, outrages the McGregors (McGregor, not Marsellus, had been Tom's friend) and is met coldly by the professor. We also learn that it was the professor's growing affection for Tom Outland that first aroused his wife's jealous sense of something dividing her from her husband. Now that there is an undefinable but unmistakable distance between the professor and his wife, we become increasingly aware of how the professor's interest in the Spanish Southwest, his feeling about his historical research, and his attitude toward Outland have combined to set him apart and to produce the crisis in the midst of which we find him when the book opens.

The book as a whole is the story of the development and resolution of this crisis, but it is also Tom Outland's story, and the fact that Miss Cather can make these two stories one with no sense of strain or structural artificiality is a tribute to the maturity of her art at this stage. Tom Outland's story, in turn, is bound up with the Southwest, with the Cliff Dwellers, and with that feeling for the impact of the past on the present which was strong in Miss Cather and which we first see in the Cliff Dweller scenes in *The Song of the Lark*. Thus the professor and Tom are linked to each other by a sensitivity to history—not academic history (which does not admit of this kind of sensitivity), but history conceived as a series of past human adventures whose implications reverberate excitingly into the present. Tom's joy in discovering and investigating Cliff City is the same kind of joy that the professor found in writing his *Spanish Adventurers in North America*. Indeed, he had gone with Tom on a journey of discovery in the Southwest using Tom's experiences as a guide in identifying places referred to in the journals of old Spanish explorers.

The new house threatens to cut the professor off from his past, from that period of his life when his daughters were children, when he was thoroughly *en rapport* with his family, when Tom Outland was a daily visitor to his home, and when he was engaged in the exciting task of getting his history under way.

> "Godfrey," his wife had gravely said one day, when she detected an ironical turn in some remark he made about the new house, "is there something you would rather have done with that money than to have built a house with it?
>
> "Nothing, my dear, nothing. If with that cheque I could have brought back the fun I had writing my history, you'd never have got your house. But one couldn't get that for twenty thousand dollars. The great pleasures don't come so cheap. There is nothing else, thank you."

The professor refuses to allow the dressmaker to remove from his old study the dress forms which she had kept there for so many years and on which so often his daughters' new party dresses had been left overnight. He keeps the shabby attic room with all its old properties as a refuge from the implications of his new house and from the brittle claims of society, a place in which to work and meditate and be alone and be himself. This sounds a tawdry enough piece of business, with its suggestions of the gloomy romantic hero or of the self-conscious Faustus in his study—but as Miss Cather handles it the theme emerges freshly and convincingly. She manipulates the professor's relations with his family very adroitly, refusing to allow herself the obvious device of a clear-cut distinction between sympathetic characters of perception and sensitivity and unsympathetic characters who lead a life of cheerful social insensitivity. Mrs. St. Peter is unsympathetic neither to the reader nor to the professor, and Louie Marsellus becomes more attractive as the book progresses. But in a sense the characters are all judged by their relation to the dead Tom Outland, and that is the principal reason why the McGregors emerge as in some undefined way superior to the Marselluses and why the professor remains an isolated figure whose isolation continues to increase until the conclusion of the story puts it suddenly but not improbably on a new basis.

Book One of *The Professor's House* is entitled "The Family" and explores the professor's relation to his wife, daughters, and sons-in-law. It concludes with the departure of Mrs. St. Peter and her daughter and son-in-law for a holiday in France; it was Louie's plan, and he is paying for everything. The professor has been warmly invited by Louie to make one of the party, but, to Louie's genuine disappointment, he refuses, finding himself unable to join in that kind of jaunt:

> That night, after he was in bed, St. Peter tried in vain to justify himself in his inevitable refusal. He liked Paris, and he liked Louie. But one couldn't do one's own things in another person's way; selfish or not, that was the truth. Besides, he could not be needed. He could trust Louie to take every care of Lillian [his wife], and nobody could please her more than her son-in-law. . . . Many people admired her, but Louie more than most. That worldliness, that willingness to get the most out of occasions and people, which had developed so strongly in Lillian in the last few years, seemed to Louie as natural and proper as it seemed unnatural to Godfrey. It was an element that had always been in Lillian, and as long as it resulted in mere fastidiousness, was not a means to an end, St. Peter had liked it, too. He knew it was due to this worldliness, even more than to the fact that his wife had a little money of her own, that she and his daughters had never been drab and a little pathetic, like

some of the faculty women. They hadn't much, but they were never absurd. They never made shabby compromises. If they couldn't get the right thing, they went without. Usually they had the right thing, and it got paid for, somehow. He couldn't say they were extravagant; the old house had been funny and bare enough, but there were no ugly things in it.

With his family away, the professor moves into the old house and more or less lives in the study. His plans are to spend the summer editing and annotating the diary kept by Tom Outland when he was investigating Cliff City. His meditations on Outland in the lonely house as he prepares to work on the diary provide Miss Cather with a perfect transition to "Tom Outland's Story," which occupies Book Two.

Earlier in the novel Scott McGregor makes a significant remark to his father-in-law. "You know, Tom isn't very real to me any more. Sometimes I think he was just a—a glittering idea." He had become "a glittering idea" to his friend McGregor; to Louie Marsellus, who had never met him, he was an adored name and the source of a fortune; to Mrs. St. Peter he was someone who had separated her in some degree from her husband: only Professor St. Peter himself remained to cherish Outland's memory, and as time went on Outland becomes a part of the professor's own history. Marsellus once suggested that he should settle some of Outland's money on the professor, since Outland had owed so much to him, but when Rosamond brings this message from her husband to her father, he repudiates the suggestion fiercely:

> Once and for all, Rosamond, understand that he owed me no more than I owed him. . . . In a lifetime of teaching, I've encountered just one remarkable mind; but for that, I'd consider my good years largely wasted. And there can be no question of money between me and Tom Outland. I can't explain just how I feel about it, but it would somehow damage my recollections of him, would make that episode in my life common-place like everything else. And that would be a great loss to me. I'm purely selfish in refusing your offer; my friendship with Outland is the one thing I will not have translated into the vulgar tongue.

By the time we reach Book Two, therefore, the professor has become in some sense identified with Outland, and the story of Outland's life is part of the professor's own background.

"Tom Outland's Story" is set in the New Mexico landscape, and description of natural scenery is employed as an almost lyrical background to the boy's adventures. That background helps to explain not only Tom, but also the quality of the professor's feeling for history. The style of this part of the narrative is simple and swinging (it is supposed to be Tom's own words, the professor's recollection of the story Tom had told him). The first description of Cliff City gives some idea of the unpretentious but effective prose:

> It was beautifully proportioned, that tower, swelling out to a larger girth a little above the base, then growing slender again. There was something symmetrical and powerful about the swell of the masonry. The tower was the fine thing that held all the jumble of houses together and made them mean something. It was red in colour, even on that grey day. In sunlight it was the colour of winter oak-leaves. A fringe of cedars grew along the edge of the cavern, like a garden. They were the only living things. Such silence and stillness and repose—immortal repose. That village sat looking down into the canyon with the calmness of eternity. The falling snow-flakes, sprinkling the piñons, gave it a special kind of solemnity. I can't describe it. It was more like sculpture than anything else. I knew at once that I had come upon the city of some extinct civilization, hidden away in this inaccessible mesa for centuries, preserved in the dry air and almost perpetual sunlight like a fly in amber, guarded by the cliffs and the river and the desert.

There is "the glory and the freshness of a dream" about much of this writing, which describes history impinging concretely on the mind of a naïve and enthusiastic youngster. Tom actually experienced what the professor has tried to distill in his writings:

> One thing we knew about these people; they hadn't built their town in a hurry. Everything proved their patience and deliberation. The cedar joists had been felled with stone axes and rubbed smooth with sand. The little poles that lay across them and held up the clay floor of the chamber above, were smoothly polished. The door lintels were carefully fitted (the doors were stone slabs held in place by wooden bars fitted into hasps). The clay dressing that covered the stone walls are tinted, and some of the chambers were frescoed in geometrical patterns, one color laid on another. In one room was a painted border, little tents, like Indian tepees, in brilliant red.
>
> But the really splendid thing about our city, the thing that made it delightful to work there, and must have made it delightful to live there, was the setting. The town hung like a bird's nest in the cliff, looking off into the box canyon below, and beyond into the wide valley we called Cow Canyon, facing an ocean of clear air. A people who had the hardihood to build there, and who lived day after day looking down upon such grandeur, who came and went by those hazardous trails, must have been, as we often told each other, a fine people. But what had become of them? What catastrophe had overwhelmed them?

In Book Three of the novel we return to the professor. He is sitting in his old study reflecting on his own past. "He had had two romances:

one of the heart, which had filled his life for many years, and a second of the mind—of the imagination. Just when the morning brightness of the world was wearing off for him, along came Outland and brought him a kind of second youth." Through Outland, he reflects, "he had been able to experience afresh things that had grown dull with use." Outland was responsible for the fact that "the last four volumes of *The Spanish Adventurers* were more simple and inevitable than those that went before." He becomes the symbol of the professor's attitude to history.

We learn of the professor's holidays in Europe, youthful trips to France and later expeditions to Spain, and these become linked in his and the reader's mind with his journeys in the American Southwest, to provide a background of warmth and color to his speculations about civilization. Here, as later in *Death Comes for the Archbishop*, Miss Cather takes her old conflicting interests in the American West and in European culture and fuses them in a new way. In her earlier novels, a character had to escape from one to achieve the other; but among the Indian and Spanish remains of the Southwest the conflict is resolved.

Meditating over his past alone in the old house the professor feels himself more and more detached from life, even from his own life. "He did not regret his life, but he was indifferent to it. It seemed to him like the life of another person." A conviction seizes him that he is near the end of his life, though his doctor assures him that there is nothing the matter with him. He falls asleep on his study couch with the gas fire lit, and a storm blows out the flame of the fire and slams the window shut. He realizes vaguely what has happened and knows that the room is filling with gas. "The thing to do was to get up and open the window. But suppose he did not get up—? How far was a man required to exert himself against accident?" He falls asleep but is discovered in time by Augusta, the sewing woman, who comes in to get the keys to open the new house, for the family is coming home from France.

The professor recovers himself in a conversation with Augusta, a practical, unimaginative woman, "seasoned and sound and on the solid earth . . . and, for all her matter-of-factness and hard-handedness, kind and loyal." Sitting quietly with Augusta, he thinks again of his past life, "trying to see where he had made his mistake."

> Perhaps the mistake was merely in an attitude of mind. He had never learned to live without delight. And he would have to learn to, just as, in a Prohibition country, he supposed he would have to learn to live without sherry. Theoretically he knew that life is possible, may be even pleasant, without joy, without passionate griefs. But it had never occurred to him that he might have to live like that.

His reluctance to meet his returning family, to become involved in a domestic and social pattern again, continues, but as a result of his involuntary near-suicide a change comes over his attitude, which enables him to face the arrival of the "Berengaria," bringing his wife and the Marselluses back across the Atlantic, without anxiety.

> His temporary release from consciousness seemed to have been beneficial. He had let something go—and it was gone: something very precious, that he could not consciously have relinquished, probably. He doubted whether his family would ever realize that he was not the same man they had said good-bye to; they would be too happily preoccupied with their own affairs. If his apathy hurt them, they could not possibly be so much hurt as he had been already. At least, he felt the ground under his feet. He thought he knew where he was, and that he could face with fortitude the *Berengaria* and the future.

So the book concludes. It is a novel which sometimes barely avoids tawdry romantic situations and a too neat pairing off of introverts and extroverts. But they *are* avoided. The professor's intellectual and imaginative qualities are linked to the life of action through the subject of his historical researches (which are themselves bound up with his character) and his association with Tom Outland. His growing aloofness fits none of the formulas of the romantic hero, while the use made of Outland's early life and his exploration of Cliff City gives a wholly original tone to the story. The full meaning of the professor's crisis and its resolution is never overtly examined, and a note of deliberate mystery remains to the end. The novel is symbolic in a way in which *O Pioneers!* and *My Ántonia* are not, though these earlier novels have their own kind of symbolism. In some respects it is closer to *Alexander's Bridge* than any of the intervening novels, but it has more substance and more conviction than that early work. The pioneering novels and even such a small-scale affair as *A Lost Lady* were relatively rough-hewn works; *The Professor's House* shows Miss Cather moving toward a more delicate kind of art.

MORTON D. ZABEL

Willa Cather:
The Tone of Time

In 1927, at fifty-four, Willa Cather, after three decades of steady and patient labor in her craft, stood at the height of her career, with fifteen years of her best work behind her and her most popular book, *Death Comes for the Archbishop*, claiming an unstinted admiration. When she died twenty years later, she had already come to appear as the survivor of a distant generation, remote from the talents and problems of the past two anxious decades. This estrangement was no surprise to her. It was of her own choice and election. In 1936, in prefacing her collection of essays then called *Not Under Forty*, she admitted that her writing could have "little interest for people under forty years of age." "The world broke in two in 1922 or thereabouts," she said, and it was to "the backward, and by one of their number," that she addressed her later books. She had, in fact, so addressed her work ever since she first found her real bearings in authorship with *O Pioneers!* in 1913. Backwardness was with her not only a matter of her material and temperament. It was the condition of her existence as an artist.

She was one of the last in a long line of commemorators and elegists of American innocence and romantic heroism that virtually dates from the beginnings of a conscious native artistry in American literature. Her books, once she found her natural voice and métier, and once she had put aside her Eastern subjects and earlier themes of rebellious protest, had become elegies, and Irving, Cooper, Hawthorne, Mark Twain, and

From *Craft and Character in Modern Fiction*. Copyright © 1940, 1947 by Morton D. Zabel. The Viking Press, 1947.

Sarah Orne Jewett figure in their ancestry. When, on rare occasions, she praised her fellow-craftsmen, from Miss Jewett to Katherine Mansfield, Thornton Wilder, or Thomas Mann (who "belongs immensely to the forward-goers . . . But he also goes back a long way, and his backwardness is more gratifying to the backward"), it was usually because they also turned to the past and rooted their values there.

She was quite aware of the false and bogus uses to which the historic sentiment had been put in American fiction. Its products surrounded her in the early 1900s when she was feeling her way toward her career: "machine-made historical novels," "dreary dialect stories," "very dull and heavy as clay"—books by John Fox, Jr., James Lane Allen, Mary Johnston, and their successful competitors, the memory of which today she likened to "taking a stroll through a World's Fair grounds some years after the show is over." She knew Miss Jewett shone like a star in that lustreless company; that Henry James's "was surely the keenest mind any American had ever devoted to the art of fiction"; that Stephen Crane "had done something real." She also had to learn the secret of their distinction the hard way: she came out of the West attracted by the prairie girl's mirage of the East—its cities, salons, opera houses, studios, Beacon Hill sanctities, the fever and excitement of New York, the lure of Atlantic liners, with the shrines of Europe beyond. Her early stories, many never collected in her books, are full of this worshipful glamour, and she was past thirty-five when she tried to make something of it in her first novel, which combined a problem out of Edith Wharton, a setting and something of a manner out of Henry James, and an outsider's clumsiness in handling them, with inevitable results in self-conscious stiffness and crudity of tone.

Only then did she remember the advice Sarah Orne Jewett had once given her: "The thing that teases the mind over and over for years, and at last gets itself put down on paper—whether little or great, it belongs to Literature." "Otherwise," as Miss Jewett had also said, "what might be strength in a writer is only crudeness, and what might be insight is only observation; sentiment falls to sentimentality—you can write about life, but never life itself." Willa Cather put Beacon Hill and Bohemia behind her. She returned to Nebraska, to a prairie town trying hard not to be blown away in the blast of a winter wind. She found the local habitation of her talent, and her serious career in art began.

From that point she began her journey into lost time, going back beyond Nebraska, Colorado, and Kansas to colonial New Mexico, to eighteenth-century Quebec, and finally to the pre-Civil War Virginia of her family, every step taking her deeper into the values and securities she set most store by. She had, to help her, her rediscovered devotion to the scenes of her early youth, the Western fields and skies she called "the grand passion of my life," her brilliant gift for rendering landscape and weather in the closest approximation to the poetic art of Turgenev and Gogol our fiction has seen, her retentive sympathy with the life of farms, small towns, prairie settlements, immigrant colonies, and Southwestern outposts and missions. In all the tales of regional America that have been produced in the past forty years nothing has exceeded her skill in evoking the place-spirit of rural America in her finest books—My Ántonia, A Lost Lady, The Professor's House, and Death Comes for the Archbishop.

The pathos of distance by which she induced her special poetry into these scenes was, of course, stimulated by her feeling that the inspiring landscape of the prairies, deserts, and mountains, no less than the gracious charms of colonial Virginia or old New York, had been obliterated by a vulgar and cheapening modernity. The garage that now stands on Charles Street in Boston on the site of the house where Mrs. James T. Fields had once held court to "Learning and Talent" was symptomatic for Willa Cather of a general and humiliating degradation. So the old wagon roads of the West, "roads of Destiny" that "used to run like a wild thing across the open prairie," had been resurveyed and obliterated to make highways for tourist and motor traffic. The railways once "dreamed across the mountains" by a race of Titans, highways in the heroic conquest of the West, were streamlined for commuters between New York and California. Wooden houses and piazza'd mansions, once landmarks of pioneer fortitude and hospitality, came down and suburban Tudor or sham Château went up in their place. The frontier universities that had once fostered a scholarship of vision and historical passion yielded to academic power plants thick with politics and careerism. She despised such a world, whose literature itself she saw as mere statistics and "sensory stimuli," and apparently she preferred to be despised by it.

The interesting thing about Miss Cather's career is that it started in protest against and flight from the very world she ended by idealizing and mourning. It recapitulates a characteristic American pattern of rebellion and return, censure and surrender. The prairie and small town, the Western hinterland and the neighborly community, as she presented them in her best early stories—"A Wagner Matinee," "Paul's Case," "The Sculptor's Funeral," "A Death in the Desert"—were objects of a moral reproach and castigation as severe as anything she later directed against the vulgarizing influences of the modern world. She was, indeed, a pioneer in the twentieth-century "revolt from the village," and she spared no scorn in describing the provincial spirit. It had created the life of a "dunghill," of petty existences, of "little people" and a small humanity, of stingy hates and warping avarice that made generous spirits shrivel and ardent natures die. The savagery of her indictment was perhaps the strongest passion she ever summoned in any of her works. Her frontier in those days was not the West; it was the East and and the world of art, with desire the goad of her heroes and heroines and the running theme of her stories, as much as it was of Drieser's.

It was in young artists—the dreaming, headstrong, fractious, or unstable young, fated to defeat or bad ends by the materialism and ugliness of their surroundings—that she first envisaged the heroic ideal. Paul, Katharine Gaylord, Harvey Merrick, and Don Hedger are the defeated or dishonored "cases" that foreshadow the triumphant lives of Alexandra Bergson, Thea Kronborg, Ántonia Shimerda, Archbishop Machebeuf, and Nancy Till, and that lend their note of desire or vision to the middle terms of Miss Cather's argument—the inspired spirits who do not succeed but who, by some force of character or apartness of nature, lend significance to the faceless anonymity around them. These characters— the "lost lady" Marian Forrester, Myra Henshawe, Tom Outland, Profes- sor St. Peter, even the slighter Lucy Gayheart in a later novel—are the most persuasive of Miss Cather's creations, her nearest claims to skill in a field where she was admittedly and obviously incompetent—complex and credible psychology. But somehow she could never bring her opposites into full play in a novel. They remained irreconcilably differentiated, dramatically hostile, morally and socially incapable of true complexity.

The full-bodied and heavily documented novel was never conge- nial to Miss Cather; she rightly understood her art to be one of elimina- tion and selection, which eventually meant that it was an art of simplification and didactic idealization. *The Song of the Lark* and *One of Ours* drag with detail. *My Ántonia* and *A Lost Lady* are her finest successes because there her selection defines, suggests, and evokes without falsely idealizing. When she seized a theme of genuine social and moral potentiality in *The Professor's House* or *My Mortal Enemy*, she pared away its substance until she produced what must always be, to her admirers, disappointingly frugal and bodiless sketches of two of the most interesting subjects in the America of her time. And when she decided to model *Death Comes for the Archbishop* on the pallid two-dimensional murals of Puvis de Chavannes, she prepared the way for the disembodied idealization, making for inert- ness and passivity, that overtook her in *Shadows on the Rock*, weakest of her books and portent of the thinness of her final volumes.

What overtook her plots and characters is the same thing that overtook her version of American life and history. She could not bring her early criticism into effective combination with her later nostalgic sentiment. She represents a case analogous to that of Van Wyck Brooks, who started by vigorously but disproportionately castigating American literature, and has ended in a sentimentalization equally unbalanced and simplistic. So Miss Cather, having never mastered the problem of desire in its full social and moral conditioning, passed from her tales of ambitious artists and defeated dreamers, worsted by provincial mediocrity or career-ism, to versions of American idealism and its defeat that never come to satisfactory grips with the conditions of society and personal morality. As her lovers, her artists, her pioneers, and her visionary Titans become disembodied of complex emotion or thought, so her America itself became disembodied of its principles of growth, conflict, and historical maturity. There obviously worked in her nature that "poetic romanticism" to which Lionel Trilling has referred her case: what Parrington called "the inferior-ity complex of the frontier mind before the old and established"; the pioneer's fear of failure but greater fear of the success which comes "when an idea becomes an actuality"; the doctrine of American individualism to which F. J. Turner credited the pioneer's failure to "understand the rich-ness and complexity of life as a whole." So to Willa Cather's early veneration for the distant goals and shining trophies of desire, ambition, and art, there succeeded a veneration for lost or distant sanctities which gradually spelled her diminution as a dramatic and poetic craftsman. The village, the prairie, the West, the New Mexican missions thus became in time abstractions as unworkable, in any critical or moral sense, as her simplified understanding of Mann's Joseph cycle. Art itself, in her versions of Flaubert, Gogol, Mann, or Katherine Mansfield, took on a remote ideality and aesthetic pathos that do much to explain her distaste for Dostoevsky or Chekhov. And the Church, to which she finally appealed as a human and historical constant, became in her unimplicated and inexpe-rienced view of it the most abstract of all her conceptions, a cultural symbol, not a human or historical actuality, and the least real of any of the standards she invoked in her judgments and criticism of the modern world.

She defended her art in an essay, "The Novel Démeublé," in 1922, which belongs among the theorizings by artists which constituted for Henry James an "accident" which is "happiest, I think, when it is soonest over." At best, it shows Miss Cather's temerity in venturing into "the dim wilderness of theory"; at its worst it must be taken as one of those ventures which justify themselves only because they tell what a restricted view of art some writers must impose on themselves in order to get their own kind of work done. In 1922 it had some value as a warning against the excesses of realism and documentation in fiction, as a preference for feeling and insight over "observation" and "description." But when it went on to assert that Balzac's material—not merely Paris and its houses but "the game of pleasure, the game of business, the game of finance"—is "unworthy of an artist," that the banking system and Stock Exchange are scarcely "worth being written about at all," and that "the higher processes of art are all processes of simplification," it set Miss Cather down as an aesthetic fundamentalist whose achievement was bound, by the nature of her beliefs, to be sharply curtailed and inhibited. She stood by the essay; she reprinted it unmodified in her later editions. And there it shows, *post factum*, how little a principle of deliberate simplification can serve its believer if he is also an artist. Willa Cather set up a standard directly opposed to Zola's program of naturalism—and similarly deluding and disabling in its literalness and crudity. For both sensibility and naturalism arrive at the same impasse when they deny art its right to richness of thought and complexity. What such principles limit is not merely crafts-manship; it is subject-matter itself. Miss Cather saw as little as Zola did that to inhibit craftsmanship or content is to inhibit or starve the sensibil-ity and insight that nourish them, and to arrive at the sterility of high-mindedness and the infirmity of an ideal. It is artists who have denied their art and theory no possible risk, challenge, or complexity who have arrived at the surer lease on creative life; it is to James and Conrad, to Yeats, Eliot, and Valéry, that we turn, in their theory no less than in their practice, for the more responsible clues to endurance and authority in modern literature.

Yet it was by such means of simplification, discipline, curtailment, that Willa Cather made her achievement possible and wrote the books of her best years—books which, if essentially minor in substance, are wholly her own, and if elegiac in their version of American history, revive a past that was once, whatever its innocence, a reality, and that required, in its own delusions as much as in the versions of it she created, the correction and resistance of a later realism. The boy who told the story of My Ántonia, finding himself transported from Virginia to the prairies of Ne-braska, said: "I had the feeling that the world was left behind, that we had got over the edge of it, and were outside man's jurisdiction. I have never before looked up at the sky when there was not a familiar mountain ridge against it." For thirty years Willa Cather found her clue to the heroic values of life in that Western world of open plains and pioneer struggle, lying, with its raw earth, untested possibilities, and summons to heroic endeavor, beyond the familiar jurisdiction of codes and laws. But when, in her last novel, *Sapphira and the Slave Girl* in 1940, she at last turned back, for the first time in her literary career, from Nebraska to the Virginia of her birth and earliest memories, to a country of older laws and severer customs—to Back Creek Valley west of the Blue Ridge and to the house of Henry Colbert, the miller, and his wire Sapphira, a Dodderidge of Loudon County—she brought the air of the more primitive Western world into it, the insistence on primary or primitive emotion.

The story offered the familiar features of her Western books—there is the retreat to the past, now 1856, when human dignity and honor were not yet outlawed by the confused motives and vulgar comforts of modern times; there is the idealizing pathos of distance and lost beauty; there is an epilogue that brings the story twenty-five years nearer—but only to 1881—when time has dissolved old conflicts, relaxed old tensions, and healed old wounds by its touch of grace and humility. There is a stoic husband, asking no questions of an unkind destiny. There is an imperious wife who finds herself exiled in the rough country over the Blue Ridge as earlier heroines like Marian Forrester and Myra Henshawe were exiled in the rough country of the West, self-confounded by her pride and fear of truth, defeating herself rather than allow victory or happiness to others. There is also a young girl, the Negro slave Nancy, on whom Sapphira vents her defeat and jealousy, another embodiment of the spirit of youth and natural grace which had already appeared in Alexandra, Thea, Ántonia, Tom Outland, and Lucy Gayheart—the pure in heart whom no evil can defeat wholly and on whom Miss Cather fixed for her faith in character in an age of warring egotisms and debasing ambition.

Willa Cather thus risked not only a repetition of characters and effects in which her expertness had already passed from mastery to formulation. She duplicated her matter and her pathos so narrowly as to make unavoidable the sensation that what was once a sincere and valid theme had been subjected to a further attenuation of sentimental argument and special pleading. This effect was emphasized by the insistent plainness and simplicity of manner to which she adhered—that conscious simplicity, fiction most decidedly and stubbornly démeublé, which at times (in My Ántonia and A Lost Lady particularly) she raised to a point of conviction and lyric poignance that must remain her one indisputable achievement as an artist, but which on other occasions (One of Ours, Shadows on the Rock) she permitted to lapse either into a kind of didactic dullness of sobriety or into a sentimentality that begs the whole question of creating and substantiating character by means of words, sensation, and observed detail.

Her devotion to the past and its perished beauty was sincere but inevitably limited by a didactic principle and threatened by the inflexibility of an idealistic convention. Only when her sentiment was toughened by personal or atmospheric realism did she bring off her pathos successfully, and only when her idealism was grounded in a hard sense of physical and regional fact was she able to avoid banality and abstraction. To reread the whole of her work is to realize how deliberately she accepted her risks and limitations in order to win her prizes. It is to see that the subtlety and scope of her themes—*The Professor's House* remains the most significant case—could readily fail to find the structure and substance that might have given them life or redeemed them from the tenuity of a sketch. It is to realize that her novels reduce to a single motive and pattern whose sincerity is undeniable but rudimentary and which eventually becomes threadbare. But it is also to admit, finally, that in her best work Willa Cather brought to a kind of climax and genuine epic vision the work of the American women who preceded her—Rose Terry Cooke, Sarah Jewett, Mrs. Freeman—and that she sublimated to its elements a conception of pioneer life and native energy which in other hands has generally lapsed into vulgar romanticism and the more blatant kind of American eloquence.

It was her honesty and persistence in rendering this quality that made possible her real contribution to contemporary, and to American, writing. She defined, like Dreiser, Scott Fitzgerald, and a few other of her contemporaries between 1910 and 1930, a sense of proportion in American experience. She knew what it meant to be raised in the hinterland of privation and harsh necessities; knew what it meant to look for escape to Chicago and the world beyond; knew how much has to be fought in one's youth and origins, what the privileges of the richer world mean when they are approached from the outposts of life, what has to be broken away from and what has to be returned to for later nourishment, and how little the world appears when its romantic distances and remote promise are curtailed to the dimensions of the individual destiny. This sense of tragic limitation forms the saving leaven of realism and moral necessity in Dreiser's novels; Scott Fitzgerald gave superb expression to the experience in the last eight pages of *The Great Gatsby* and in *Tender Is the Night*; Katherine Anne Porter has given another and classic version of it in her work. Willa Cather unquestionably had something to do with preserving for such artists that proportion and perspective in American experience.

The space of seventy years is too short in human history, even in modern history, to permit anyone to claim that he saw the world break in two during it. The measure of the human fate is not to be calculated so conveniently, even in a century of disturbance like the twentieth, and least of all in the moral perspective to which the artist or serious moralist must address himself. To do so is to impose a personal sentiment on something too large to contain it. It was to such sentiment, with its attendant didacticism and inflexibility, that Willa Cather came to submit. But it must also be granted that she lived through a cleavage and a crisis in something more than American life; that she saw "the end of an era, the sunset of the pioneer"; that it "was already gone, that age; nothing could ever bring it back"; and she defined the pathos, if not the challenge and moral imperative, its passing imposed on every survivor and writer concerned with it. She did not succeed in surmounting the confines of her special transition and the resentment it induced in her, and she did not write the kind of books that assure the future or the energy of a literature. That opportunity she consciously rejected. Talents who came after her have written books that surpass hers in conflict and comprehension, as in difficulty and courage—*The Enormous Room, The Sun Also Rises, Tender Is the Night, None Shall Look Back, All the King's Men, A Curtain of Green* and *Delta Wedding, Flowering Judas* and *Pale Horse, Pale Rider, The Sound and the Fury* and *Light in August*. Yet she did something in a time of distraction and cultural inflation to make the way clear for them, as much by the end she defined for one tradition as by the example of tenacity and personal scruple she set for herself. No one who read her books between 1915 and 1930 can forget their poetry of evocation and retrospective beauty—no sensitive reader can miss it today—particularly if he shared, as most Americans have shared, whether intimately or by inheritance, any part of the experience that went into their making. And Willa Cather also did something the aspirant to permanent quality rarely achieves: she wrote a few books—*My Ántonia* and *A Lost Lady* chief among them—that are not only American elegies but American classics, and that can still tell us, in a time of sanctified journalism and irresponsible sophistication, how much of a lifetime it costs to make that rare and expensive article.

JAMES E. MILLER, JR.

"My Ántonia":
A Frontier Drama of Time

Critics of Willa Cather have long been confronted with the baffling persistence in popularity of a novel apparently defective in structure. My Ántonia may well turn out to be Willa Cather's most fondly remembered and best loved novel, while the perfectly shaped, brilliantly executed A Lost Lady continues unread. It does seem strange that one who wanted to unclutter the novel by throwing the furniture out the window should have bungled so badly the structure of one of her most important works.

René Rapin blames Cather for transplanting Ántonia from the country to Black Hawk: "only in her own natural habitat can she hold our attention and capture our emotion." And Rapin censures Cather severely for losing sight of Ántonia completely in the closing books of the novel. David Daiches discovers the source of the defect in Cather's point of view. The "narrator's sensibility," he says, "takes control; and this raises problems which Willa Cather is never quite able to solve." Like Daiches, E. K. Brown is disturbed by the disappearance of Ántonia for pages at a time, and says in the novel's defense: "Everything in the book is there to convey a feeling, not to tell a story, not to establish a social philosophy, not even to animate a group of characters."

Most critics, like Brown, have felt the unified emotional impact of My Ántonia and have grappled with the puzzling problem of the book's actual lack of consistent central action or unbroken character portrayal. It is indeed a fine creative achievement to give the effect of unity when

From American Quarterly 4, vol. 10 (1958). Copyright © 1958 by the Trustees of the University of Pennsylvania.

there apparently is none, and there are those who would claim that the nature of Cather's accomplishment is beyond the critic's understanding, an inscrutable mystery of the artist's miraculous creative process.

The action in My Ántonia is episodic, lacks focus and abounds in irrelevancies (consider the inserted wolf-story of Pavel and Peter, for example). Indeed, there is in the novel no plot in the accepted sense of the word. And further, there is not, as there usually is in the plotless story, a character who remains consistently on stage to dominate the obscurely related events. In the second and third books, entitled respectively "The Hired Girls" and "Lena Lingard," Ántonia fades gradually but completely from view, and the reader becomes engrossed, finally, in the excitingly sensual but abortive relationship of the narrator, Jim Burden, and the voluptuous hired girl turned seamstress, Lena Lingard.

But there is that quality of evoked feeling which penetrates the pages of the book, inhering even in the scenes omitting Ántonia, and which gathers finally to a profound and singular focus which constitutes the emotional unity of the book. We sense what we cannot detect— structural elements subtly at work reinforcing and sharpening the aroused feeling.

Jim Burden's assertion in the "Introduction" that he supposes the manuscript he has written "hasn't any form" should not deceive the reader too readily. He also states of Ántonia, "I simply wrote down pretty much all that her name recalls to me." If these confessions reveal that neither action nor character gives unity to the novel, they also suggest, indirectly, that a feeling—the emotion attached to Ántonia's name—informs the novel structurally. When Jim Burden, dissatisfied with "Ántonia" as his title, prefixes the "My," he is informing the reader in advance that the book is not about the real Ántonia, but rather about Ántonia as personal and poignant symbol. For Jim, Ántonia becomes symbolic of the undeviating cyclic nature of all life: Ántonia is the insistent reminder that it is the tragic nature of time to bring life to fruition through hardship and struggle only to precipitate the decline and, ultimately, death, but not without first making significant provision for new life to follow, flower and fall. The poignancy lies in the inability of the frail human being to rescue and retain any stage, no matter how beautiful or blissful, of his precious cycle. When Jim Burden asserts at the close of My Ántonia that he and Ántonia "possess" the "incommunicable past," he does not convince even himself. It is precisely this emotional conviction that neither they nor anyone else can possess the past, that the past is absolutely and irrevocably "incommunicable" even to those who lived it—which constitutes the novel's unity.

The "feeling" of My Ántonia is not the divorced and remote and discomforting "feeling" of the author, nor the displayed or dramatized "feeling" of a character, but the evoked feeling of the reader. And the element in the novel which produces and controls this feeling exists in the sensibility of the narrator, Jim Burden. It is in the drama of his awakening consciousness, of his growing awareness, that the emotional structure of the novel may be discovered.

It is Jim Burden's sensibility which imposes form on My Ántonia and, by that form, shapes in the reader a sharpened awareness of cyclic fate that is the human destiny. The sense of cyclic fate finds expression first in an obsessive engagement with the colorful, somber and varied seasons of the year, next in an unfolding realization of the immutable and successive phases of human life, and, finally, in an engrossing but bewildering encounter with the hierarchic stages of civilization, from the primitive culture to the sophisticated.

"The Shimerdas," the first book of My Ántonia, introduces from the start the drama of time in the vivid accounts of the shifting seasons. The book encompasses one year, beginning with the arrival in Autumn of the Shimerdas and Jim Burden on the endless Nebraska prairie, portraying the terrible struggle for mere existence in the bleakness of the plains' Winter, dramatizing the return of life with the arrival of Spring, and concluding with the promise of rich harvest in the intense heat of the prairie's Summer. This is Jim Burden's remembered year, and it is his obsession with the cycle of time that has caused him to recall Ántonia in a setting of the changing seasons.

Almost every detail in "The Shimerdas" is calculated to shrink the significance of the human drama in contrast with the drama of the seasons, the drama of nature, the drama of the land and sky. The struggle becomes, then, not merely a struggle for a minimum subsistence from the stubborn, foreign soil, but also even more a struggle to re-create and assert existence in a seemingly hostile or indifferent land. No doubt all of the Nebraska pioneers experienced Jim Burden's sensation on arriving on the prairie: "Between that earth and that sky I felt erased, blotted out."

The drama of "The Shimerdas" is the drama of the human being at the mercy of the cyclic nature of the universe. The "glorious autumn" of their arrival on the treeless prairie contributes to that acute sense that "the world was left behind" and that they "had got over the edge of it." The autumn is not the autumn of bountiful nature but the autumn of vast distances and approaching death. The descent of the winter snows heightens the vast primitive beauty of the undisturbed plains: "The sky was brilliantly blue, and the sunlight on the glittering white stretches of prairie was almost blinding." But even innate to the sharp-colored beauty is an apparent hostility. The whiteness not only blinds but brings in its wake despair and death. When, after the first primitive struggle is over, Ántonia cries out to Jim in the midst of summer, "I wish my papa live to see this summer. I wish no winter ever come again," she displays intuitive insight into the relation of her father's suicide to the cosmic order of time which decrees that the death of winter must unfailingly follow the ripening autumn.

Like autumn, spring when it comes to the prairie is not so much manifest in visible nature as it is a hovering presence compellingly alive and dominant: "There was only—spring itself; the throb of it, the light restlessness, the vital essence of it everywhere: in the sky, in the swift clouds, in the pale sunshine, and in the warm, high wind." It is only with the arrival of spring, at its appointed time, that the Shimerdas and the Burdens, Ántonia and Jim, can emerge from the enforced retreat of winter to look forward to some benevolence from the enduring land. But as the winter shaped, and even took, the life of the prairie pioneer, so the spring imposes a cruelly exacting ritual of tilling and tending the virgin land. Life is hard and the soil close and unyielding without its due. And the "breathless, brilliant heat" of summer, when it descends with fiery fury on the empty lands, brings with its devastation also fertility: "The burning sun of those few weeks, with occasional rains at night, secured the corn."

Throughout the first book of My Ántonia, it is the world of nature rather than the human world which dominates, and even the human beings tend to identify themselves with the things of the land. One of Jim Burden's first vivid sensations in the new land is in his grandmother's garden: "I was something that lay under the sun and felt it, like the pumpkins, and I did not want to be anything more. I was entirely happy." During their first year on the prairie the rotation of the decreed seasons imposes a primitive existence not far different from that of the plains' animals, and impresses on the pioneers a keenly felt truth: "In a new country a body feels friendly to the animals." If in the garden Jim imagined himself a pumpkin, there were other times when he and the rest felt a sympathetic resemblance to the gopher, in their intimate dependence on the land for sustenance and home. At the end of this first year's struggle with the land, Ántonia emerges with an essential and profound wisdom that only the cyclic seasons in their cruelty and their beneficence could bestow. She reveals to Jim, "Things . . . will be hard for us."

As Ántonia and Jim are shaped and "created" by the successive seasons, so their lives in turn are cycles of a larger order in time, and shape and create the nation. It is in the dramatization of Ántonia from the girlhood of the opening pages through her physical flowering in the middle books to, finally, her reproduction of the race in a flock of fine boys in the final pages of the book that her life is represented, like the year with its seasons, as a cycle complete in its stages of birth, growth, fruition and decline. Although Ántonia's life represents a greater cycle than that of the year, the pattern remains the same in both. The year, of course, is merely a term for the designation of a unit of time, and its resemblance to the life-cycle suggests that life, too, is a physical representation of time.

As the seasons of fall, winter, spring and summer impose a structure on the first book of Willa Cather's novel, the successive stages of Ántonia's life assist in imposing a structure on the total work. We may trace these stages through the various books into which the novel is subdivided. Some critics have called Ántonia an earth goddess. She is a re-creation of an archetypal pattern—woman as the embodiment of self-assured if not self-contained physical fertility which insures the endurance of the race. Ántonia never despairs, not even in the first book of the novel in which the hostility of the first prairie winter deprives her of her father; but throughout she works and lives with an innate dignity which springs from her intuitive knowledge of her appointed function in the continuation of the species. Even in the second book, called "The Hired Girls," Ántonia feels no sense of an enforced inferiority but rather a supreme reliance on the hidden resources bestowed upon her by the hard physical struggles of her past.

As Ántonia stands out sharply in the first book, in the second she merges with many "hired girls" in Black Hawk who are of her kind, and in the third, called "Lena Lingard," she does not even appear except as a remembered presence in the talks about the past between Lena and Jim Burden in Lincoln. In these conversations there is a foreshadowing of Ántonia's fate which is the subject of the fourth book, entitled "The Pioneer Woman's Story." If in Book I Ántonia represents the eternal endurance under supreme hardship of woman appointed propagator of the race, and in Book II she represents the overflowing liveliness and energetic abundance of physical woman come to the flower, in Books III and IV she symbolizes the calm and faithful endurance of woman eternally wronged. In Ántonia's fierce love for her fatherless child exists the full explanation of mankind's continuing to be. But Willa Cather insists on Ántonia's appearing in a double role, not only as woman wronged, but also as woman fulfilled in her destiny. In the last book of the novel, "Cuzak's Boys," Ántonia is glimpsed in her declining years surrounded by the "explosive life" of her many children. When Jim Burden sees her after the absence of all those years, he recognizes in her the persistence of that quality he had sensed when they roamed the prairie as boy and girl: "She was there, in the full vigor of her personality, battered but not diminished, looking at me, speaking to me in the husky, breathy voice I remembered so well."

In the closing books of My Ántonia ("The Pioneer Woman's Story" and "Cuzak's Boys"), Ántonia emerges as vividly as she did in the first. For an explanation of the fading of Ántonia in Books II and III ("The Hired Girls" and "Lena Lingard"), we must turn to a third principle of structure operating in the book, another cycle greater in scope than either a year or a life. For a foreshadowing of this cycle we may turn to Frederick Jackson Turner and his famous essay, "The Significance of the Frontier in American History." Turner asserted, in the late nineteenth century, that the distinguishing feature of America's development was the cyclic character of her movement westward, conquering over and over again a new wilderness. There was, Turner said, "a recurrence of the process of evolution in each western area reached in the process of expansion."

My Ántonia exemplies superbly Turner's concept of the recurring cultural evolution on the frontier. There is first of all the migration from the East, in the case of the Shimerdas from Czechoslovakia, in Jim Burden's case from Virginia, both lands of a high cultural level. In the West these comparatively sophisticated people are compelled literally to begin over again, on a primitive level, shedding their cultural attainment like an animal its skin, and, like animals, doing battle with the land and the elements for the meanest food and shelter.

The books of My Ántonia reflect the varying stages of this evolutionary process in cultural development. On this level of structure, not the seasons of the year, nor the phases of Ántonia's life, but the successive cultural plateaus of the nation operate as ordering elements in the novel. And it is on this level of significance and in the dramatization of this epic archetypal cycle of the country that justification for those sections of the book, so frequently condemned because they lose focus on Ántonia, may be found.

In the first book, "The Shimerdas," the newly arrived pioneers from the East discover nothing but their strength and the prairie's stubborn soil out of which to create for themselves a new world in their own image. In this primitive struggle with the prairie, on a level with the struggle of prehistoric man in the dawn of time, some lose their lives, some their spirit, and all lose that overlay of softening civilization which they brought from the East. There is not only the primitive struggle, but these pioneers become primitive men in the harshness of the struggle. Ántonia's father, sad for the old country, dies; and Ántonia takes a man's place behind the plow. On the prairie the elements, the sky and the land impose a communal democracy in all of the meager human institutions.

"The Hired Girls," the second book of My Ántonia, portrays a higher stage in the cultural evolution of the frontier: the small town comes to the wilderness. If Jim Burden discovers his own hidden courage and becomes a man in the snake-killing incident of Book I, in Book II he discovers the genuine complexity of adulthood, especially in a social context which the bare prairie does not afford. Jim is puzzled by the stratification of society in Black Hawk, a stratification that could not exist on the virgin prairie, and which does not tally with Jim's moral judgment: the "hired girls" are for Jim the most interesting, the most exciting and the liveliest of all possible companions, far superior to the dull conformists of the town. It is the strong lure of the hired girls, however, which precipitates Jim's first crucial decision: in spite of the strong spiritual and physical attraction of these girls, Jim turns to the study which will prepare him for college and which, in Black Hawk, culminates in the triumph of his high school commencement oration. Already there has come to the frontier prairie that element whose absence caused Ántonia's father to despair. After Ántonia has heard Jim's speech, she tells him: "there was something in your speech that made me think so about my papa." In her instinctive way Ántonia dimly understands her father's sacrifice of his life and Jim's yearning for higher intellectual achievement, even though her own destiny, centered in the physical reproduction of the race, may be and is to be fulfilled on the innocent and unsophisticated prairie.

Jim's discoveries, both intellectual and emotional, of Book II, are continued and intensified in the next book, "Lena Lingard." Lincoln, Nebraska, is as far above Black Hawk culturally as Black Hawk is above the empty, untouched prairie, and though the university has the limitations imposed by the isolation of the plains, there is "an atmosphere of endeavour, of expectancy and bright hopefulness" which prevails. It is Jim's good fortune to develop a close association with Gaston Cleric, the intellectually alive and intense head of the Latin Department, who introduces Jim to the exciting world of ideas. Jim discovers that "when one first enters that world everything else fades for a time, and all that went before is as if it had not been." But the climax of Jim's awakening is a realization of the persistence of the past: "Yet I found curious survivals; some of the figures of my old life seemed to be waiting for me in the new." Jim's awareness of the crucial impingement of his prairie heritage on his involvement in a received culture seems an instinctive artistic confirmation of Turner's frontier thesis.

Culture does come to the Nebraska prairie, not only in the form of a world of ideas via Gaston Cleric, but also in the form of music and theater. The nature of the curious impact is revealed brilliantly when Jim describes his and Lena's reaction to the traveling "Camille": "A couple of jack rabbits, run in off the prairie, could not have been more innocent of what awaited them." Throughout Book III of the novel, there is a delightful rediscovery by the children of the pioneer generation of a cultural world forsaken by their parents for the hard and isolated life of the prairie. But the pioneer values of freshness and courage and integrity—and many more—survive and condition the responses.

Lincoln, Nebraska, though it offers much, offers a mere token of what waits in the rich and glittering East. Lured on by bright dreams of intellectual achievement, Jim Burden follows Gaston Cleric to Harvard, which, in the book's developing hierarchy, is to Lincoln as Lincoln is to Black Hawk and Black Hawk to the barren prairie. But with the dramatization of three stages of civilization as it comes to the wilderness, and with the suggestion of the future destiny by the "invocation" of "ancient" Harvard and by the suggestion of greater cultural riches farther East, Willa Cather shifts the focus from the dream of the nation and, indeed, of civilization, back to Ántonia of the prairies. The novel has, in a sense, come full circle when Jim, in the last book, finds himself in the midst of that very culture the nostalgic remembrance of which drove Ántonia's father to despair: "Once when I was abroad I went into Bohemia, and from Prague I sent Ántonia some photographs of her native village." By this casual visit, the return to the point of origin, the cycle of cultural movement is symbolically completed. And when the sophisticated, world-traveled, perhaps even world-weary, Jim Burden returns to the prairie scenes of his boyhood and discovers Ántonia and her houseful of boys, he discovers at the same time the enduring quality of those values not dependent on cultural level, but accessible on the untutored prairies. Ántonia, "in the full vigour of her personality, battered but not diminished," not only endures but achieves an emotionally and physically fulfilled life. Her boys are her triumphant creative achievement.

My Ántonia closes with the dominant image of the circle, a significant reminder of the general movement of all the structural elements in the book. After his visit with Ántonia, Jim confesses, "I had the sense of coming home to myself, and of having found out what a little circle man's experience is." This vivid image reinforces the cyclic theme which pervades the book: the cycle of the seasons of the year, the cycle of the stages of human life, the cycle of the cultural phases of civilization. My *Ántonia* is, then, ultimately about time, about the inexorable movement of future into present, of present into past. Against the backdrop of this epic drama of the repetitive movement of time, man poignantly plays out his role. Ántonia, when she cries out to Jim, "I wish no winter ever come again," more nearly expresses the essence of the book's theme than does Jim when he asserts at the end, "whatever we had missed, we possessed together the precious, the incommunicable past." *Optima dies . . . prima fugit*, translated by Jim as "the best days are the first to flee," stands as the book's epigraph. This intensely felt awareness of the past *as past* is the emotional heart of the novel, and is evoked and sustained by the book's several levels of structure and their involvement with the revolving cycles of time.

JOHN H. RANDALL III

The Protestant Past:
"Sapphira and the Slave Girl"

During the course of my studies I have tried to trace Willa Cather's development, to show how she started out by portraying heroic individualists who struggle successfully to master their environment, then, under the influence of personal and social events in the twenties and thirties, gradually evolved a way of looking at the world which was traditional and hierarchic. I have also tried to show how she was unable to maintain this latter view for any length of time and kept drifting back from an affirmation of feudal social arrangements to an exaltation of the individual, although in such stories as *Lucy Gayheart* and "The Best Years" the individualist view she expresses is a sentimentalized and debased version of that which had formed the basis of her prairie novels. Now, at the end of her career, she writes a novel in which both versions of the ideal life and society are inconsistently mixed. For *Sapphira and the Slave Girl* starts out as an affirmation of individualism; then it completely reverses its values and ends up by strongly affirming both feudal hierarchy and the authority of the group.

I have suggested earlier that after her parents' deaths Willa Cather seemed to be shocked out of her preoccupation with Catholic culture; at any rate, following her father's death and the completion of *Shadows on the Rock* she never treated Catholic themes again. The break-up of her family carried her mind back to her own past and reawakened an interest in the scenes of her childhood and adolescence, as we saw in the short stories of *Obscure Destinies* and in *Lucy Gayheart*. But, apparently feeling that she had worked that vein out (certainly a reader feels so), in the autumn of

---

1937 she began a new novel which was entirely different from any other she had written, with a setting which went back even farther into her past, to her very early childhood, to the mountains of Virginia which she had left at the age of eight. The story takes place in her grandparents' time before the Civil War, and is about that radical Protestant movement, abolitionism. She had long intended to write a story about her Virginia memories as a favor to her father. At about the same time as the publication of the book she told a newspaper reporter who questioned her about what religion she held, "I'm an Episcopalian and a good one, I hope!" Thus it seems quite likely that Willa Cather intended the book to be a tribute to her family's Protestant heritage.

The story tells how Sapphira Dodderidge, a Loudoun County aristocrat who is afraid of becoming an old maid, takes "a long step downward" to marry Henry Colbert, who is a miller by profession, a "foreigner" by extraction (his grandfather came from Flanders), and a democrat in his manners. To escape from the stigma that must ensue from such a poor match she and her husband move across the mountains to a farm she owns on the edge of the wilderness. There they resume their separate occupations, he being the only miller in the district, and she the only practicing aristocrat.

A lapse of twenty-five years finds them somewhat estranged from each other: Henry now sleeps down at the millhouse, while Sapphira stays on at the manor. Because she is afflicted with dropsy and has been unable to get out of a wheelchair alone for four years, Sapphira's suspicions are easily aroused, and she becomes extremely jealous of the young yellow girl Nancy who keeps Henry's room down at the mill for him. Thinking that Nancy and her husband are having an affair, she determines to ruin the girl. She invites Henry's wild young nephew Martin Colbert, "the worst rake in the country," to visit them and then takes every opportunity possible to throw Nancy in Martin's way. Harried beyond endurance, Nancy finally appeals to Sapphira's daughter Rachel Blake, who never has been sympathetic with her mother's slaveholding mentality and autocratic temperament. Rachel helps Nancy escape to Canada via the Underground Railroad. The money needed for the venture is supplied by the miller, but, although he is firmly convinced that slavery is wrong, he does not think he has the right to interfere with his wife's personal property. Instead of facing the issue squarely and realizing he must make a decision, he adopts the equivocal course of leaving his coat hanging overnight by an open window with a hundred dollars in its pocket, telling Rachel in advance that he is going to do so. Nancy escapes successfully and returns twenty-five years later after the Civil War to visit with her old friends, who include Willa Cather's father and mother. For some reason Willa Cather includes herself in the story as a child of five who is all agog to see the yellow girl she had heard so much about. Later she rightly considered this to be an artistic error, and regretted having included the episode.

The main conflict in the book is that between Sapphira on the one hand and her husband and daughter on the other, arising from the former's jealous persecution of the slave girl Nancy; a persecution which outrages every moral feeling the other two possess. She is able to undertake her cruel scheme only because of the abuses possible under the institution of slavery. This is not the first time she has abused her position as mistress of her establishment; she had done wrong to Nancy's mother Till a generation earlier by marrying her to a "capon man" because Till was a lady's maid and because, in the words of the Negro cook, she didn't want a lady's maid to be "havin' chillun all over de place,—always a-carryin' or a-nussin' 'em." Now she inflicts grievous wrong on the daughter Nancy by forcing her into a position where her rights as a human being are completely abrogated. The situation is well summed up by Rachel's reflections at a crucial point just before she makes up her mind to help Nancy escape:

> Mrs. Colbert had turned on Nancy; that was well known. Now she had the worst rake in the country staying in her house, and she was sending the girl up into the woods alone, after giving him fair warning. Did her mother really want to ruin Nancy? Could her spite go so far as that?
>
> Rachael Blake closed her eyes and leaned her head and arms forward on her dresser top. She had known her mother to show great kindness to her servants, and, sometimes, cold cruelty. But she had never known her to do anything quite so ugly as this, if Nancy's tale were true.

This is not the only criticism of the "peculiar institution" voiced in the book. Willa Cather informs us that Rachel had been openly opposed to slavery since the time she was twelve years old and had overheard a conversation between the abolitionist postmistress of their village and her father, who had wanted to buy a slave for her. Miss Cather writes:

> A feeling long smothered had blazed up in her—had become a conviction. She had never heard the things said before, never put into words. It was the *owning* that was wrong, the relation itself, no matter how convenient or agreeable it might be for master or servant. She had always known it was wrong. It was the thing that made her unhappy at home, and came between her and her mother. How she hated her mother's voice in sarcastic reprimand to the servants! And she hated it in contemptuous indulgence.

And later in the book:

Ever since she could remember, she had seen her mother show shades of kindness and cruelty which seemed to her purely whimsical.

The miller, being of Flemish extraction and thus an alien to the Loudoun County aristocracy from which his wife came, does not share her slaveholding views, and the daughter takes after him rather than her mother. But there is another level of conflict between husband and wife which has to do with religious differences; Sapphira is an Anglican, while her husband and daughter have strong Baptist connections. Willa Cather makes this clear very early in the book when describing the miller's courtship.

With his father he regularly attended a dissenting church supported by small farmers and artisans. He was certainly no match for Captain Dodderidge's daughter.

And later, in speaking of Sapphira's attendance at the Anglican communion, she remarks:

The miller, of course, did not accompany her. Although he had been married in Christ Church, by an English rector, he had no love for the Church of England.

So the conflict between Henry Colbert and his wife is among other things a conflict of social and religious traditions: between the Episcopalian slaveholding hierarchy of Virginia and a radical Protestant egalitarianism and abolitionism.

The struggle between Henry and Sapphira is apparent from the very first chapter. In a scene which serves as a trope for the whole novel the miller is having breakfast with his wife when she casually mentions the possibility of selling Nancy to a friend. Immediately a strong feeling of resentment and hostility appears beneath the customary veneer of good manners and domestic courtesy:

Her husband pushed back his plate. "Nancy least of all! Her mother is here, and old Jezebel. Her people have been in your family for four generations. You haven't trained Nancy for Mrs. Grimwood. She stays here."

The icy quality, so effective with her servants, came into Mrs. Colbert's voice as she answered him.

"It's nothing to get flustered about, Henry. As you say, her mother and grandmother and great-grandmother were all Dodderidge niggers. So it seems to me I ought to be allowed to arrange Nancy's future. Her mother would approve. She knows that a proper lady's maid can never be trained out here in this rough country."

The miller's frown darkened. "You can't sell her without my

name on the deed of sale, and I will never put it there. You never seemed to understand how, when we first moved up here, your troup of niggers was held against us. This isn't a slave-owning neighbourhood. If you sold a good girl like Nancy off to Winchester, people hereabouts would hold it against you. They would say hard things."

The same kind of hostility is discernible in the relations between Rachel and Sapphira. A strong undercurrent of antagonism existed between Rachel and her mother; she had always been unhappy as long as she had lived at home, and Willa Cather reflects: "Rachel had always been difficult,—rebellious toward the fixed ways which satisfied other folk. Mrs. Colbert had been heartily glad to get her married and out of the home at seventeen." Their conflicting attitudes are dramatized in the passage in which Rachel is identified with the spirit of radical Protestantism, so important in the abolition movement:

> Her daughter sometimes felt a kind of false pleasantness in the voice. Yet, she reflected as she listened to the letter, it was scarcely false—it was the only kind of pleasantness her mother had,—not very warm.
>
> As Mrs. Colbert finished, Mrs. Blake said heartily: "That is surely a good letter. Aunt Sarah always writes a good letter."
>
> Mrs. Colbert took off her glasses, glancing at her daughter with a mischievous smile. "You are not put out because she makes fun of your Baptists a little?"
>
> "No. She's a right to. I'd never have joined with the Baptists if I could have got to Winchester to our own Church. But a body likes to have some place to worship. And the Baptists are good people."
>
> "So your father thinks. But then he never did mind to forgather with common people. I suppose that goes with a miller's business."
>
> "Yes, the common folks hereabouts have got to have flour and meal, and there's only one mill for them to come to." Mrs. Blake's voice was rather tart. She wished it hadn't been, when her mother said unexpectedly and quite graciously:
>
> "Well, you've surely been a good friend to them, Rachel."
>
> Mrs. Blake bade her mother good-bye and hurried down the passage. At times she had to speak out for the faith that was in her; faith in the Baptists not so much as a sect (she still read her English Prayer Book every day), but as well-meaning men and women.

So far so good; *Sapphira and the Slave Girl* starts out to be a very readable and powerful novel. But then Willa Cather does a disconcerting thing. About three-quarters of the way through she completely reverses the values upon which the book is based, so that instead of the democratic Rachel being the heroine, the protagonist now becomes the autocratic and imperious Sapphira. Sticking up for the underdog gives way to acceptance of a social system which Willa Cather has already admitted to be unjust. The result is a blurring and a complete loss of definition of the moral issues involved. For the first two hundred and thirty pages the book's main center of interest is Nancy, and the story is concerned with her growth from slavery to freedom, from innocence to experience. She is another in the long line of Cather protagonists who have to struggle to free themselves from a hostile environment:

> She was to go out from the dark lethargy of the cared-for and irresponsible; to make her own way in this world where nobody is altogether free, and the best that can happen to you is to walk your own way and be responsible to God only. Sapphira's darkies were better cared for, better fed and better clothed than the poor whites in the mountains. Yet what ragged, shag-haired, squirrel-shooting mountain man would change places with Sampson, his trusted head miller?

Here slavery is clearly equated with being cared for and freedom with taking care of oneself. This is exactly the attitude of Thea Kronborg and other early Cather heroines for whom the process of growing up includes breaking away from the family; it is at once self-reliant, Puritan, and individualistic. But later in the same book Willa Cather includes episodes which completely contradict this attitude. She shows Nancy going to pieces as a result of persistent molestation by Martin ("I'm goin' to throw myself into the millpawnd, I am!" she makes her say at one point) and later has her doze off in the wagon in which she is being rescued because, as she says, "The girl seemed worn out and dulled by the day's excitement." Later still Willa Cather makes Nancy lose her courage completely and beg to be taken back to her family and friends.

> "Oh, Miz' Blake, please mam, take me home! I can't go off amonst strangers. It's too hard. Let me go back an' try to do better. I don't mind Miss Sapphy scoldin'. Why, she brought me up, an' now she's sick an' sufferin'. Look at her pore feet. I ought-a borne it better. Miz' Blake, please mam, I want to go home to the mill an' my own folks."
> "Now don't talk foolish. What about Martin?"
> "I kin keep out-a his way, Miz' Blake. He won't be there always. I can't bear it to belong nowheres!"

After building her character up in the first part of the novel, Willa Cather whittles it down again. Actions such as these diminish Nancy's stature, and completely disrupt what seems to be the original moral purpose of the story.

The same process of building up a character only to undercut her later on can be seen in the characterization of Rachel Blake. In the early part of the book Rachel is the only one with a mind of her own, who is not afraid to speak out against injustice and who stands up for Nancy's rights as a human being when the latter is being persecuted by Martin and Sapphira. But toward the end of the book we hear strangely little of her. After her part in the escape has become known there is a complete break between her mother and her. She receives a letter containing the following message:

> Mistress Blake is kindly requested to make no further visits at the Mill House.
>
> Sapphira Dodderidge Colbert

Then Willa Cather, apparently at a loss as to how to resolve the conflict she has set up, has recourse to a *deus ex machina* once more. A diphtheria epidemic comes along and carries off one of Rachel's children; Sapphira hears about it and invites Rachel and the remaining child to spend the winter at her house, and then, strangely enough, it is the mother who forgives the daughter instead of the other way around. The miller, who had formerly been at least passively on Rachel's side, switches around and comes to admire Sapphira. Then we suddenly discover that family insubordination is wrong and that Willa Cather is all for autocracy:

> He seemed in a moment to feel sharply so many things he had grown used to and taken for granted: her long illness, with all its discomforts, and the intrepid courage with which she had faced the inevitable. He reached out for her two hands and buried his face in her palms. She felt his tears wet on her skin. For a long while he crouched thus, leaning against her chair, his head on her knees.
>
> He had never understood his wife very well, but he had always been proud of her. When she was young, she was fearless and independent, she held her head high and made this Mill House a place where town folks liked to come. After she was old and ill, she never lowered her flag; not even now, when she knew the end was not far off. He had seen strong men quail and whimper at the approach of death. He, himself, dreaded it. But as he leaned against her chair with his face hidden, he knew how it would be with her; she would make her death easy for everyone, because she would meet it with that composure which he had sometimes called heartlessness, but which now seemed to him strength. As long as she was conscious, she would be mistress of the situation and of herself.
>
> After this long silence, in which he seemed to know that she followed his thoughts, he lifted his head, still holding fast to her hands, and spoke falteringly. "Yes, dear wife, do let us have Rachel here. You are a kind woman to think of it. You are good to a great many folks, Sapphy."

"Not so good as Rachel, with her basket!" She turned it off lightly, tweaking his ear.

"There are different ways of being good to folks," the miller held out stubbornly, as if this idea had just come to him and he was not to be teased into letting go of it. "Sometimes keeping people in their place is being good to them."

As a work of art the book, however interesting, is a failure. Henry Colbert's final acceptance of his wife's ethical and social ideas is, of course, a complete espousal of hierarchy and "the great principle of subordination" and completely undercuts the novel's chief significant action, the freeing of Nancy by Rachel Blake. As it stands, the book simply will not hold together. Willa Cather starts the book as if it were a novel of her early period and ends up writing in her later vein. The shift from emphasis on the individual (Rachel) to emphasis on the group (Sapphira's feudal establishment) here occurs within the confines of a single novel, thus recapitulating the author's entire development. But however convenient this complete inversion of values may be for the literary historian, it completely wrecks the story as a work of art by knocking out its moral center. We are presented with two contradictory views of human nature: one, having Rachel as its exponent, consists in the belief that equality is a moral requirement and that some measure of dignity and respect is due to every man as a human right; the other, represented by Sapphira, holds that equality consists of treating equals as equals and unequals as unequals. There is a complete confusion of values between a feudal Episcopalian hierarchy and a democratic Puritan individualism. The two are clearly incompatible, and Willa Cather makes no effort to show that the state of tension between the two is a tension which exists in life itself. Instead she veers from all-out rugged individualism to complete group conformity, and we are left in no doubt as to the fact that it is Sapphira who gets Willa Cather's final approval.

The necessity which Willa Cather apparently felt for a happy ending, however unbelievable, for a reconciliation between mother and daughter and restoration of peace within the family fold, completes the ruin of what starts out to be a powerful and dramatic novel. Everything in the novel points to a tragic ending, for the way its structure is set up there can be no reconciliation if Nancy is to go free. But Willa Cather does not have the courage to follow out the logical implications of the situation and bring the story to its inevitable conclusion. It is evident that her later view of life definitely interfered with her handling of the novel, and by undercutting its moral realism, reduced its artistic worth.

Miss Elizabeth Sergeant, in her remarks about the writing of the novel, throws some interesting light on its curious reversal of values. She says of Willa:

> She was then [1939] engaged with Sapphira, and told us that she had discarded some six pounds of manuscript dealing with the Shenandoah Valley background.
>   . . . in her zest for the novel démeublé, she threw out many pages and chapters to give Sapphira the central place.

So it seems that Willa Cather herself had trouble making up her mind who the real heroine was, although she finally decided in favor of the authoritarian Sapphira. There must have been complete confusion in her mind as to which of the opposing value systems claimed her final allegiance. In this book more than in any other the conflict between value systems destroys her vision of reality and makes a hash of her art. It seems clear that all the ambiguities and uncertainties implicit in her view of life come out in her treatment of Sapphira. For Sapphira is a projection of Willa Cather's own mother, the gay, laughing, imperious Virginia Boak Cather; the early Rachel is the young Willa Cather striving to break away from the family and find a place of her own in the world; the later Rachel is the older Willa Cather who, filled with remorse at her parents' deaths, wanted nothing so much as to be accepted back again into the now nonexistent family group; and the older Willa Cather is also seen in Henry Colbert, who buries his face in the palms of his wife's hands and doggedly admits that she is right. For whether consciously or not, in this story Willa Cather has given us an allegory of her whole life, from the young adolescent's departure from the bosom of her parents to the frustrated elderly lady's defeated return. If she ends the novel with the triumph of the mother-figure, it is because for her that was the only ending that was psychologically possible, however unconvincing it may appear to the reader.

DOROTHY VAN GHENT

Willa Cather

It is customary to speak of Willa
Cather as an "elegist" of the American pioneer tradition. "Elegy" suggests
celebration and lament for a lost and irrecoverable past; but the boldest
and most beautiful of Willa Cather's fictions are characterizied by a sense
of the past not as an irrecoverable quality of events, wasted in history, but
as persistent human truth repossessed—salvaged, redeemed—by virtue of
memory and art.

Her art is a singular one. The prose style is suave, candid, transparent, a style shaped and sophisticated in the great European tradition; her
teachers were Homer and Virgil, Tolstoi and Flaubert. But the creative
vision that is peculiarly hers is deeply primitive, psychologically archaic in
an exact sense. In that primitivism was her great strength, for it allowed
the back door of her mind to keep open, as it were, to the rumor and
movement of ancestral powers and instinctive agencies.

Closely related to this gift was her sensitivity to the land, its
textures, horizons, weathers. "Whenever I crossed the Missouri River
coming in to Nebraska," she said, "the very smell of the soil tore me to
pieces. . . . I almost decided to settle down on a quarter section of land
and let my writing go." Elizabeth Sergeant, her friend and a discerning
critic of her work, wrote, "I saw that her intimacy with nature lay at the
very root . . . of her power to work at all." She had been brought to
Nebraska, from Virginia, when she was nine. This was in 1883, when
Nebraska was still frontier territory, almost bare of human landmarks; the
settlers lived in sod houses, scarcely distinguishable from the earth, or in
caves in the clay bluffs; roads were faint wagon trails in a sea of red grass.
The removal from an old, lush, settled country to a virtual wilderness was
undoubtedly the determinative event of Willa Cather's life; occurring when

From *Willa Cather* (Pamphlets on American Writers) no. 36 (1964). Copyright © 1964 by
University of Minnesota.

the child was entering puberty and most sensitive to change, the uprooting from the green valley of her grandparents' home in Virginia, and the casting out upon a limitless wild prairie, opened her sensibility to primordial images and relationships that were to be the most powerful forces in her art.

After a year of homesteading, Charles Cather moved his family into the little town of Red Cloud, where he opened an office dealing in farm loans and mortgages. They lived in a house much like that of the Kronborgs in *The Song of the Lark*, with seven children crowded in a narrow boxcar arrangement of rooms and a leaky attic where the older ones slept. Willa started going to school here; on the farm, her grandmother had begun teaching her Greek and Latin, and she continued these studies now with an old man who kept a general store down the street. Years later her friend Edith Lewis wrote of that Nebraska girlhood, which she too had known: "I remember how lost in the prairies Red Cloud seemed to me, going back to that country after a number of years; as if the hot wind that so much of the time blew over it went on and left it behind, isolated, forgotten by the rest of the world . . . And I felt again that forlornness, that terrible restlessness that comes over young people born in small towns in the middle of the continent." That aridity and drabness formed another decisive pattern in the girl's emotional nature, a traumatic one that reappears in the stories and novels as a desperate impulse of "escape" from a surrounding and voracious mediocrity. Her own resistances took the form of rebellion against conventionality; she cut her hair short like a boy's, wore boy's clothes, created scandal by setting up a laboratory for zoological experiments, hung around listening to the conversation of the older men of the town.

Her "escape" was slow, uneven, costing years of drudgery. From 1891 to 1895, a period of crop failures and financial depression, she attended the state university at Lincoln, meeting many of her expenses by writing for the Sunday issue of the *State Journal*; at a dollar a column, by writing a tremendous number of columns she was able to scrape through. For the next decade, from her twenty-third to her thirty-third year, she worked at various jobs in Pittsburgh: for five years as a newspaperwoman, at first on the *Home Monthly*, a suffocatingly parochial "family magazine," then on the *Daily Leader*, where she read copy, edited telegraphic news, and wrote dramatic criticism; and five years as a teacher of English and Latin in the Pittsburgh high schools. In 1903 she published a book of poems, *April Twilights*, slight pieces of imitative cadence; and in 1905 her first book of stories, *The Troll Garden*, was published by S. S. McClure— who immediately offered her a post in New York on his then brilliant magazine. Her work on *McClure's Magazine* was highly successful—she

rapidly became managing editor—and exhausting; probably the most valu-
able experience during this period was her brief friendship with the writer
Sarah Orne Jewett (Miss Jewett died within the year), whose sensitive
criticism seems to have reoriented her writing, away from "literary" models
and toward the material and the voice which were genuinely her own. In
1912, the year of the publication of her first novel, *Alexander's Bridge*, she
resigned from *McClure's*, and from that time on was able to live the quiet
and dedicated life of her craft.

Miss Cather said frequently that the only part of her life which
made a lasting impression on her imagination and emotion was what
happened before she was twenty. No doubt the remark overcondenses and
oversimplifies, but one finds an impressive truth in it when one looks at
those early years in the light of her mature work. There was the deprived
adolescence in the sterile little midwestern town; there were the traumatic
tensions leading to "escape." She was never able to free herself from this
negative theme, and under its warping tendency she was led frequently to
substitute strained personal emotion and belief for creative intuition. But
another, far more subtle, essentially mysterious theme was also an effect of
that adolescent deprivation: this was the theme of a "self" at once more
generic and more individual than the self allowed to live by the constric-
tions of American adulthood. It is as if the aridities of her girlhood, and
the drudgery that followed, had left her with a haunting sense of a "self"
that had been effaced and that tormented her for realization. She was to
search for it in elusive ways all her life, and sometimes, in her greatest
novels, when she left off searching for it she found it.

Connected with that search was a quest for "ancestors." One
thinks of that great faceless prairie, stretching empty to the jumping-off
places of the earth, where the nine-year-old child was thrust to find its
identity. Where were the beginnings? Where the human continuities, the
supporting and enfolding "past," the streets, the houses, the doors, the
images of care and contact? Even trees were so rare, and had such a hard
fight to grow, that one visited them anxiously as if they were persons. One
felt instinctively, in that shoreless emptiness, a special charism in the
secretive animals—snakes and badgers—that warned one to be friendly
with them; one might need their help. When Willa Cather first visited the
ancient cliff-dweller ruins of Arizona, in 1912, she experienced a shock of
recognition as intense, troubling, and exalting as that felt by Keats when
he first saw the Elgin marbles. Here, in these desolate little cities,
"mountain built with peaceful citadel," were the places of the ancestors,
their streets and doorways, their hanging gardens of cactus, their inner
chambers, the signs of their care and contact in traces of the potter's

thumb on shards of clay vessels. She was to write of them again and again, and make many pack trips back to that country. Like the theme of the lost self, this too was a theme of recovery: to recover the ancestors, to redeem them from their forgotten places, to make them speak. A great loneliness—the American loneliness—invests these themes: and something else, the need of a form of integration between the self and the human past, in order that life may be affirmed and celebrated. She was to achieve that celebratory form most fully in the two late great novels, *Death Comes for the Archbishop* and *Shadows on the Rock*.

She started late. Her first book of fiction, the seven stories collected in *The Troll Garden*, was published when she was thirty-two; *Alexander's Bridge*, her first novel, when she was thirty-nine; and *O Pioneers!*, the first of her pastoral novels, where the essential nature of her gift began to realize itself, when she was forty. But behind this late start were the years of discipline in which she had been learning how to handle what she knew, and learning what it was that she knew. A number of the stories in *The Troll Garden* are no more than finger exercises in technique and gropings for subject—in a somewhat tenuous Jamesian vein which she was soon to turn away from. But the *novella*-length tale "Paul's Case" is an accomplished piece of workmanship, showing her long discipleship to Flaubert. It is done with his scrupulosity of detail and something of his shaping, tragic poetry.

Paul is a Pittsburgh high school boy, dandyish, anathema to his teachers because they feel his contempt for them, amounting to physical aversion. He comes to their aggrieved and rancorous sitting on his expulsion from school with a "scandalous red carnation" in his buttonhole. His life with his fellow students is one of lies: he tells them about his acquaintance with soloists in visiting opera companies, suppers with them, sending them flowers; when these lies lose effect, desperately he bids his classmates good-bye, saying he is going to travel to Naples, Venice, Egypt. Paul has no channeled talents; he suggests no particular capabilities at all; he is merely an amorphously longing teen-ager, "different" from others in the exclusiveness of his devotion to glamour in the teeth of the brutal body of fate. His existence is a continuous fracture of spirit, between his home in a lower middle class slum on Cordelia Street ("the cold bathroom with the grimy zinc tub, the cracked mirror, the dripping spiggots") and the theater, where he has an actor friend whom he visits behind the scenes, Carnegie Hall where he ushers, and the street outside the Schenley Hotel where he watches at night, in a debauch of envy and longing, the goings and comings of the theatrical crowd.

One has constantly in the back of one's mind the image of

Flaubert's Emma Bovary, for Paul, too, is a creature of *les sens*, isolated in the terrifying hebetude of his environment. And like Emma's, his fate comes running to him with his own features, but more eagerly and swiftly than hers; with his adolescent prescience, he prepares his fate like a diva. His father and the school principle having taken away his "bone" (forbidden him entrance to his aesthetic haunts) and put him to work as a bank messenger, he quietly absconds with a thousand dollars to New York. There he takes a suite at the Waldorf, buys with "endless reconsidering and great care" a frock coat and dress clothes, visits hatters and a shoe house, Tiffany's for silver and a new scarf pin, sends for flowers and champagne, and in his new silk underwear and red robe contemplates his glittering white bathroom. "The nerve-stuff of all sensations was whirling about him like the snow flakes. He burnt like a faggot in a tempest."

He is run down almost immediately. In the newspapers he sees how they are closing in on him (with promises from his father of total forgiveness), and "all the world had become Cordelia Street." Despite a poisonous champagne hangover, he does not flinch from the logic of his dilemma: he takes a cab to the ferry, and in Newark drives out of town to the Pennsylvania tracks. In his coat are some drooping red carnations, and before lying down on the track, "Paul took one of the blossoms carefully from his coat and scooped a little hole in the snow, where he covered it up."

"Paul's Case," is a brilliant adolescent analogue of the "cases" of Faust and Quixote. He has the Faustian hunger for magical experience transcending the despised soil of his animal milieu; he has Quixote's fanatic heroism in facing to the death, with his poor brave sword of pasteboard and forgery, the assaults of the swinish herd whose appetite is for violation. But most of all—because of his modern and reduced mimetic range—he has Emma Bovary's ineffably romantic sensuality, lusting like a saint for ecstasies that can be embodied only in vulgar artifice—until projected, inevitably, upon death. Within the formal sectors of Willa Cather's fiction, Paul is her earliest model of the young, artistically or merely sensitively gifted person in western America, whose inchoate aspiration is offered no imago by the environment, and no direction in which to develop except a blindly accidental one. The ironic detachment of the story gives it the purity and polish of a small classic.

Two of the shorter pieces in *The Troll Garden*, "A Wagner Matinee" and "The Sculptor's Funeral," take firm grip on the fatality of deprivation which was an inherent part of Miss Cather's native Nebraska material. "A Wagner Matinee" is a bleakly effective *récit*, holding in concentration the terrible spiritual toll taken by frontier life, especially upon women. An old aunt of the narrator, grizzled and deformed, comes to visit her nephew in New York; she had been a music teacher at the Boston Conservatory, and marriage had taken her to a Nebraska homestead fifty miles from a railroad, to live at first in a dugout in a hillside. He takes her to a concert. At the *Tannhäuser* overture, she clutches his coat sleeve. "Then it was I first realized that for her this broke a silence of thirty years; the inconceivable silence of the plains. . . . There came to me an overwhelming sense of the waste and wear we are so powerless to combat; and I saw again the tall, naked house on the prairie, black and grim as a wooden fortress; the black pond where I had learned to swim, its margin pitted with sun-dried cattle tracks; the rain gullied clay banks about the naked house, the four dwarf ash seedlings where the dishcloths were always hung to dry before the kitchen door."

"The Sculptor's Funeral" suffers from a somewhat ponderous use of the Jamesian-Balzacian reflector, but its observation of the working of the frontier curse, the habit of deprivation—horrifyingly at home in the Protestant mentality—is ferocious. The dead master-sculptor is taken home to Kansas to be buried. There, over the corpse, the observer sees the mother, the voracious mother with "teeth that could tear," frenzied in her sterility, and all the "raw, biting ugliness" that had been the portion of the artist in youth. He understands now the real tragedy of the man's life—not dissipation, as the town-folk say, but "a blow which had fallen earlier and cut deeper . . . a shame not his, and yet so inescapably his, to hide in his heart from his very boyhood." A drunken lawyer makes the final accusing tirade, against the town's suspicion and hatred of excellence, by which the most promising of its children have been harried to exile, degradation, or suicide. One remembers that, about a hundred years earlier, Stendhal's Julien Sorel had, in the shadow of the guillotine, made a similar accusation of his provincial fathers.

The story "The Garden Lodge" is composed on the motif of the lost instinctive self that has been compromised or frozen into a ghost by the complicated successes of American adulthood. The story's protagonist is a sophisticated woman who patronizes the arts in her suburban home. Her own childhood background had been a slummy, bohemian one, her father an indigent violinist, her mother acquiescent to his futile idealism, the unpaid bills, the mess. She had rejected all that, aiming to make her life a soberly rational and emotionally economic success. After entertaining as house guest a distinguished pianist, whose music had charmed her, she is haunted by "an imploring little girlish ghost that followed her about, wringing its hands and entreating for an hour of life." During a storm, she spends a night in the studio, fingering the piano and at last falling to sleep on the floor, disturbed in dream by that lost and violated child. "There was a moment between world and world, when neither asleep nor awake, she felt her dream grow thin, melting away from her, felt the warmth under her heart growing cold. Something seemed to slip from the clinging hold of her arms, and she groaned protestingly through her parted lips, following it a little way with fluttering hands. . . . The horror was that it had not come from without, but from within. The dream was no blind chance; it was the expression of something she had kept so close a prisoner that she had never seen it herself; it was the wail from the donjon deeps when the watch slept."

Alexander's Bridge (1912) is a distinguished first novel, but Miss Cather almost immediately repudiated it as "literary"—which had become a bad word for her—with a just recognition of what was contrived in its framework and stylish in its situation. Bartley Alexander is a famous engineer of bridges, married to a Bostonian heiress, leading in the "dead calm" of his middle age a gracious life that he loves, but nervously squirming under the constraints of his success—positions on boards of civic enterprise and committees of public welfare, the obligations of his wife's fortune. On his business trips to Europe he occasionally seeks, or tells himself he is seeking, the affectionately gay inconsequence of a mistress of his student years, Hilda Burgoyne, who has now become a distinguished actress. But he is intuitive enough to know that it is not really Hilda whom he seeks, but a more shadowy companion, "some one vastly dearer to him than she had ever been—his own young self," a youth who waits for him at the places he used to meet Hilda, links his arm in his, walks with him. He projects this entity upon Hilda and entoils her in its charm, which he makes her think is her own. With this acquiescence, the ghostly companion grows younger and more vigorous and importunate: "He remembered how, when he was a little boy and his father called him in the morning, he used to leap from his bed into the full consciousness of himself. That consciousness was Life itself. Whatever took its place, action, the power of concentrated thought, were only functions of a mechanism useful to society; things that could be bought in the market. There was only one thing that had an absolute value for each individual, and it was just that original impulse, that internal heat, that feeling of one's self in one's own breast." Even when he is most conscious of the satisfactions of his home, his friends, the wife whom he loves, the "thing" breaks loose out of an unknowable darkness, "sullen and powerful," thrilling him with a sense of quickened life and stimulating danger. He sacrifices Hilda to it, and finally is sacrificed to it himself—by the story's contrivance, he is drowned from one of his own bridges, because of a collapse in its faulty structure.

The finger-pointing symbolism (Alexander fell because of a flaw in his character, like the flaw in the bridge) is trite and specious, falsifying the troubled perception which is the story's strength and truth. Alexander's situation is that of the woman in "The Garden Lodge," except that the blocked, imprisoned self approached her only in a dream, attentuated to a child's shape, and she was able when she awoke to force it back into the "donjon deeps" forever; while Alexander's demonic visitor had broken past the watches of the ego and could not be exorcised, although there was no way to establish it, licitly, within the cultural pattern that had trapped his habits.

It would be possible to sketch a kind of allegory of motives between this situation and what happened to Willa Cather when she wrote her next book, O Pioneers! (1913). For with O Pioneers! the natural forces of her gift—the unknown, unpredictable "self"—suddenly broke through her carefully trained literary habits. If there is a literary precursor, it is Thomas Hardy, but only in the sense that, like Hardy, she had found her subject in her own tribal country, in its ancient geological recalcitrance and its tragic face of blessing. Here she herself was the pioneer, of whom it might be said, as she says of Alexandra, the Swedish farm girl who is the heroine of the book: "For the first time, perhaps, since that land emerged from the waters of geologic ages, a human face was set toward it with love and yearning." But she brought to this discovery a voice that held and used its earlier disciplines, melodically and resonantly.

She scarcely knew what to do with the material, for the way it had put itself together, as a two-part pastoral, seemed to have no formal rationale, and the longer part—the story of Alexandra—had no backbone of structure at all, was as fluid and featureless as the high, oceanic grassland where Alexandra made her farm: the author could only mourn over the "foolish endeavor" she had somehow got on her hands. Ten years later, when she understood better that dark logic which Keats called "Negative Capability," she wrote of her experience with O Pioneers!: "When a writer begins to work with his own material, he realizes that, no matter what his literary excursions may have been, he has been working with it from the beginning—by living it. With this material he is another writer. He has less and less power of choice about the moulding of it. It seems to be there of itself, already moulded. . . . In working with this material he finds that he need have little to do with literary devices; he comes to depend more and more on something else—the thing by which our feet find the road home on a dark night, accounting of themselves for roots and stones which we had never noticed by day."

Alexandra Bergson's parents had come from Sweden to take up land in Nebraska, and their death leaves her, in her early twenties, the head of a family of three brothers. The patch of land, won by homestead rights, is the only survival relationship they have. It is the high, dry, prairie country of the Divide, between two rivers, the coarse, incalculable, primitively resistant ground of an action so ancient in character it might have taken place in neolithic times and in that other austere land between two rivers. "The record of the plow was . . . like the feeble scratches on stone left by prehistoric races, so indeterminate that they may, after all, be only the markings of glaciers, and not a record of human strivings." In winter "it is like an iron country . . . One could easily believe that in that dead landscape the germs of life and fruitfulness were extinct forever." Alexandra faces the exigence of that destiny in the almost unconscious spirit of a person driven by uranian and chthonic gods, and makes her heroic peace with them. "Her personal life, her own realization of herself, was almost a subconscious existence; like an underground river that came to the surface only here and there, at intervals months apart, and then sank again to flow on under her own fields."

She had a recurrent dream, usually on Sunday mornings when she is able to lie abed late—a dream as archaic as the whole action of her story. The subject of the dream is an authentic god straight out of the unconscious, one of those vegetation and weather gods by whose urgencies she is compelled and whose energies sustain her. "Sometimes, as she lay thus luxuriously idle, her eyes closed, she used to have an illusion of being lifted up bodily and carried lightly by some one very strong. It was a man, certainly, who carried her, but he was like no man she knew; he was much larger and stronger and swifter, and he carried her as easily as if she were a sheaf of wheat. She never saw him, but, with eyes closed, she could feel that he was yellow like the sunlight, and there was the smell of ripe cornfields about him. She could feel him approach, bend over her and lift her, and then she could feel herself being carried swiftly off across the fields. . . . As she grew older, this fancy more often came to her when she was tired than when she was fresh and strong. . . . Then, just before she went to sleep, she had the old sensation of being lifted and carried by a strong being who took from her all her bodily weariness." Like Adonis, Attis, and Thammuz, this Eros of the corn and sunlight is a life principle, extending infinitely beyond the human subject, but appearing in the beneficent image of a guardian god to the subject strong enough and obedient enough to attend it.

In a sense, that divine being is the unconscious itself, assuming the image of a strength greater than the personal. Because of the primitive authenticity of the image, it seems right to see reflected here, also, something of the instinctive process by which the book came to be written, as well as those others of Willa Cather's works whose structure obeys laws more obscure and fundamental than literary precepts or even than her own ideas of her purposes: it is the "something else—the thing by which our feet find the road home on a dark night"—a power like that which carried Alexandra in her dream, "larger and stronger and swifter" than conscious intent. The two parts of the Nebraska pastoral—Alexandra's part and that called "The White Mulberry Tree"—are wrought into one form by an instinct as sure as the cycle of seasons, a cycle which itself seems to be the natural commanding form of the novel. The story of Alexandra engages the whole work in the rhythms of the land, powerful tidal urgencies of weather and seasons and their erosions of human life, while the episode of "The White Mulberry Tree"—the love story of Alexandra's young brother Emil and the Bohemian girl Marie Shabata—flashes across those deeper rhythms like a swift springtime, lyrical, brilliant, painful. The episode is saturated with light, bronze and gold on the wide warm fields of grain that smell like baking bread, and gold and green under the leaves of the orchard where Emil and Marie meet their sudden doom, murdered as they lie in first embrace; so that the light ripening the land seems the one great reality, and the blood of the two young lives poured dark into the earth a sacrifice to it.

The Song of the Lark (1915) is a ponderously bulky novel that suffers from autobiographic compulsion. Ostensibly it is modeled on the career of the Swedish opera singer Olive Fremstad. However, Willa Cather's friend Elizabeth Sergeant wrote that she "was deeply—by her own account—identified with her character [Thea Kronborg], who had many of her traits and had undergone many of her own experiences." The setting is changed to Moonstone, Colorado, a small town in the desert west of Denver. Thea, a gifted child in a suffocatingly crowded and brutally inept family, takes her first music lessons from a pathetic, drunken old German; for proper lessons in Chicago she is financed by a brakeman on the Denver train, who is in love with her and who is shortly killed in an accident; from Chicago she goes on to supreme success in New York, where her promoter is a wealthy young dandy, also in love with her. The end of Thea's story explores both the splendors and penalties of success, the bleak asceticism which the artist pays for the presumptions of his gift. The naturalistic, circumstantial form to which the subject lent itself carried its usual vulnerability to "thesis" writing, a weakness inherent also in Miss Cather's attraction to the subject of the artist's struggle. The result is invented plot situations, sagging proportions, made-up dialogue, and a prose that often goes lax. In her preface to a later edition, she wrote·that the book should have ended before the successful phase of Thea's career: "What I cared about, and still care about, was the girl's escape; the play of blind chance, the way in which commonplace occurrences fell together to liberate her from commonness." But this too is a thesis, indicating the way in which traumatic personal memory—of her own "escape"—turned into obsessive idea.

"Life began for me," she said, "when I ceased to admire and began to remember." But there is more than one kind of remembering. There is personal memory bound up with the chronology of one's own life and with ego-tensions and resistances. There is what Proust called "bodily memory," which, because it is physical and sensory, may be at once personal and more than personal, for the impulses of the senses register common qualities of experience, timeless as sun and earth, breath and flesh. And there is what the Greeks call *anamnesis*, memory of "important" things, matters whose significance is part of one's heritage—a kind of *commemoration* since it involves other and profounder memories than one's own, buried perhaps as deep as instinct and aroused mysteriously as instinct. There is still a great deal in *The Song of the Lark* that is of the older orders of memory, more broadly based than that of the ego, more essential and more original—in that sense of the word which implies "origins." Toward the end of *O Pioneers!* when Alexandra is almost broken by young Emil's death, she goes to his grave in the night during a storm, and is found there in the morning, drenched, icy, and nearly unconscious, by Crazy Ivar, an old man who lives in a clay bank like a coyote and who can talk with animals and heal them. He and Alexandra have always understood each other. She tells him: "After you once got cold clear through, the feeling of the rain on you is sweet. . . . It carries you back into the dark, before you were born; you can't see things, but they come to you, somehow, and you know them and aren't afraid of them. Maybe it's like that with the dead. If they feel anything at all, it's the old things, before they were born . . ." In *The Song of the Lark*, Thea, an adolescent only beginning to break through the ugliness and mediocrity surrounding her, hears in a symphony a voice immensely ancient and yet sounding within herself: "a soul new and yet old, that had dreamed something despairing, something glorious, in the dark before it was born; a soul obsessed by what it did not know, under the cloud of a past it could not recall."

Thea tries to hold that "soul" under her cloak, as if it were a child or another self that must be protected in tenderness and darkness lest it be snatched from her before it could grow: "There was some power abroad in the world bent upon taking away from her that feeling with which she had come out of the concert hall. Everything seemed to sweep down on her to tear it out from under her cape. If one had that, the world became one's enemy; people, buildings, wagons, cars, rushed at one to crush it under, to make one let go of it." Like Alexandra's, Thea Kronborg's nature had been formed close to the land, and toughened and simplified in that matrix. She is able to harbor the instinctive self, with its ancient gifts like those a child receives in fairy tales from dwarfs and witches constrained to bless him, because she recognizes both its transcendence and the personal disciplines needed to redeem it from "the cloud of a past it would not recall," to give it feature, to bring it to birth by her own labor.

The voice heard in the symphony is associated with the western desert of her childhood. The desert had moved mysteriously with apparitions older than history, mirages of silver lakes where one saw reflected the images of cattle magnified to a preposterous height and looking like mammoths, "prehistoric beasts standing solitary in the waters that for many thousands of years actually washed over that desert: the mirage itself may be the ghost of that long-vanished sea." Further south were the ruined dwellings of "the Ancient People." Here, in miniature cities honeycombed into clefts of the canyons, were human features of a past extending "back into the dark," a racial history speaking of immemorial experience with a voice of silence: steep trails worn deep into the rock by the Ancient People's generations carrying water up the canyon wall to their hanging gardens, signs of their mysteries, their food, their fire. "Food, fire, water, and something else—even here, in this crack in the world, so far back in the night of the past! Down here at the beginning, that painful thing was already stirring; the seed of sorrow, and of so much delight . . . A vanished race; but along the trails, in the stream, under the spreading cactus, there still glittered in the sun the bits of their frail clay vessels, fragments of their desire." The discovery of the cliff-dwellings is for Thea Kronborg—as it was for her author—a materialized revelation of something unknown and yet remembered, something ancestral and legendary yet recognizable as an image responding from within the self, an *anamnesis* borne directly to the senses by external forms. Her own gift as a singer seems to her the same impulse that made those forms, given to her in order to salvage their meaning.

In Miss Cather's next book, *My Ántonia* (1918), there occurs a majestic, mysterious image that suggests, in another way, the timeless aspect of the subject matter which seems most naturally her own. Jim Burden (the narrator of the story) and some "hired girls" from the little

Nebraska town of Black Hawk have spent a lazy afternoon by the river, ending with a picnic supper. "Presently we saw a curious thing: There were no clouds, the sun was going down in a limpid, gold-washed sky. Just as the lower edge of the red disk rested on the high fields against the horizon, a great black figure suddenly appeared on the face of the sun. We sprang to our feet, straining our eyes toward it. In a moment we realized what it was. On some upland farm, a plough had been left standing in the field. The sun was sinking just behind it. Magnified across the distance by the horizontal light, it stood out against the sun, was exactly contained within the circle of the disk; the handles, the tongue, the share—black against the molten red. There it was, heroic in size, a picture writing on the sun. Even while we whispered about it, our vision disappeared; the ball dropped and dropped until the red tip went beneath the earth. The fields below us were dark, the sky was growing pale, and that forgotten plough had sunk back to its own littleness somewhere on the prairie." The image could have been carved, as a sacred life-symbol, on the stones of a lost temple of Yucatan, or in a tomb of the Valley of Kings. The plow itself, forgotten on that upland farm, could have been left there by some farmer of Chaldea.

   The story is as much Jim Burden's as it is Ántonia's. The two children share the initiatory experiences of the wild land to which their parents have brought them. Jim's family, like Willa Cather's, are from Virginia; Ántonia Shimerda's family are Bohemians who have come to take up homestead rights in the new country. Jim's family live in a house, Ántonia's in a cave in a clay bank, the children sleeping in holes tunneled into the gumbo mud. Around them is "nothing but land: not a country at all, but the material out of which countries are made." It is like the sea, featureless and barren, but running with obscure, unaccountable movement as of the rushing of theromorphic gods: "I felt that the grass was the country, as the water is the sea. The red of the grass made all the great prairie the colour . . . of certain seaweeds when they are first washed up. And there was so much motion in it; the whole country seemed, somehow, to be running . . . as if the shaggy grass were a sort of loose hide, and underneath it herds of wild buffalo were galloping, galloping . . ." The ends of the earth are very near. "The light air about me told me that the world ended here": one had only to walk straight on through the red grass to the edge of the world where there would be only sun and sky left.

   Out of homely American detail are composed certain friezelike entablatures that have the character of ancient ritual and sculpture. There is the suicide and funeral of Mr. Shimerda, Ántonia's father, a gifted musician who could, finally, not bear the animal life to which the first generation of pioneers was subjected. For his suicide he dressed himself fastidiously in the fine clothes of the concert hall, went out to the cow barn, and shot himself. It was dead winter, and his corpse had got frozen to the ground before it was discovered. It was left there safely till the day of the funeral, when the hired men from the Burden farm "went ahead on horseback to cut the body loose from the pool of blood in which it was frozen fast to the ground." The Shimerdas were Roman Catholic, an anomaly in that predominantly Protestant neighborhood of farmers, and as a suicide he could not be buried in Catholic ground, so his grave was made at a crossroads in the age-old superstition clinging to the suicide. But no roads ever crossed over his grave. "The road from the north curved a little to the east just there, and the road from the west swung out a little to the south; so that the grave, with its tall red grass that was never mowed, was like a little island." And Jim Burden says, "I loved the dim superstition, the propitiatory intent, that had put the grave there; and still more I loved the spirit that could not carry out the sentence—the error from the surveyed lines, the clemency of the soft earth roads along which the home-coming wagons rattled after sunset."

There are the hired men on the farm, Jake and Otto, who, with the "sag of their tired shoulders against the whitewashed wall," form a mute memorial as dignified and tender in outline as a Greek stele— nomadic figures who bear with them the ancient pathos of mysterious coming and mysterious departure, "without warning . . . on the west-bound train one morning, in their Sunday clothes, with their oilcloth valises—and I never saw them again." And there are the hired girls, girls who like Ántonia came from the farming community to take domestic work in the town of Black Hawk; robust, exuberant, and held in contempt by the townspeople, these girls appear like a sunlit band of caryatids, or like the succession of peasant girls who loved generously and suffered tragically in old ballads, or like the gay interlinked chain of girls in Proust's À l'ombre des jeunes filles en fleurs. "When I closed my eyes," Jim Burden says, "I could hear them all laughing—the Danish laundry girls and the three Bohemian Marys. . . . It came over me, as it had never done before, the relation between girls like those and the poetry of Virgil. If there were no girls like them in the world, there would be no poetry. I understood that clearly, for the first time."

Jim Burden, who goes away to the city and returns to the Nebraska farmland only after long intervals, is able to register that Chekhovian "suffering of change" which enters Willa Cather's work during this period. On his last return both he and Ántonia are middle-aged, Jim a weary intellectual nomad, Ántonia married to a Bohemian farmer with a brood of children about her, gay in her orchards and her kitchen. With scarcely a tooth in her head, save for some broken brown snags, she is still able to leave "images in the mind that did not fade—that grew stronger with time . . . She lent herself to immemorial human attitudes which we recognize by instinct as universal and true." The suffering of change, the sense of irreparable loss in time, is one polarity of the work; the other polarity is the timelessness of those images associated with Ántonia, with the grave of the suicide at the crossroads, with the mute fortitude of the hired men and the pastoral poetry of the hired girls, and most of all with the earth itself, carrying in mysterious stroke, like the plow hieroglyphed on the sun, signs of an original and ultimate relationship between man and cosmos.

TERENCE MARTIN

The Drama of Memory
In "My Ántonia"

In Willa Cather's novels of the West,
the land, raw and unsubdued, stands out as the initial force to be
confronted. "The great fact was the land itself," she says in describing the
milieu of O Pioneers! (1913), "which seemed to overwhelm the little
beginnings of human society that struggled in its sombre wastes." The far
different world of Death Comes for the Archbishop (1927), with its vast
distances and arid wastes, seems older, earlier, yet equally a "great fact" as
Miss Cather emphasizes its primeval quality: the mesa, she writes, "had an
appearance of great antiquity, and of incompleteness; as if, with all the
materials for world-making assembled, the creator had desisted, gone away
and left everything on the point of being brought together, on the eve of
being arranged into mountain, plain, plateau." Here, too, "the country
was still waiting to be made into a landscape."

Such statements recall Jim Burden's initial reaction to the Nebraska prairie in My Ántonia (1918). As he rattles out to his grandparents'
house at night, he peers over the side of the wagon. "There seemed to be
nothing to see; no fences, no creeks or trees, no hills or fields. If there was
a road, I could not make it out in the faint starlight. There was nothing
but land: not a country at all, but the material out of which countries are
made." Unformed, incomplete, lacking fences, trees, and hills, the land
gives Jim Burden the feeling of being "over the edge" of the world,
"outside man's jurisdiction."

From PMLA 84, no. 2 (March 1969). Copyright © 1969 by Modern Language Association
of America.

To this land Willa Cather brings the people who will struggle to make it give them first a subsistence, then a livelihood. In *O Pioneers!* the process is exemplified in the life of Alexandra Bergson, whose family had come to Nebraska when she was a child, whose faith and determination virtually force the land into yielding the riches which she so passionately believes it to possess. The early sections of *O Pioneers!* pose the question of survival sharply; the novel turns on the ultimately successful attempt of the pioneers to wrest a living from the land. In *My Ántonia*, Jim Burden's grandparents have achieved a degree of stability as the novel begins; it is the Shimerdas, the Bohemians, who move onto the prairie and make the early, elemental struggle that is the prerequisite of survival and success. With the efforts of her characters to subdue, to form, to complete the land, Willa Cather's novels of the prairie may properly be said to begin. Necessarily, then, Miss Cather writes about change, for if the people are not to be annihilated or forced into retreat by the land, the land must be altered by the efforts of the people.

The land, still menacing to the newcomer in its intransigence; the people of various backgrounds, whose object is to humanize, even domesticate, this land; the change, physical, economic, and social, consequent upon their efforts—such staple elements of Willa Cather's novels of the prairie go into the making of *My Ántonia*. But the novel has, of course, a special character of its own, an individuality that comes in large part from the Shimerdas; from their daughter Ántonia, who becomes a symbol of battered but undiminished human value; from Lena Lingard, soft, enticing, sensually eloquent; and, finally, from the narrator, Jim Burden, whose point of view defines the theme and structure even as it controls the tone of the novel.

From the time of the composition of *My Ántonia*, the role of Jim Burden has invited attention. Perhaps feeling the need to define that role more specifically, Willa Cather revised the preface of the novel for the reissue of 1926, making changes that altered Jim Burden's relation to the story he tells. In the 1918 preface, for example, Jim agrees to record his memories of Ántonia, which he has not thought of doing before; in the second preface, however, he is already at work on the manuscript before the meeting and conversation that supposedly take place with Willa Cather on the train. Such a change implies that something private and personal has been at work in the mind of Jim Burden, that the manuscript has taken initial shape because of an inner need to articulate the meaning of a valued, ultimately treasured, memory. Willa Cather has amended her first (prefatory) thoughts by bringing her narrator closer emotionally to the substance of the narrative.

Readers have continued to assess the role of Jim Burden because of its relevance to the structure of the novel as a whole. David Daiches, for example, believes that "the narrator's development goes on side by side with Ántonia's" and finds the symbolism uncertain at the conclusion: "The final suggestion that this is the story of Jim and Ántonia and their relation is not really borne out by the story as it has developed. It begins as that, but later the strands separate until we have three main themes all going—the history of Ántonia, the history of Jim, and scenes of Nebraska life." The result, Daiches feels, and no mean achievement, is "a flawed novel full of life and interest and possessing a powerful emotional rhythm in spite of its imperfect structural pattern." E. K. Brown sees a potential problem in the choice of a man as narrator: Jim Burden "was to be fascinated by Ántonia as only a man could be, and yet he was to remain a detached observer, appreciative but inactive, rather than take a part in her life." The consequence of Willa Cather's effort to achieve those two not fully compatible effects is an emptiness "at the very center" of Jim's relation to Ántonia, "where the strongest emotion might have been expected to obtain." Stressing the function of the narrator, James E. Miller, Jr., believes that the "emotional structure of the novel may be discovered" in the drama of Jim Burden's "awakening consciousness," which "shapes in the reader a sharpened awareness of cyclic fate that is the human destiny." John H. Randall, III, in his impressive study of Willa Cather, would seem to agree with the implications of some of the previous arguments when he says that Jim Burden is more than "a first-person onlooker who is relating someone else's story." Randall develops the idea of a double protagonist, part Ántonia, who faces the future, part Jim Burden, who faces the past. Together, Jim and Ántonia make a complete, albeit "Janus-faced," personality.

If structural coherence is to be found in My Ántonia, the character of Jim Burden seems necessarily to be involved. As the story of Ántonia, the novel is quite rightly found inadequate; and even as the story of Ántonia and Jim Burden, the narrative strands, as Mr. Daiches indicates, tend to separate. For it is the story of Jim's Ántonia, and the meaning and implications of that term must somehow subsume the various elements of the novel. As I see it, the substance and quality of the narrative itself—at once evolving toward and conditioned by the image of Jim's Ántonia—provide a principle of unity that takes the special form of a drama of memory.

Jim Burden's drama of memory begins with his portrayal of the Shimerda family, who have arrived on the prairie from Bohemia at the same time Jim has come from Virginia to live with his grandparents after the death of his mother and father. The conditions of the agricultural frontier in Nebraska force the Shimerdas into a bleak, defensive existence. They take up residence in a kind of cave, in front of which is a flimsy shed thatched with the wine-colored grass of the prairie. To Jim's grandmother the dwelling seems "no better than a badger hole; no proper dugout at all." But it is where the new family must live if they are to have shelter. On the fringe of civilization, overpowered by the utter strangeness of their environment, the Shimerdas face a contest for survival more in bewilderment than in desperation. For they have come unprepared. Mr. Shimerda, as Jim says, "knew nothing about farming"; a weaver by trade, he "had been a skilled workman on tapestries and upholstery materials" in his native land. We sense his confusion, his loss of identity, in his new surroundings. Awed by the magnitude of nature on the prairie, Jim Burden admits that "between that earth and that sky I felt erased, blotted out"; his statement evinces a deep feeling of insignificance, a sense of the radically diminished importance of the human being and his endeavors. This Jim can accept with the stoicism of youth: "I did not say my prayers that night," he writes; "here, I felt, what would be would be." Mr. Shimerda, however, can neither attain nor afford the luxury of resignation. For the prairie threatens him in subtle and profound ways. "Of all the bewildering things about a new country," writes Willa Cather in O Pioneers!, "the absence of human landmarks is one of the most depressing and disheartening." A citizen of the Old World, Mr. Shimerda cannot survive the loss of a society that was characterizied by intellectual and artistic "landmarks." Faced with the necessity of making a new start from a point prior to any he had ever imagined, Mr. Shimerda has nothing with which to begin but his fiddle and an old gun given to him long ago for playing at a wedding. He dies from a lack of history; his suicide a testimony to the grim reality of the struggle imposed by frontier conditions.

In portraying the remaining Shimerda family, Willa Cather steadfastly avoids the trap of sentimentality. It would be a simple matter to resolve their problems with a rush of pity and a flood of tears, and the Burdens stand willing (almost determined) to help. But the Shimerdas (Mrs. Shimerda and Ambrosch particularly, but Ántonia also, to a degree) prove difficult to help. Embittered by their lot, they are shown to be unpleasant, ungrateful, and boastful; they brag of the old country and make comparisons invidious to the new. The sullen duplicity of Ambrosch leads finally to the harness incident, in which Ambrosch kicks at Jake Marpole and is felled by a blow from Jake's solid American fist. "They ain't the same, Jimmy," Jake says afterward, "these foreigners ain't the same. You can't trust 'em to be fair. It's dirty to kick a feller. You heard how the women turned on you—and after all we went through on account of 'em last winter! They ain't to be trusted. I don't want to see you get too thick with any of 'em." To which Jim responds with emotion: "I'll never be friends with them again, Jake."

Although such antipathy fades completely with time and understanding (the latter supplied principally by Mr. Burden), it typifies in a muted way some of the tensions implicit in American history. Earlier, on the train heading for Nebraska, Jake Marpole has approved Jim Burden's reluctance to go into the car ahead and talk with the little girl with "pretty brown eyes," as the conductor describes Ántonia; you are "likely to get diseases from foreigners," he tells Jim. Jake is a Virginian, an old American, showing his distrust of the newcomer. But a similar feeling could exist between immigrant groups. Otto Fuchs tells Jim's grandmother that "Bohemians has a natural distrust of Austrians." When she asks why, he replies: "Well, ma'am, it's politics. It would take me a long while to explain." Religion, too, could obviously provide a source of tension, though, again, the subdued tone of the narrative resolves such tensions quietly, and, in one case, with a final note of humor. When the Catholic Mr. Shimerda kneels and crosses himself before the Burdens' religiously decorated Christmas tree (decorated with candles and with a nativity scene sent to Otto Fuchs from Austria), Jim and his grandmother are apprehensive. Mr. Burden is staunchly Protestant, no friend to the pomps of Popery: "He was rather narrow in religious matters," says Jim, "and sometimes spoke out and hurt people's feelings." The moment of crisis dissolves, however, when grandfather, as Jim says, "merely put his fingertips to his brow and bowed his venerable head, thus Protestantizing the atmosphere."

An unsentimental portrait of the Shimerdas thus is not only valid psychologically; it also allows us to glimpse the prejudices that were part of the human situation on the Nebraska prairie. Such feelings, however, are consistently set in a larger context of generosity; in March the Shimerdas occupy a new four-room house which their neighbors have helped them to build. They were now "fairly equipped," says Jim, "to begin their struggle with the soil." *Struggle* is, of course, the key word, for the Shimerdas' position can be made reasonably secure only by unremitting labor. Much of the necessary work, as we know, falls to Ántonia, whose fortunes in the Shimerda household are distinctly subordinate to those of Ambrosch, the oldest son. (It is for Ambrosch, Ántonia tells Jim Burden, that they have come to the United States.) Through Jim's eyes we see her as she grows coarse and muscular doing the work of a man on the farm. "She was too proud of her strength," he says, annoyed because Ántonia talks constantly to him about how much she can "lift and endure." Ambrosch gives her hard jobs and dirty ones as well, some of them "chores a girl ought not to do"; and Jim knows that "the farm-hands around the country joked in a nasty way about it." At the dinner table "Ántonia ate so noisily now, like a man, and she yawned often . . . and kept stretching her arms over her head, as if they ached." Jim's grandmother had said, "Heavy field work'll spoil that girl. She'll lose all her nice ways and get rough ones." To Jim, if not to his grandparents, "she had lost them already." Work has hardened his playmate of the previous autumn; virtually harnessed to the plow, developing a "draught-horse neck." she has little time for him. "I ain't got time to learn," she says when he informs her of the beginning of a new school term: "School is . . . for little boys." But the knowledge that her father would have been hurt by such an answer, and even more by the necessity for such an answer, brings tears to her eyes. Ántonia's determination to work for the immediate needs of her family molds her to the land. Fit material for a symbol, she is, I think we must in candor admit, already a bit too muscular for conventional romantic purposes.

The pace and emphases of the narrative in My Ántonia come of course from Jim Burden. As we know, the point of view is retrospective, and despite his disclaimer in the preface, Jim has both the perspective and the inclination to shape his material with care. Accordingly, Book One has a definite pattern, that of the seasons: beginning with the autumn of his arrival, Jim takes us through the year to the fullness and heat of the following summer. Moreover, he portrays himself predominantly in terms of his reactions to the seasons during his first year on the prairie. The first section of the novel thus operates as a kind of rehearsal for nostalgia. For this year lives at the center of Jim's memory, never to be relived, never to be forgotten. It has for him an idyllic quality, a quality of tenderly remembered freedom and happiness resulting from his surrender to the forces of nature with which everyone else must contend. On the night of his arrival in Nebraska, we recall, Jim adopts an attitude of resignation: "here . . . what would be would be." The next day in his grandmother's garden he relaxes against a "warm yellow pumpkin," crumbles earth in his fingers, and watches and listens to nature. "Nothing happened," he says. "I did not expect anything to happen. I was something that lay under the sun and felt it, like the pumpkins, and I did not want to be anything more. I was entirely happy." He thinks of death (his parents, we remember, have recently died) and wonders if death makes us "a part of something entire." "At any rate," he concludes, "that is happiness; to be dissolved into something complete and great."

Jim Burden, in short, makes an immediate surrender to nature in this garden with its ripe pumpkins. And his feeling of immersion in nature has a significant and permanent effect upon him, for he never loses his ability to appreciate the prairie in a personal way or his need to find happiness amid the ripeness and fulfillment of life. Though he must tell us of human hardship, Jim reveals his sense of rapture as he recalls and describes the seasons. "All the years that have passed," he says, "have not dimmed my memory of that first glorious autumn." The new country lay open before him, leading him to celebrate the splendor of the prairie in the last hour of the afternoon:

> All those fall afternoons were the same, but I never got used to them. As far as we could see, the miles of copper-red grass were drenched in sunlight that was stronger and fiercer than at any other time of the day. The blond cornfields were red gold, the haystacks turned rosy and threw long shadows. The whole prairie was like the bush that burned with fire and was not consumed. The hour always had the exultation of victory, of triumphant ending, like a hero's death—heroes who died young and gloriously. It was a sudden transfiguration, a lifting-up of day.

Jim's tone is reverential, replete with wonder, the product of a deep respect for the prairie and for the sunlight that brings it to ripeness.

Winter becomes primarily a time of taking refuge. Snow disguises the prairie with an insidious mask of white, leaving one, as Jim says later, with "a hunger for color." He is convinced that "man's strongest antagonist is the cold," though, in the security of his grandmother's basement kitchen, which "seemed heavenly safe and warm in those days," he can hardly experience its bitterness in the manner of the Shimerdas, who have only one overcoat among them and take turns wearing it for warmth. On cold nights, he recalls, the cry of coyotes "used to remind the boys of wonderful animal stories." A sense of adventure pervades Jim's life: by comparison, the life represented in books seems prosaic: the Swiss family Robinson, for example, "had no advantage over us in the way of an adventurous life"—and, later, Robinson Crusoe's life on the island "seemed dull compared with ours." If winter means taking refuge, it also satisfies the needs of Jim's young imagination and contributes the memory of adventure, a feeling of hardship happily domesticated by the company, the kitchen, and the stove "that fed us and warmed us and kept us cheerful."

Spring with the reawakening of the prairie and summer with its sense of fruition complete the cycle of the seasons. The pervasive lightness of spring delights Jim: "If I had been tossed down blindfold on that red prairie, I should have known that it was spring." And July brings the "breathless, brilliant heat which makes the prairies of Kansas and Nebraska the best corn country in the world. It seemed as if we could hear the corn growing in the night; under the stars one caught a faint crackling in the dewy, heavy-odored cornfields where the feathered stalk stood so juicy and green." These are to become the world's cornfields, Jim sees in retrospect; their yield will underlie "all the activities of men in peace or war."

A sense of happiness remembered pervades Book One, softening and mellowing the harsher outlines of the story Jim Burden has to tell. We are never really on the prairie with Jim, nor does he try to bring us there. Rather, he preserves his retrospective point of view and tells us what it was like for him on the prairie. "I used to love to drift along the pale-yellow cornfield," he says; and (as we have seen) "All the years that have passed have not dimmed my memory of that first glorious autumn"; and, again, though she is four years his senior and they have arrived on the prairie at the same time, Ántonia "had come to us a child, and now she was a tall, strong young girl." Such statements, and numerous devices of style throughout the novel, make a point of narrative distance and deliver the story to us in an envelope of memory. The style, that is to say, makes a deliberate—and almost total—sacrifice of immediacy in favor of the afterglow of remembrance. Even the scenes of violence are kept at a distance by having someone else tell them to Jim Burden; indeed, they are not so much scenes as inset stories, twice removed from the reader. Pavel's story of the wolves in Russia, Ántonia's story of the tramp who jumped into the threshing machine, the story of Wick Cutter's death (told by one of Ántonia's children)—all these contain a terror and a violence that is subdued by having them related to Jim as part of his story to us. In a similar indirect way we learn of Mr. Shimerda's death and of the seduction of Ántonia by Larry Donovan (whom we never meet). Only when Jim kills the snake, thus, in a sense, making the prairie safe for Ántonia, and when for Ántonia's sake he decoys himself in Wick Cutter's bedroom, are terror and violence (and in the latter case a mixture of comedy) brought close; and, in keeping with the retrospective point of view, these episodes, too, come to us through the spectrum of Jim's memory.

Defining the mode of Jim Burden's relation to his narrative leads us to see the special character of the novel itself and to judge it on its own terms rather than on any we might inadvertently bring to it. The statement of one critic that "something precious went into American fiction with the story of Ántonia Shimerda" is meant as a tribute to Willa Cather's novel; but it seems to me a misdirected tribute. For the novel does not present the *story* of Ántonia; it does, I believe, present a drama of memory by means of which Jim Burden tells us how he has come to see

Ántonia as the epitome of all he has valued. At the time he writes, Jim Burden has made sense of his experience on the prairie, has seen the meaning it has and will have in his life. The early sections of My Ántonia present in retrospect the substance of meaning, conditioned throughout by Jim's assurance of that meaning. The latter sections justify his right to remember the prairie in the joyous manner of his youth. And the process of justification involves, most importantly, the image of Ántonia. This image acquires symbolic significance for Jim; embodying and justifying his memories, it validates nostalgia by giving his feeling for the past a meaning in the present.

By common consent, the "I" of the preface is taken to be Willa Cather. In the preface we learn that both to Jim Burden and Willa Cather, Ántonia, "more than any other person we remembered, . . . seemed to mean . . . the country, the conditions, the whole adventure of our childhood." Miss Cather says that she had lost sight of Ántonia, but that Jim "had found her again after long years." The preface thus establishes a relation between Jim Burden and Willa Cather outside the narrative that is important to the relationship of Jim and Ántonia within the narrative. Jim Burden becomes the imaginative instrument by means of which Willa Cather reacquaints herself with Ántonia: "He made me see her again, feel her presence, revived all my old affection for her." Her narrator, in short, serves Miss Cather as the vehicle for her own quest for meaning and value; his success measures her success; his symbol becomes her symbol; for his Ántonia is the Ántonia she has created for him.

If Jim Burden is to be made more than a heuristic phantom of the imagination, however, he must be given some kind of autonomy as a fictional character. Some drama, however quiet it may appear in retrospect, must play itself out in his life; some resolution must come inherently from the narrative. If we are to have a drama of memory, Jim's memory must somehow be challenged before it is vindicated in and by the image of Ántonia. The offstage challenges, those involved, for example, when Jim explains his twenty-year absence from the Nebraska prairie by saying "life intervened," afford little but material for conjecture and inference. The onstage challenge, however, affording material for analysis, enters Jim's room in Lincoln in Book Three in the very pretty form of Lena Lingard.

Lena Lingard first appears as one of the hired girls in Book Two, along with Tiny Soderball, lesser characters such as the Bohemian Marys and the Danish laundry girls, and, of course, Ántonia, who has come to Black Hawk to work for the Harlings. The move to Black Hawk does take Ántonia away from the prairie temporarily and tends to merge her importance with that of a group of girls. But by placing Ántonia and Lena Lingard together, as friends, Willa Cather can begin to suggest the different roles each of them will play in the life of Jim Burden. Moreover, Black Hawk provides a canvas on which Miss Cather can portray social consciousness and burgeoning social change in the Nebraska of this time. Despite the domestic vitality of the Harling family, readily available for Jim Burden (now living next door with his grandparents) to draw on, Black Hawk seems increasingly dull to Jim during his high-school years. Small and very proper, the town makes life for young men an initiation into monotony. Except, of course, for the presence of the hired girls. These young women, all of foreign families, bring vivacity to Black Hawk; lighthearted, gay, and unpretentious, at the dances they are in great demand. More often than not, however, the proper young men must meet them surreptitiously, for the hired girls enjoy a lower social status than do the girls of the older American families in the town. Remarking on the social distinction, Jim Burden says that

> the daughters of Black Hawk merchants had a confident, uninquiring belief that they were 'refined,' and that the country girls, who 'worked out,' were not. The American farmers in our county were quite as hard-pressed as their neighbors from other countries. All alike had come to Nebraska with little capital and no knowledge of the soil they must subdue. All had borrowed money on their land. But no matter in what straits the Pennsylvanian or Virginian found himself, he would not let his daughters go out into service. Unless his girls could teach a country school, they sat home in poverty.

Kept from teaching by their inadequate knowledge of English, yet determined to help their families out of debt, the hired girls took domestic or similar employment. Some remained serious and discreet, says Jim, others did not. But all sent home money to help pay "for ploughs and reapers, brood-sows, or steers to fatten." Jim frankly admires such family solidarity, as a result of which the foreign families in the county were "the first to become prosperous." Today, he says, former hired girls are "managing big farms of their own; their children are better off than the children of the town women they used to serve." Pleased with their success, Jim feels paternal toward the entire group of girls and applauds the social change which accompanies their prosperity.

A single generation serves to bring about the kind of change Jim describes. In the Black Hawk of his youth, however, "the country girls were considered a menace to the social order." And surely none of them represented more of a menace than Lena Lingard. Demure, soft, and attractive, Lena radiates sexual charm without guile or effort. Before Jim has finished high school, both the married Ole Benson and the proper young bachelor Sylvester Lovett have become driven, obsessed men because of her. Later, in Lincoln, her landlord, Colonel Raleigh, and the Polish violin teacher, Mr. Ordinski, are entranced by Lena and suspicious of Jim on her account. A blonde, Norwegian, Nebraskan Circe, Lena is a temptress who "gave her heart away when she felt like it," as Jim says, but "kept her head for business." If she does not literally turn her admirers into swine, she cannot prevent their appetites from giving them at times hardly less graceful postures. When dancing, says Jim, Lena moved "without exertion rather indolently." If her partner spoke to her, she would smile, but rarely answer. "The music seemed to put her into a soft, waking dream, and her violet-colored eyes looked sleepily and confidingly at one from under her long lashes. . . . To dance 'Home, Sweet Home' with Lena was like coming in with the tide. She danced every dance like a waltz, and it was always the same waltz—the waltz of coming home to something, of inevitable, fated return."

This is the Lena Lingard who walks into Jim's room in Lincoln, who dominates Book Three and seems very close to taking command of the novel. Like Ántonia, she has come from off the prairie; like Ántonia, too, she is generous and forthright. But unlike Ántonia, she makes a success of herself in business, as a fashion designer, first in Lincoln, later in San Francisco. And unlike Ántonia, she is determined not to marry, not to have a family. Lena's unconscious power to distract a man from whatever he may or should be doing exerts its influence on Jim during his final year at the University of Nebraska. He begins to drift, as he says, to neglect academic life, to live from day to day languidly in love with Lena. His mentor, Gaston Cleric, tells him to "quit school and go to work, or change your college and begin again in earnest. You won't recover yourself while you are playing about with this handsome Norwegian." To Gaston Cleric, Lena seems "perfectly irresponsible." In the light of her successful career, the judgment seems only partially valid, but Cleric is near the mark; Lena induces irresponsibility in the men who know her. And Jim is coming to know her well.

No overt antagonism exists between Lena and Ántonia, who are friends with a great deal in common. Yet Ántonia warns Jim in good-natured seriousness not to see too much of Lena; and when Ántonia discovers the manner in which Jim kisses Lena, she exclaims, "If she's up to any of her nonsense with you, I'll scratch her eyes out." Jim's dreams suggest the different roles the girls have in his life. At times he dreams of Ántonia and himself, "sliding down strawstacks as we used to do; climbing up the yellow mountains over and over, and slipping down the smooth sides into soft piles of chaff." He has also a recurrent dream of Lena coming toward him barefoot across a field, "in a short skirt, with a curved reaping-hook in her hand." "She was flushed like the dawn," he continues, "with a kind of luminous rosiness all about her. She sat down beside me, turned to me with a soft sigh and said, 'Now they are all gone, and I can kiss you as much as I like'." Jim says, "I used to wish I could have this flattering dream about Ántonia, but I never did."

Jim's dream of Ántonia, we note, is based on the memory of shared childhood experiences, its sexual significance sublimated in terms of youthful fun and adventure. In Black Hawk, Ántonia has forbidden Jim to kiss her as he apparently kisses Lena, thereby rejecting his tentative gesture toward a relationship of adolescent sexuality. If he is to dream of Ántonia, he must put her in a context of their youth. His dream of Lena, however, more frankly sexual (with the reaping-hook suggestive of such things as fulfillment, castration, and the negation of time), has no context; it can take place only because "they are all gone." Jim's wish that he could have such a dream about Ántonia is part of his larger desire to have some definite, some formal relationship with her. As he says to her later, "I'd have liked to have you for a sweetheart, or a wife, or my mother or my sister—anything that a woman can be to a man." With Lena he drifts into a hedonistic relationship which carries with it the peril of irresponsibility. Somehow Lena always seemed fresh, new, like the dawn: "she wakened fresh with the world everyday," Jim says, and it was easy to "sit idle all through a Sunday morning and look at her." (Ántonia, of course, would be worshipping, not being worshipped, on a Sunday morning.) Like all enchantresses, Lena inspires a chronic forgetfulness. In an ultimate dramatic sense she would be fatal to memory. Consequently, she stands opposed to Ántonia, who will come to bear and to justify the burden of Jim's memory.

The structure of the narrative in Book Three suggests the charm that Lena exercises on Jim. Her entrance into his room, we recall, interrupts his study of Virgil. After she leaves, Jim thinks of all the country girls of Black Hawk and sees a relation between them and the poetry of Virgil: "If there were no girls like them in the world, there would be no poetry. I understood that clearly, for the first time. This revelation seemed to me inestimably precious. I clung to it as if it might suddenly vanish." The country girls are the raw material of poetry; and Jim feels that without them there can be no valid life of the mind. But when he sits down to his lesson for the following day, his newly acquired insight into the relation of "life" and "art" yields up his old dream of Lena, "like the memory of an actual experience." "It floated before me on the page like a picture," he recalls, "and underneath it stood the mournful line: 'Optima dies . . . prima fugit'—the best days are the first to flee." Since this quotation from the Georgics serves as the epigraph of the novel, one has here, I believe, a sense of being close to the emotional center of Jim Burden's narrative. And yet Lena, not Ántonia, inspires the melancholy reflection. In the light of Jim's return to the prairie in Book Four, and, especially, in Book Five, one must conclude that, however tender, this is an unproductive nostalgia, an indulgence in romantic melancholy. Jim's dream of Lena only *seems* "like the memory of an actual experience." And the reality of memory rather than the artificiality of dream will finally serve him as a basis for happiness. Ultimately, the epigraph of the novel comes, as it must, to have fuller and deeper reference to the memory of Ántonia than to the dream of Lena.

Lena Lingard, it is important to see, retards the drama of memory. She represents in the novel not so much an anti-theme as a highly diversionary course of inaction. Promising repose, a blissful release from time, she can be identified by Jim with nothing but herself—which is to say that she does not, as does Ántonia, lend herself "to immemorial human attitudes which we recognize by instinct as universal and true."

Returning to Black Hawk after an absence of two years, Jim is "bitterly disappointed" that Ántonia, betrayed by Larry Donovan, has become "an object of pity," whereas Lena commands wide respect. Having gone to school with Lena, Jim has little immediate sympathy for one who cannot give her heart and keep her head for business. But he responds once again to the country, and its changes seem to him "beautiful and harmonious": "it was like watching the growth of a great men or a great idea." He goes to his old house on the prairie to hear about Ántonia from the Widow Stevens, sleeps in his old room, and confronts his only source of disappointment when he meets Ántonia working in the fields. While they talk, near Mr. Shimerda's grave, he perceives a "new kind of strength in the gravity of [her] face" and confesses that the idea of her is part of his mind. His old feeling for the earth returns, and he wishes he "could be a little boy again." Committed to his early definition of happiness, and thus to the idea of the prairie, and thus to that of Ántonia, he looks hard at her face, which, as he says, "I meant always to carry with me; the closest realest face, under all the shadows of women's faces, at the very bottom of my memory." The drama of memory has been resolved; Jim's memories will take form around the image of Ántonia.

Having placed so much value on a single memory, Jim feels both impelled and afraid to test its validity by a return to the prairie after an absence of many years. Throughout these years he has apparently maintained a kind of inner life; the image of Ántonia, suggesting youth and early happiness, has hardened into a reality which he fears to see shattered. But his visit to the Cuzaks in Book Five vindicates and fulfills the memory he has treasured. "Ántonia had always been one to leave images in the mind that did not fade—that grew stronger with time," he says; "in my mind there was a succession of such pictures." To indicate the value of the past to her, Ántonia produces for him her collection of photographs—of Jim, Jake Marpole, Otto Fuchs, the Harlings, even of Lena Lingard—as part of her family's heritage. Together they look through these photographs of old times, but in such a rich, lively context of the present, with children of all sizes laughing and crowding around to show that they, too, know of the early days, that past and present tend to merge in a dynamic new image of happiness that makes the future possible. Amid Ántonia's large family Jim feels like a boy again, but—and this I feel measures the final success of his return—he does not *wish* that he were a boy again, as he did in Book Four. He has no more need to cling to the past, for the past has been transfigured like the autumn prairie of old. He has "not been mistaken" about Ántonia: "She was a rich mine of life, like the founders of early races." "She had only to stand in the orchard, to put her hand on a little crab tree and look up at the apples, to make you feel the goodness of planting and tending and harvesting at last." The somewhat contrived scene of Ántonia's children scrambling and tumbling up out of their new fruit cave, "a veritable explosion of life out of the dark cave into the sunlight" which makes Jim dizzy for a moment, proclaims the relationship between Ántonia and the prairie: both have yielded life in abundance; both have prevailed.

The unity of My *Ántonia* thus derives, I believe, from a drama of memory fulfilled in the present. Clearly the novel does not give us the story of Ántonia's life nor that of Jim's. Rather, it brings us to see the meaning of Ántonia to a man whose happiest days have been those of his youth, who, in the apotheosis of Book Five, becomes reconciled to the present because of the enduring value of the past, even as he comes to possess that past anew because of the promise and vitality of the present. Jim's image of Ántonia has proved fruitful; his drama of memory is not only resolved but fulfilled. He has atained a sense of meaning in his narrative by confronting in retrospect the elements of his early world: from Jim we have learned of the land, the various people who work the land, and the change which the passing of a generation brings about; from Jim, too, we have had the portrait of the Shimerdas and that of Lena Lingard; and from Jim we have the triumphant image of Ántonia, "battered but not diminished," as his personal symbol of the value of human experience. The elements of the novel cohere in Jim Burden's drama of memory. And in Jim's Ántonia they are all subsumed.

BLANCHE H. GELFANT

The Forgotten Reaping-Hook: Sex in "My Ántonia"

Our persistent misreading of Willa Cather's My Ántonia rises from a belief that Jim Burden is a reliable narrator. Because we trust his unequivocal narrative manner, we see the novel as a splendid celebration of American frontier life. This is the view reiterated in a current critique of My Ántonia and in a recent comprehensive study of Cather's work: "My Ántonia shows fertility of both the soil and human beings. Thus, in a profound sense My Ántonia is the most affirmative book Willa Cather ever wrote. Perhaps that is why it was her favorite." Critics also elect it *their* favorite Cather novel: however, they regret its inconclusive structure, as did Cather when she declared it fragmented and unsatisfactory in form. David Daiches's complaint of twenty years ago prevails: that the work is "flawed" by "irrelevant" episodes and material of "uncertain" meaning. Both critical positions—that My Ántonia is a glorious celebration of American life and a defective work of art—must be reversed once we challenge Jim Burden's vision of the past. I believe we have reason to do so, particularly now, when we are making many reversals in our thinking. As soon as we question Jim's seemingly explicit statements, we see beyond them myriad confusions which can be resolved only by a totally new reading. This would impel us to reexamine Jim's testimony, to discover him a more disingenuous and self-deluded narrator than we supposed. Once we redefine his role, My Ántonia begins to resonate to new and rather shocking meanings, which

From *American Literature* 43, no. 1 (March 1971). Copyright © 1971 by Duke University Press.

implicate us all. We may lose our chief affirmative novel, only to find one far more exciting—complex, subtle, aberrant.

Jim Burden belongs to a remarkable gallery of characters for whom Cather consistently invalidates sex. Her priests, pioneers, and artists invest all energy elsewhere. Her idealistic young men die prematurely; her bachelors, children, and old folk remain "neutral" observers. Since she wrote within a prohibitive genteel tradition, this reluctance to portray sexuality is hardly surprising. What should intrigue us is the strange involuted nature of her avoidance. She masks sexual ambivalence by certainty of manner, and displays sexual disturbance, even the macabre, with peculiar insouciance. Though the tenor of her writing is normality, normal sex stands barred from her fictional world. Her characters avoid sexual union with significant and sometimes bizarre ingenuity, or achieve it only in dreams. Alexandra Bergson, the heroine of O Pioneers!, finds in recurrent reveries the strong transporting arms of a lover; and Jim Burden in My Ántonia allows a half-nude woman to smother him with kisses only in unguarded moments of fantasy. Their dreams suggest the typical solipsism of Cather's heroes, who yield to a lover when they are most solitary, most inverted, encaptured by their own imaginations. As Alexandra dispels such reveries by a brisk cold shower, their inferential meaning becomes almost comically clear. Whenever sex enters the real world (as for Emil and Marie in O Pioneers!), it becomes destructive, leading almost axio- matically to death. No wonder, then, that Cather's heroes have a strong intuitive aversion to sex which they reveal furtively through enigmatic gestures. In A Lost Lady, when young Niel Herbert, who idealizes the Forrester's sexless marriage, discovers Mrs. Forrester's love affair, he vents his infantile jealousy and rage the only way he can—symbolically. While the lovers are on the phone, he takes his "big shears" and cuts the wires, ostensibly to prevent gossip, but also to sever a relationship he cannot abide. Ingenious in rationalizing their actions, Cather's heroes do not entirely conceal an underlying fear of physical love; and the connection between love and death, long undiscerned in Cather's work, can be seen as its inextricable motif. Even in her first novel, Alexander's Bridge, the hero's gratuitous death—generally thought to flaw the work—fulfills the inherent thematic demand to show physical passion as disastrous. Here, as in O Pioneers!, a later work, illicitness is merely a distracting irrelevance which helps conceal the fear of sexuality in all relationships. O Pioneers! reduces the interval between love and death until they almost coincide. At three o'clock, Emil races "like an arrow shot from the bow" to Marie; for the first time they make love; by evening, they are dead, murdered by the half-demented husband.

In My Ántonia, Jim Burden grows up with an intuitive fear of sex, never acknowledged, and in fact, denied: yet it is a determining force in his story. By deflecting attention from himself to Ántonia, of whom he can speak with utter assurance, he manages to conceal his muddied sexual attitudes. His narrative voice, reinforced by Cather's, emerges firm and certain; and it convinces. We tend to believe with Jim that his authoritative recitation of childhood memories validates the past and gives meaning to the present even though his mature years stream before him emptied of love, intimacy, and purpose. Memory transports him to richer and happier days spent with Ántonia, the young Bohemian girl who signifies "the country, the conditions, the whole adventure of . . . childhood." Because a changing landscape brilliantly illumines his childhood—with copper-red prairies transformed to rich wheatfields and corn—his personal story seems to epitomize this larger historical drama. Jim uses the coincidence of his life-span with a historical era to imply that as the country changed and grew, so did he, and moreover, as his memoirs contained historical facts, so did they hold the truth about himself. Critics support Jim's bid for validity, pointing out that "My Ántonia exemplifies superbly [Frederick Jackson] Turner's concept of the recurring cultural evolution on the frontier."

Jim's account of both history and himself seems to me disingenuous, indeed, suspect; yet it is for this very reason highly pertinent to an understanding of our own uses of the past. In the introduction, Jim presents his memoirs as a spontaneous expression—unselected, unarranged, and uncontrolled by ulterior purpose: "From time to time I've been writing down what I remember . . . about Ántonia. . . . I didn't take time to arrange it; I simply wrote down pretty much all that her name recalls to me. I suppose it hasn't any form, . . . any title, either." Obviously, Jim's memory cannot be as autonomous or disinterested as he implies. His plastic powers reshape his experience, selecting and omitting in response to unconscious desires and the will. Ultimately, Jim forgets as much as he remembers, as his mind sifts through the years to retrieve what he most needs—a purified past in which he can find safety from sex and disorder. Of "a romantic disposition," Jim substitutes wish for reality in celebrating the past. His flight from sexuality parallels a flight from historical truth, and in this respect, he becomes an emblematic American figure, like Jay Gatsby and Clyde Griffiths. Jim romanticizes the American past as Gatsby romanticizes love, and Clyde money. Affirming the common, the prototypical, American dream of fruition, all three, ironically, are devastated—Gatsby and Clyde die violently, while Jim succumbs to immobilizing regressive needs. Their relationship to the dream they could not survive must strike us oddly, for we have reversed their situation by surviving to see the dream shattered and the Golden Age of American history impugned. Out of the past that Jim idealized comes our present stunning disorder, though Jim would deny such continuity, as Cather did. Her much-quoted statement that the world *broke* in 1922 reveals historical blindness mistaken for acuity. She denied that "the beautiful past" transmitted the crassness, disorder, and violence which "ruined" the present for her and drove her to hermitic withdrawal. She blamed villainous men, such as Ivy Peters in *A Lost Lady*, for the decline of a heroic age. Like her, Jim Burden warded off broad historical insight. His mythopoeic memory patterned the past into an affecting creation story, with Ántonia a central fertility figure, "a rich mine of life, like the founders of early races." Jim, however, stalks through his myth a wasteland figure who finds in the present nothing to compensate him for the loss of the past, and in the outer world nothing to violate the inner sanctum of memory. "Some memories are realities, are better than anything that can ever happen to one again"—Jim's nostalgic conclusion rationalizes his inanition. He remains finally fixated on the past, returning to the vast and ineffaceable image that dominates his memoirs— the Nebraska prairie yielding to railroad and plough. Since this is an impersonal image of the growth of a nation, and yet it seems so personally crucial to Jim, we must be alerted to the special significance it holds for him. At the very beginning of the novel, we are told that Jim *"loves with a personal passion the great country through which his railway runs."* The symbolism of the railroad penetrating virgin fields is such an embarrassingly obvious example of emotional displacement, it seems extraordinary that it has been so long unnoted. Like Captain Forrester, the unsexed husband of *A Lost Lady*, Jim sublimates by traversing the country, laying it open by rail; and because he sees the land grow fertile and the people prosper, he believes his story to be a celebration.

But neither history's purely material achievement, nor Cather's aesthetic conquest of childhood material, can rightfully give Jim Burden personal cause to celebrate. Retrospection, a superbly creative act for Cather, becomes for Jim a negative gesture. His recapitulation of the past seems to me a final surrender to sexual fears. He was afraid of growing up, afraid of women, afraid of the nexus of love and death. He could love only that which time had made safe and irrefragable—his memories. They revolve not, as he says, about the image of Ántonia, but about himself as a child. When he finds love, it seems to him the safest kind—the narcissistic love of the man for himself as a boy. Such love is not unique to Jim Burden. It obsesses many Cather protagonists from early novels to late: from Bartley Alexander in *Alexander's Bridge* to Godfrey St. Peter in

The Professor's House. Narcissism focuses Cather's vision of life. She valued above all the inviolability of the self. Romantically, she saw in the child the original and real self; and in her novels she created adult characters who sought a seemingly impossible reunion with this authentic being—who were willing to die if only they could reach somehow back to childhood. Regression becomes thus an equivocal moral victory in which the self defies change and establishes its immutability. But regression is also a sign of defeat. *My Ántonia*, superficially so simple and clear a novel, resonates to themes of ultimate importance—the theme of identity, of its relationship to time, and of its contest with death. All these are subsumed in the more immediate issue of physical love. Reinterpreted along these lines, *My Ántonia* emerges as a brilliantly tortuous novel, its statements working contrapuntally against its meanings, its apparently random vignettes falling together to form a pattern of sexual aversion into which each detail fits—even the reaping-hook of Jim's dream:

> One dream I dreamed a great many times, and it was always the same. I was in a harvest-field full of shocks, and I was lying against one of them. Lena Lingard came across the stubble barefoot, in a short skirt, with a curved reaping-hook in her hand, and she was flushed like the dawn, with a kind of luminous rosiness all about her. She sat down beside me, turned to me with a soft sigh and said, "Now they are all gone, and I can kiss you as much as I like."

In Jim's dream of Lena, desire and fear clearly contend with one another. With the dreamer's infallibility, Jim contains his ambivalence in a surreal image of Aurora and the Grim Reaper as one. This collaged figure of Lena advances against an ordinary but ominous landscape. Background and forefigure first contrast and then coalesce in meaning. Lena's voluptuous aspects—her luminous glow of sexual arousal, her flesh bared by a short skirt, her soft sighs and kisses—are displayed against shocks and stubbles, a barren field when the reaping-hook has done its work. This landscape of harvest and desolation is not unfamiliar; nor is the apparitional woman who moves across it, sighing and making soft moan; nor the supine young man whom she kisses and transports. It is the archetypal landscape of ballad, myth, and drama, setting for *la belle dame sans merci* who enchants and satisfies, but then lulls and destroys. She comes, as Lena does, when the male is alone and unguarded. "Now they are all gone," Lena whispers, meaning Ántonia, his threshold guardian. Keeping parental watch, Ántonia limits Jim's boundaries ("You know you ain't right to kiss me like that") and attempts to bar him from the dark unexplored country beyond boyhood with threats ("If I see you hanging around with Lena much, I'll go tell your grandmother"). Jim has the insight to reply, "You'll always treat me like a kid"; but his dream of past childhood games with Ántonia suggests that the prospect of perpetual play attracts him, offering release from anxiety. Already in search of safety, he looks to childhood, for adolescence confronts him with the possibility of danger in women. Characteristically, his statement that he will prove himself unafraid belies the drift of his unconscious feelings. His dream of Lena and the reaping-hook depicts his ambivalence toward the cycle of growth, maturation, and death. The wheat ripens to be cut; maturity invites death.

Though Jim has declared his dream "always the same," it changes significantly. When it recurs in Lincoln, where he goes as a university student, it has been censored and condensed, and transmuted from reverie to remembrance:

> As I sat down to my book at last, my old dream about Lena coming across the harvest-field in her short skirt seemed to me like the memory of an actual experience. It floated before me on the page like a picture, and underneath it stood the mournful line: "Optima dies . . . prima fugit."

Now his memory can deal with fantasy as with experience: convert it to an image, frame it, and restore it to him retouched and redeemed. Revised, the dream loses its frightening details. Memory retains the harvest-field but represses the shocks and stubbles; keeps Lena in her short skirt, but replaces the sexual ambience of the vision. Originally inspired by the insinuative "hired girls," the dream recurs under the tranquilizing spell of Gaston Cleric, Jim's poetry teacher. As his name implies, Cleric's function is to guide Jim to renunciation of Lena, to offer instead the example of desire sublimated to art. Voluptuous excitement yields to a pensive mood, and poetry rather than passion engages Jim: "It came over me, as it had never done before, the relation between girls like those [Lena and "the hired girls"] and the poetry of Virgil. If there were no girls like them in the world, there would be no poetry." In his study, among his books, Lena's image floats before him on a page of the Georgics, transferred from a landscape of death to Virgil's bucolic countryside; and it arouses not sensual desire but a safer and more characteristic mood: nostalgia—"melancholy reflection" upon the past. The reaping-hook is forgotten. Lena changes from the rosy goddess of dawn to an apparition of evening, of the dimly lit study and the darkened theater, where she glows with "lamplight" rather than sexual luminosity.

This preliminary sublimation makes it possible for Jim to have an affair with Lena. It is brief and peculiar, somehow appropriating from the theaters they frequent an unreal quality, the aspect of play. In contrast to the tragic stage-lovers who feel exquisitely, intone passionately, and love enduringly, they seem mere unengaged children, thrilled by make-believe people more than each other. "It all wrung my heart"; "there wasn't a nerve left in my body that hadn't been twisted"—Jim's histrionic (and rather feminine) outbursts pertain not to Lena but to *Marguerite Gauthier* as impersonated by "an infirm old actress." Camille's "dazzling loveliness," her gaiety and glitter—though illusory—impassion him far more than the real woman's sensuality. With Lena, he creates a mock-drama, casting himself in the stock role of callow lover pitted against Lena's older suitors. In this innocuous triangle, he "drifts" and "plays"—and play, like struggle, emerges as his memoirs' motif. Far from being random, his play is directed toward the avoidance of future responsibilities. He tests the role of lover in the security of a make-believe world where his mistress is gentle and undemanding, his adversaries ineffectual, and his guardian spirit, Cleric, supportive. Cleric wants him to stop "playing with this handsome Norwegian," and so he does, leaving Lena forever and without regret. Though the separation of the stage-lovers Armand and Camille wracks them—"Lena wept unceasingly"—their own parting is vapid. Jim leaves to follow Cleric to Boston, there to study, and pursue a career. His period of enchantment has not proved one of permanent thrall and does not leave him, like Keats's knight, haggard and woebegone.

Nevertheless, the interim in Lincoln has serious consequences, for Jim's trial run into manhood remains abortive. He has not been able to bypass his circular "road to Destiny," that "predetermined" route which carries him back finally to Ántonia and childhood. With Lena, Jim seems divertible, at a crossroad. His alternatives are defined in two symbolic titles symbolically apposed: "Lena Lingard" and "Cuzak's Boys." Lena, the archetypal Woman, beckons him to full sexuality. Ántonia, the eternal Mother, lures him back through her children, Cuzak's boys, to perennial childhood.

If Jim cannot avoid his destiny, neither can he escape the "tyrannical" social code of his small town, Black Hawk, which permits its young men to play with "hired girls" but not to marry them. The pusillanimous "clerks and bookkeepers" of Black Hawk dance with the country girls, follow them forlornly, kiss them behind bushes—and run. "Respect for respectability" shunts them into loveless marriages with women of money or "refinement" who are sexless and safe. "Physically a race apart," the country girls are charged with sensuality, some of them considered "dangerous as high explosives." Through an empty conformist marriage, Jim avoids danger. He takes a woman who is independent and masculine, like Ántonia, who cannot threaten him as Lena does by her sheer femininity. Though Lena may be "the most beautiful, the most *innocently* sensuous of all the women in Willa Cather's works," Jim is locked into his fantasy of the reaping-hook.

Jim's glorification of Lena as the timeless muse of poetry and the unattainable heroine of romance requires a closer look. For while he seems to exalt her, typically, he works at cross-purposes to demean her—in his own involuted way. He sets her etherealized image afloat on pages of poetry that deal with the breeding of cattle (his memoirs quote only the last line here):

> So, while the herd rejoices in its youth
> Release the males and breed the cattle early,
> Supply one generation from another.
> For mortal kind, the best day passes first.
> (*Georgics*, Book III)

As usual, Jim remembers selectively—only the last phrase, the novel's epigraph—while he deletes what must have seemed devastating counsel: "Release the males." Moreover, the *Georgics* has only factitious relevance to Lena (though I might point out that it undoubtedly inspired Cather by suggesting the use of regional material and the seasonal patterning of Book I of My *Ántonia*). If anything, the allusion is downright inappropriate, for Virgil's poem extols pastoral life, but Lena, tired of drudgery, wants to get away from the farm. Interested in fashion and sensuous pleasure, settling finally in San Francisco, she is not really the muse for Virgil.

Jim's allusion does have a subtle strategic value: by relegating Lena to the ideal but unreachable world of art, it assures their separation. Mismatched lovers because of social class, they remain irreconcilable as dream and reality. A real person, Jim must stop drifting and study; he can leave the woman while possessing Lena, the dream, in remembered reverie. Though motivated by fear and expediency (as much as Sylvester Lovett, Lena's fearful suitor in Black Hawk), he romanticizes his actions, eluding the possibility of painful self-confrontation. He veils his escape by identifying secretly with the hero Armand Duval, also a mismatched lover, blameless, whose fervid affair was doomed from the first. But as a lover, Jim belongs as much to comedy as to melodrama. His affair fits perfectly within the conventions of the comedy of manners: the sitting-room, Lena's "stiff little parlour"; the serving of tea; the idle talk of clothes and fashion; the nuisance pet dog Prince; the minor crises when the fatuous elder lovers intrude—the triviality. Engaged with Lena in this playacting, Jim has much at stake—nothing less than his sexuality. Through the more serious drama of a first affair, he creates his existential self: an adult male who fears a sexual woman. Through his trivial small-town comedy of manners, he keeps from introspection. He is drifting but busy, too much preoccupied with dinner parties and theater dates to catch the meaning of his drift. His mock romance recalls the words he had used years earlier to describe a childhood "mock adventure": "the game was fixed." The odds are against his growing up, and the two mock episodes fall together as *pseudo*-initiations which fail to make him a man.

Jim's mock adventure occurs years back as he and Ántonia explore a series of interconnected burrows in prairie-dog-town. Crouched with his back to Ántonia, he hears her unintelligible screams in a foreign tongue. He whirls to discover a huge rattler coiling and erecting to spring. "Of disgusting vitality," the snake induces fear and nausea: "His abominable muscularity, his loathsome, fluid motion, somehow made me sick." Jim strikes violently and with revulsion, recognizing even then an irrational hatred stronger than the impulse for protection. The episode—typically ignored or misunderstood—combines elements of myth and dream. As a dragon-slaying, it conforms to the monomyth of initiation. It has a characteristic "call to adventure" (Ántonia's impulsive suggestion); a magic weapon (Peter's spade); a descent into a land of unearthly creatures (prairie-dog-town); the perilous battle (killing the snake); the protective tutelary spirit (Ántonia); and the passage through the rites to manhood ("You now a big mans"). As a test of courage, Jim's ordeal seems authentic, and critical opinion declares it so: "Jim Burden discovers his own hidden courage and becomes a man in the snake-killing incident." But even Jim realizes that his initiation, like his romance later, is specious, and his accolade unearned: "it was a mock adventure; the game . . . fixed . . . by chance, as . . . for many a dragon-slayer."

As Jim accepts Ántonia's praise, his tone becomes wry and ironic, communicating a unique awareness of the duplicity in which he is involved. Ántonia's effect upon Jim seems to me here invidious because her admiration of his manhood helps undermine it. Pronouncing him a man, she keeps him a boy. False to her role as tutelary spirit, she betrays him from first to last. She leads him into danger, fails to warn him properly, and finally, by validating the contest, closes off the road to authentic initiation and maturity.

Jim's exploration "below the surface" of prairie-dog-town strikes me as a significant mimetic act, a burrowing into his unconscious. Who is he "below the surface"? In which direction do his buried impulses lead?

He acts out his quest for self-knowledge symbolically: if he could dig deep enough he would find a way through this labyrinth and learn the course of its hidden channels—whether "they ran straight down, or were horizontal . . . whether they had underground connections." Projecting upon the physical scene his adolescent concern with self, he speaks an analytic and rational language—but the experience turns into nightmare. Archetypal symbol of "the ancient, eldest Evil," the snake forces him to confront deeply repressed images, to acknowledge for the only time the effect of "horrible unconscious memories."

The sexual connotations of the snake incident are implicit. Later in Black Hawk they become overt through another misadventure—Wick Cutter's attempted rape of Jim, whom he mistakes for Ántonia. This time the sexual attack is literal. Wick Cutter, an old lecher, returns in the middle of the night to assault Ántonia, but meanwhile, persuaded by Ántonia's suspicions, Jim has taken her place in bed. He becomes an innocent victim of Cutter's lust and fury at deception. Threatened by unleashed male sex—the ultimate threat—he fights with primordial violence, though again sickened with disgust. Vile as the Cutter incident is—and it is also highly farcical—Jim's nausea seems an overreaction, intensified by his shrill rhetoric and unmodulated tone. Unlike the snake episode, this encounter offers no rewards. It simply reduces him to "a battered object," his body pommeled, his face swollen. His only recognition will be the laughter of the lubricious "old men at the drugstore." Again Ántonia has lured him into danger and exposed him to assault. Again he is furious: "I felt that I never wanted to see her again. I hated her almost as much as I hated Cutter. She had let me in for all this disgustingness." Through Wick Cutter, the sexual urge seems depraved, and more damning, ludicrous. No male in the novel rescues sex from indignity or gives it even the interest of sheer malevolence (as, for example, Ivy Peters does in A Lost Lady).

Also unexempt from the dangers of sex, Ántonia is seduced, exploited, and left with an illegitimate child. When finally she marries, she takes not a lover but a friend. To his relief, Jim finds husband and wife "on terms of easy friendliness, touched with humour." Marriage as an extension of friendship is Cather's recurrent formula, defined clearly, if idiosyncratically, by Alexandra in O Pioneers!: "I think when friends marry, they are safe." Turning words to action, Alexandra marries her childhood friend, as does Cecile in Shadows on the Rock—an older man whose passion has been expended on another woman. At best, marriage has dubious value in Cather's fiction. It succeeds when it seems least like marriage, when it remains sexless, or when sex is only instrumental to procreation. Jim accepts Ántonia's marriage for its "special mission" to bring forth children.

Why doesn't he take on this mission? He celebrates the myth of creation but fails to participate. The question has been raised bluntly by critics (though left unanswered): "Why had not Jim and Ántonia loved and married?" When Ántonia, abandoned by Donovan, needs Jim most, he passionately avers, "You really are a part of me": "I'd have liked to have you for a sweetheart, or a wife, or my mother or my sister—anything that a woman can be to a man." Thereupon he leaves—not to return for twenty years. His failure to seize the palpable moment seems to one critic responsible for the emotional vacuum of Jim's life: "At the very center of his relation with Ántonia there is an emptiness where the strongest emotion might have been expected to gather." But love for a woman is not Jim's "strongest emotion," cannot mitigate fear, nostalgia, or even simple snobbery. Nothing in Jim's past prepares him for love or marriage, and he remains in effect a pseudobachelor (just as he is a pseudolover), free to design a future with Ántonia's family that excludes his wife. In his childhood, his models for manhood are simple regressive characters, all bachelors, or patently unhappy married men struggling, like Mr. Shimerda, Chris Lingard, and Ole the Swede, for and against their families. Later in Black Hawk, the family men seem merely vapid, and prophetically suburban, pushing baby-carriages, sprinkling lawns, paying bills, and driving about on Sundays. Mr. Harling, Ántonia's employer in Black Hawk, seems different; yet he only further confuses Jim's already confused sense of sexual roles, for he indulges his son while he treats his daughter as a man, his business partner. With Ántonia, his "hired girl," Mr. Harling is repressive, a kind of superego, objecting to her adolescent contacts with men—the dances at Vannis's tent, the evening walks, the kisses and scuffles on the back porch. "I want to have my fling, like the other girls," Ántonia argues, but Harling insists she quit the dances or his house. Ántonia leaves, goes to the notorious Cutter, and then to the seductive arms of Larry Donovan—with consequences that are highly instructive to Jim, that can only reinforce his inchoate fears. Either repression of sex or disaster: Jim sees these alternatives polarized in Black Hawk, and between them he cannot resolve his ambivalence. Though he would like Ántonia to become a woman, he wants her also to remain asexual.

By switching her sexual roles, Ántonia only adds to his confusion. As "hired girl" in Black Hawk and later as Cuzak's wife, she cooks, bakes, sews, and rears children. Intermittently, she shows off her strength and endurance in the fields, competing with men. Even her name changes gender—no adventitious matter, I believe; it has its masculine variant,

Tony, as Willa Cather had hers, Willie. Cather's prototype for Ántonia, Annie Pavelka, was a simple Bohemian girl; though their experiences are similar, Ántonia Shimerda is Cather's creation—an ultimately strange bisexual. She shares Cather's pride in masculinity and projects both her and Jim's ambivalent sexual attitudes. Cather recalled that "much of what I knew about Annie came from the talks I had with young men. She had a fascination for them." In the novel, however, Lena fascinates men while Ántonia toils alongside them. "I can work like mans now," she announces when she is only fifteen. In the fields, says Jim, "she kept her sleeves rolled up all day, and her arms and throat burned as brown as a sailor's. Her neck came up strongly out of her shoulders like the bole of a tree out of the turf. One sees that draught-horse neck among the peasant women in all old countries." Sailor, tree, draught-horse, peasant—hardly seductive comparisons, hardly conducive to fascination. Ántonia's illegitimate pregnancy brutalizes her even more than heavy farmwork. Her punishment for sexual involvement—and for the breezy pleasures of courtship—is thoroughgoing masculinization. Wearing "a man's long overcoat and boots, and a man's felt hat," she does "the work of a man on the farm," plows, herds cattle. Years later, as Cuzak's wife, her "inner glow" must compensate for the loss of her youthful beauty, the loss, even, of her teeth. Jim describes her finally as "a stalwart, brown woman, flat-chested, her curly brown hair a little grizzled"—his every word denuding her of sensual appeal.

This is not to deny that at one time Jim found Ántonia physically desirable. He hints that in Black Hawk he had kissed her in a more than friendly way—and had been rebuffed. But he is hardly heartbroken at their impasse, for his real and enduring love for her is based not on desire but on nostalgia. Childhood memories bind him more profoundly than passion, especially memories of Mr. Shimerda. In their picnic reunion before Jim departs for Lincoln, Ántonia recounts her father's story of transgression, exile, and death. Her miniature tale devolves upon the essential theme of destructive sex. As a young man, her father succumbs to desire for the family's servant girl, makes her pregnant, marries her against his parents' wishes, and becomes thereby an outcast. His death on the distant prairie traces back to an initial sexual act which triggers inexorable consequences. It strips him of all he values: his happy irresponsible bachelor life with the trombone-player he "loves"; his family home in beautiful Bohemia; his vocation as violinist when he takes to homesteading in Nebraska; and his joy in life itself. For a while, a few desultory pleasures could rouse him from apathy and despair. But in the end, he finds the pattern of his adult life, as many Cather characters do, unbearable, and he longs for escape. Though Ántonia implies that her poppa's mistake was to marry, especially outside his social class (as Jim is too prudent to do), the marriage comes about through his initial sexual involvement. Once Mr. Shimerda acts upon sexual impulse, he is committed to a woman who alienates him from himself; and it is loss of self, rather than the surmountable hardships of pioneer life, which induces his despair. Suicide is his final capitulation to destructive forces he could have escaped only by first abnegating sex.

Though this interpretation may sound extreme—that the real danger to man is woman, that his protection lies in avoiding or eliminating her—it seems to me the essence of the most macabre and otherwise unaccountable episode in My Ántonia. I refer to that grisly acting out of male aversion, the flashback of Russian Pavel feeding the bride to the wolves. I cannot imagine a more graphic representation of underlying sentiments than we find here. Like most of the episodes in Jim's memoirs, this begins innocently, with the young bride drawing Peter, Pavel, and other guests to a nearby village for her wedding. But the happy evening culminates in horror; for the wolves are bad that year, starving, and when the guests head for home they find themselves rapidly pursued through a landscape of terror. Events take on the surreality of nightmare as black droves run like streaks of shadows after the panicking horses, as sledges overturn in the snow, and mauled and dying wedding guests shriek. Fast as Pavel drives his team, it cannot outrun the relentless "back ground-shadows," images of death. Pavel's murderous strategy to save himself and Peter is almost too inhuman to imagine: to allay the wolves and lighten his load, he wrests the bride from the struggling groom, and throws her, living bait, to the wolves. Only then does his sledge arrive in safety at his village. The tale holds the paradigm for Mr. Shimerda's fate—driven from home because of a woman, struggling for survival against a brutal winter landscape, pursued by regret and despair to death. The great narrative distance at which this episode is kept from Jim seems to me to signify its explosiveness, the need to handle with care. It is told to Jim by Ántonia, who overhears Peter telling it to Mr. Shimerda. Though the vignette emerges from this distance—and through Jim's obscuring nostalgia—its gruesome meaning focuses the apparently disjunct parts of the novel, and I find it inconceivable that critics consider it "irrelevant." The art of My Ántonia lies in the subtle and inevitable relevance of its details, even the most trivial, like the picture Jim chooses to decorate a Christmas book for Ántonia's little sister: "I took 'Napoleon Announcing the Divorce to Josephine' for my frontispiece." In one way or another, the woman must go.

To say that Jim Burden expresses castration fears would provide a facile conclusion: and indeed his memoirs multiply images of sharp instruments and painful cutting. The curved reaping-hook in Lena Lingard's hands centralizes an overall pattern that includes Peter's clasp-knife with which he cuts all his melons; Crazy Mary's corn-knife (she "made us feel how sharp her blade was, showing us very graphically just what she meant to do to Lena"); the suicidal tramp "cut to pieces" in the threshing machine; and wicked Wick Cutter's sexual assault. When Lena, the essence of sex, appears suddenly in Black Hawk, she seems to precipitate a series of violent recollections. First Jim remembers Crazy Mary's pursuit of Lena with her sharpened corn-knife. Then Ántonia recalls the story of the crazy tramp in details which seem to me unconsciously reverberating Jim's dream. Like Jim, Ántonia is relaxed and leaning against a strawstack; similarly, she sees a figure approach "across the stubble"—significantly, his first words portend death. Offering to "cut bands," within minutes he throws himself into the threshing machine and is "cut to pieces." In his pockets the threshers find only "an old penknife" and the "wish-bone of a chicken." Jim follows this anecdote with a vignette of Blind d'Arnault, a black musician who, as we shall see, represents emasculation; Jim tells how children used to tease the little blind boy and try "to get his chicken-bone away." Such details, I think, should not be considered fortuitous or irrelevant; and critics who have persisted in overlooking them should note that they are stubbornly there, and in patterned sequence.

I do not wish to make a case history of Jim Burden or a psychological document of My Ántonia, but to uncover an elusive underlying theme—one that informs the fragmentary parts of the novel and illuminates the obsession controlling Cather's art. For like most novelists, Cather writes out of an obsessive concern to which her art gives various and varied expression. In My Ántonia, her consummate work, that obsession has its most private as well as its most widely shared meanings. At the same time that the novel is highly autobiographical, it is representatively American in its material, mood, and unconscious uses of the past. In it, as in other novels, we can discover that Cather's obsession had to do with the assertion of self. This is the preoccupation of her protagonists who in their various ways seek to assert their identity, in defiance, if necessary, of others, of convention, of nature, of life itself. Biographers imply that Cather's life represented a consistent pursuit of autonomy, essential, she believed, to her survival as an artist. Undoubtedly, she was right; had she given herself to marriage and children, assuming she could, she might have sacrificed her chance to write. Clearly, she identified writing with masculinity, though which of the two constituted her fundamental drive is a matter of pyschological dynamics we can never really decide. Like Ántonia, she displayed strong masculine traits, though she loved also feminine frilleries and the art of cuisine. All accounts of her refer to her "masculine personality"—her mannish dress, her deep voice, her energetic stride; and even as a child she affected boyish clothes and cropped hair. Too numerous to document, such references are a running motif throughout the accounts of Mildred Bennett, Elizabeth Sergeant, and E. K. Brown. Their significance is complex and perhaps inescapable, but whatever else they mean, they surely demonstrate Cather's self-assertion: she would create her own role in life, and if being a woman meant sacrificing her art, then she would lead a private and inviolate life in defiance of convention.

Her image of inviolability was the *child*. She sought quaintly, perhaps foolishly, to refract this image through her person when she wore a schoolgirl costume. The Steichen photograph of her in middy blouse is a familiar frontispiece to volumes of her work; and she has been described as characteristically "at the typewriter, dressed in a childlike costume, a middy blouse with navy bands and tie and a duck skirt." In life, she tried to hold on to a childhood through dress; in art, through a recurrent cycle of childhood, maturity, and childhood again: the return effected usually through memory. Sometimes the regressive pattern signalized a longing for death, as in *The Professor's House* and *Death Comes for the Archbishop*; always it revealed a quest for reunion with an original authentic self. In *My Ántonia*, the prologue introduces Ántonia and the motif of childhood simultaneously, for her name is linked with *"the country, the conditions, the whole adventure of . . . childhood."* The memoirs proper open with the children's journey into pristine country where men are childlike or project into life characters of the child's imagination: like Jake who "might have stepped out of the pages of 'Jesse James.' " The years of maturity comprise merely an interim period—and in fact, are hardly dealt with. For Jim, as for Cather, the real meaning of time is cyclical, its purpose to effect a return to the beginning. Once Jim finds again "the first road" he traveled as a wondering child, his story ends. Hardly discernible, this road returns him to Ántonia, and through her, to his real goal, the enduring though elusive image of his original self which Cather represents by his childhood shadow. Walking to Ántonia's house with her boys—feeling himself almost a boy again—Jim merges with his shadow, the visible elongation of self. At last, his narcissistic dream comes to fulfillment: "It seemed, after all, so natural to be walking along a barbed-wire fence beside the sunset, toward a red pond, and to see my shadow moving along at my right, over the close-cropped grass." Just as the magnified shadow of plow against sky—a blazing key image—projects his romantic notion of the West, so "two long shadows [that] flitted before or followed after" symbolize his ideal of perennial children running through, imaged against, and made one with the prairie grass.

Jim's return "home" has him planning a future with Cuzak's boys that will recapitulate the past: once more he will sleep in haylofts, hunt "up the Niobrara," and travel the "Bad Lands." Play reenters as his serious concern, not the sexual play of imminent manhood, but regressive child's play. In a remarkable statement, Jim says: "There were enough Cuzak's to play with for a long while yet. Even after the boys grew up, there would always be Cuzak himself!" A current article on My Ántonia misreads this conclusion: "[though] Jim feels like a boy again . . . he does not *wish* that he were a boy again. . . . He has no more need to cling to the past, for the past has been transfigured like the autumn prairie of old." Such reasoning falls in naively with Jim's self-deception, that the transformation of the land to country somehow validates his personal life. Jim's need to reenter childhood never relents, becomes even more urgent as he feels adult life vacuous. The years have not enriched him, except with a wealth of memories—"images in the mind that did not fade—that grew stronger with time." Most precious in his treasury of remembered images is that of a boy of ten crossing the prairie under "the complete dome of heaven" and finding sublimity in the union of self and earth and sky. An unforgettable consummation, never matched by physical union, he seeks to recreate it through memory. Jim's ineffable desire for a child more alive to him than his immediate being vibrates to a pathetic sense of loss. I believe that we may find this irretrievable boy in a photograph of young *Willie Cather*, another child who took life from imagination and desire.

In a later novel, *The Professor's House*, Cather rationalizes her cathexis on childhood through the protagonist's musings, at which we might glance briefly. Toward the end of his life, Professor Godfrey St. Peter discovers he has two identities: that of his "original" self, the child; and of his "secondary" self, the man in love. To fulfill himself, "the lover" creates a meretricious "design" of marriage, children, and career, now, after thirty years, suddenly meaningless. The Professor's cyclic return to his real and original self begins with solitary retrospection. All he wants is to "be alone"—to repossess himself. For, having yielded through love to another, he has lost "the person he was in the beginning." Now before he dies, he longs for his original image as a child, an image that returns to him in moments of "vivid consciousness" or of remembrance. Looking back, the Professor sees the only escape from a false secondary life to be through premature death: death of the sexual man before he realizes his sexuality and becomes involved in the relationships it demands. This is the happy fate of his student Tom Outland, who dies young, remaining inviolate, pure, and most important, self-possessed: "He seemed to know . . . he was solitary and must always be so; he had never married, never been a father. He was earth, and would return to earth."

This Romantic mystique of childhood illuminates the fear of sex in Cather's world. Sex unites one with another. Its ultimate threat is loss of self. In Cather's construct, naively and of course falsely, the child is asexual, his love inverted, his identity thus intact. Only Ántonia manages to grow older and retain her original integrity. Like Tom Outland, her affinity is for the earth. She "belongs" to the farm, is one with the trees, the flowers, the rye and wheat she plants. Though she marries, Cuzak is only "the instrument of Ántonia's special mission." Through him she finds a self-fulfillment that excludes him. Through her, Jim hopes to be restored to himself.

The supreme value Jim and other Cather characters attribute to "old friendships" reflects a concern with self. Old friends know the child immanent in the man. Only they can have communion without causing self-estrangement, can marry "safely." They share "the precious, the incommunicable past"—as Jim says in his famous final words. But to keep the past so precious, they must romanticize it; and to validate childhood, they must let memory filter its experiences through the screen of nostalgia. Critics have wondered whether Jim Burden is finally the most suitable narrator for My Ántonia. I submit that Cather's choice is utterly strategic. For Jim, better than any other character, could control his memories, since only he knows of but does not experience the suffering and violence inherent in his story. And ultimately, he is not dealing with a story as such, but with residual "images in the mind." My Ántonia is a magnificent and warped testimony to the mind's image-making power, an implicit commentary on how that creative power serves the mind's need to ignore and deny whatever is reprehensible in whatever one loves. Cather's friend and biographer said of her, "There was so much she did not want to see and saw not." We must say the same of Jim Burden, who held painful and violent aspects of early American life at safe distance, where finally he could not see them.

Jim's vignette of Blind d'Arnault, the black piano player who entertains at Black Hawk, is paradigmatic of his way of viewing the past. Its factual scaffolding (whether Cather's prototype was Blind Boone, Blind Tom, or a "composite of Negro musicians") seems to me less important than its tone. I find the vignette a work of unconscious irony as Jim paints d'Arnault's portrait but meanwhile delineates himself. The motif of blindness compounds the irony. D'Arnault's is physical, as though it is merely

futile for him to see a world he cannot enter. Jim's is moral: an unaware-
ness of his stereotyped, condescending, and ultimately invidious vision.
Here, in his description of the black man, son of a slave, Jim's emblematic
significance emerges as shamefully he speaks for himself, for Cather, and
for most of us:

> [His voice] was the soft, amiable Negro voice, like those I remembered
> from early childhood, with the note of docile subservience in it. He had
> the Negro head, too; almost no head at all, nothing behind the ears but
> the folds of neck under close-cropped wool. He would have been repul-
> sive if his face had not been so kindly and happy. It was the happiest face
> I had seen since I left Virginia.

Soft, amiable, docile, subservient, kindly, happy—Jim's image, as
usual, projects his wish-fulfillment; his diction suggests an unconscious
assuagement of anxiety, also. His phrase of astounding insult and
innocence—"almost no head at all"—assures him that the black man
should not frighten, being an incomplete creature, possessed, as we would
like to believe, of instinct and rhythm, but deprived of intellect. Jim's
final hyperbole registers his fear of this alien black face saved from
repulsiveness only by a toothy servile smile (it might someday lose). To
attenuate his portrait of d'Arnault, Jim introduced innuendoes of sexual
incompetence. He recognizes d'Arnault's sensuality but impugns it by his
image of sublimation: "all the agreeable sensations possible to creatures of
flesh and blood were heaped up on those black-and-white keys, and he
[was] gloating over them and trickling them through his yellow fingers."
Jim's genteel opening phrase connotes male sexuality, which he must
sublimate, displace from the man to the music, reduce to a *trickle*.
D'Arnault "looks like some glistening African god of pleasure, full of
strong, savage blood"; but super-imposed is our familiar Uncle Tom "all
grinning," "bowing to everyone, docile and happy."

Similarly, consider Jim's entrancing image of the four Danish girls
who stand all day in the laundry ironing the townspeople's clothes. How
charming they are: flushed and happy; how fatherly the laundryman
offering water—no swollen ankles; no boredom or rancor; no exploitation:
a cameo image from "the beautiful past." Peter and Pavel, dreadful to any
ordinary mind for their murderous deed, ostracized by everyone, now
disease-ridden and mindless, are to Jim picturesque outcasts: Pavel spitting
blood; Peter spitting seeds as he desperately eats all his melons after
kissing his cow goodbye, the only creature for him to love. And Mr.
Shimerda's suicide. Jim reconciles himself to the horror of the mutilated
body frozen in its own blood by imagining the spirit released and home-

ward bound to its beloved Bohemia. Only the evocative beauty of Cather's language—and the inevitable validation as childhood memory—can romanticize this sordid death and the squalor in which it takes place. Violence is as much the essence of prairie life as the growth of the wheat and blossoming of the corn. Violence appears suddenly and inexplicably, like the suicidal tramp. But Jim gives violence a cameo quality. He has the insistent need—and the strategy—to turn away from the very material he presents. He can forget the reaping-hook and reshape his dream. And as the novel reveals him doing this, it reveals our common usage of the past as a romance and refuge from the present. *My Ántonia* engraves a view of the past which is at best partial; at worst, blind. But our present is continuous with the whole past, as it was, despite Jim Burden's attempt to deny this, and despite Cather's "sad little refrain": "Our present is ruined— but we had a beautiful past." Beautiful to one who recreated it so; who desperately needed it so; who would deny the violence and the destructive attitudes toward race and sex immortalized in his very denial. We, however, have as desperate a need for clarity of vision as Jim had for nostalgia; and we must begin to look at *My Ántonia*, long considered a representatively American novel, not only for its beauty of art and for its affirmation of history, but also, and instructively, for its negations and evasions. Much as we would like to ignore them, for they bring painful confrontations, we must see what they would show us about ourselves—how we betray our past when we forget its most disquieting realities; how we begin to redeem it when we remember.

DONALD SUTHERLAND

Willa Cather:
The Classic Voice

In the spring of 1901 Willa Cather taught a term of Latin in a Pittsburgh high school. By the end of the term she had lost twenty pounds. Or so she wrote to some friends. Even if the twenty pounds are an exaggeration, that is how she felt about it. She could not bring herself without agony to a scholar's meticulous care for the details of Latin grammar, which verbs take the dative and so on. Toward people who devote their lives to that kind of thing her feeling is not amusement so much as dismay at the waste of precious time which might be spent on some larger or livelier purpose. Latin grammar was not only painful to her, it was nothing to her very large purposes as a writer of English, and her grasp of it remained weak.

In *The Song of the Lark* (1915), Fred Ottenburg says of Dr. Archie, *"Lupibus vivendi non lupus sum."* Though the meaning is apparent—"Living with wolves I am not myself a wolf"—it is somewhat beclouded by at least four mistakes in the first two words. Fred Ottenburg has been drinking, which might account for the state of his Latin, but I am afraid I think the Latin is Willa Cather's.

In *Death Comes for the Archbishop* (1927) she uses the motto *Auspice Maria*, which is good enough Latin, like the formula on Spanish coins, *Auspice Deo.* Grammatically it is a kind of ablative absolute, "with the verb understood," as they say, or two nouns in the ablative case in apposition, a construction altogether alien to English, but the sense is

From *The Art of Willa Cather,* edited by Bernice Slote and Virginia Faulkner. Copyright © 1974 by University of Nebraska Press.

roughly "with Mary as favorer" or, less literally still, "by the favor of Mary." The motto is used as a chapter heading, and it sits handsomely, except for the exclamation point after it: *Auspice Maria!*, which seems an undue emphasis until, in the course of the chapter you find Father Joseph murmuring, "*Auspice*, comma, *Maria!* exclamation point!" Then it is clear that Willa Cather took *Auspice* for a verb in the imperative, *Maria* for a vocative, and the two words together to mean something like "Be auspicious, Mary!" or perhaps "Watch out for us, Mary!" I suspect she heard, unconciously, the German word *aus* in *Auspice*.

In another story she quotes the beginning of the Lord's prayer in Latin—"*Pater noster, qui in coelum est*"—which is pretty bad and I shall not dwell on it, nor shall I, on her centenary of all occasions, make a list of her mistakes, though it would not be long. These few are enough to show that her Latin was not scholarly. But they do not at all mean that her mind and style were not deeply influenced by Latin, by the language itself as well as by the literature, the content of which can be had in translation, and by the Latin mentality or temperament, which is not confined to the ancient Romans. It can be found alive in certain qualities of the French, the Italians, and the Spanish, all of whom she studied with care and wrote about, though primarily the French. Taking Latinity that generally, as a mentality distinct from the Gothic, the Anglo-Saxon, the Judaic, and even the Greek, one may say that while Latin grammar has something to do with its formation it is hardly the essential, and Willa Cather could largely do without it.

Her relation to music is comparable. She was not a musician and had little or no knowledge of counterpoint and the rest of it, so to say the grammar of music, but, as Richard Giannone has abundantly and subtly shown in his book *Music in Willa Cather's Fiction*, her work is very frequently guided if not dominated by a kind of musicality, in style and sometimes in structural procedures, along with being so often about musicians. The results are ordinarily too splendid or too charming to be even slightly discredited by her lack of musicology.

The question of the Latin language itself, within her Latinity, is not quite so easy. If something very like the essential expression of an aria can be caught and strongly felt by a listener who has no idea of what key it is in, what metric, or what the intervals are, can the essential expression of a Latin poem be caught by a reader who has only an approximate knowledge of its grammar, upon which not only the literal meaning but the rhetorical effect greatly depends? A good deal is lost on him, of course, but perhaps not the essential expression; he misses many details of the style but perhaps not the style itself, the substance or hang of it.

Some properties of Latin which have little to do with grammar are clear to anybody: its sonority, and its solemnity, which make it so good for inscriptions on monuments or for the mass, and its concision, its way of formulating a great deal in a very few words, as in *suum cuique*, or *carpe diem*, or *lacrimae rerum*. Though Willa Cather's vocabulary is usually very plain English and sparing of all but the simplest Latin derivatives, those and other properties of the Latin language at large do appear frequently in her prose, especially the concision and a certain round finality of assertion. She is said to have been influenced by Virgil in particular, and I have no doubt she was, but the style of a particular author, the Vigilian style, or the Tibullan, or the Tacitean, is not easily apprehended by everybody, not even by scholars as such. It takes an acute literary sensibility to catch these rather irrational inflections and the precise "verbal mood"—as Willa Cather calls it—of an actual poem, and that sensibility can be disconcertingly inattentive to the grammar. The great example in our time was Ezra Pound whose mistakes are more painful than those of Willa Cather because of his far more scholarly habit of mind, but who did catch the manner of Propertius, or something very close to it, I believe, more clearly than anyone had done for centuries. He did the same for our sense of many other authors, forcing upon us what was their modernity in their time. His defective Latin did not keep his general Latinity from being vast and aspiring even to a sort of imperial administration of a conglomerate world, its money as well as all its cultures and their history. I wish he had never written such a word as *opusculus*, but at least it startles an academic mind into looking beyond grammar to something more essential, if less articulate. One has to recognize that in many qualities of style and mind Willa Cather may quite well be as "steeped in the Classics" and as Virgilian, specifically, as she has been said to be.

If Latin grammar was even physically too much for her, how did the language get into her? The answer is simple, and much the same as for music: through her extremely attentive ears. When Latin is quoted or mentioned in her work it is, not always but ordinarily, being recited aloud rather than read in silence. It can be murmured, as by Father Joseph, and it can even be sung, as when in an early story (*A Son of the Celestial* [1893]) a white man is shipping the body of his Chinese crony back to China and sings—to what music I have no idea—part of an ode of Horace to his friend Maecenas.

A more telling instance is Tom Outland, in *The Professor's House* (1925). When Tom is alone on his mesa he commits to memory "fifty lines or more" from the second book of the *Aeneid*, and recites them aloud to himself, in the high solitude of the Indian ruins. The lines are about the Trojan Horse, the beginning of the fall of Troy, and no doubt they enlarge his feeling, as well as the reader's, about the Indian ruins and the fall of that civilization. Later he recites the lines to the Professor with " 'a good pronunciation and good intonation,' " but they are primarily inside Tom Outland, as they were first recited to himself alone, not for the Professor's ear. At this rate Latin is something assimilated into the organism, mentally by memory and physically by the muscles of the mouth and throat. The vocal performance for the Professor, however correct externally, belongs to a vital interior which has become somewhat Virgilian in feeling.

The voices of characters in Willa Cather's work, whether singing, speaking, or laughing, even snoring, are personal behavior and can characterize more intimately than gesture or action. This may also be the way with her own prose, in straight narrative, which would be, as much as dialogue, what she calls expression or utterance, something proceeding like a voice from an appreciable inside, outward.

This is all very easily said but not easily realized by people like myself, for whom writing, especially in the dead or foreign languages, is an existence in space, on the page, and though it takes time to read and is in sequence, one word after another, its existence is not primarily temporal, not vocal unless you happen to read it aloud. It is an objective continuity, a verbal object, and one need not feel there is a subjectivity out of which it is issuing. It just extends itself along its flat or two-dimensional space like a frieze or an inscription. This question, of the essentially written or inscribed word, as against the essentially spoken or sung word, cannot be settled in theory to anybody's satisfaction, certainly not in the case of the novel, whose theory is notoriously unsettled and which can ally itself with almost any other art it pleases, music, painting, drama, epic poetry or lyric, even letters. The problem is practical: how, if you are eye-minded, to learn to read works written primarily in a vocal mode. Or, how to apply the auditory imagination at least equally with the visual imagination. It is not a question of euphony, not even of rhythm, so much as of meanings and expression proceeding in time. Even at a particular tempo, if you please, as when the story "Uncle Valentine" (1925) has, under its title, the notation *adagio non troppo*.

Willa Cather's attention to the expressive qualities of the voice going on was extraordinary, but not quite so extraordinary when you consider that her youth was spent in a terribly vocal era. It was the end of a great age of opera, there were the unbelievable divas and tenors and child prodigies, but the speaking voice too was having a great age, in the theatre and also in oratory. Sarah Bernhardt, one of Willa Cather's heroines and exemplars of a certain style, was, whatever else, a golden voice, and there is an interesting story about that. It was not a singing voice, though it behaved very like one, just as her style of acting was operatic but had to be confined to melodrama. She was the great star of *Tosca*, but when it was a play and not yet an opera. The limitation bothered her and she got the idea, which she proposed to Coquelin, another great speaking voice, of a *spoken* opera, presumably something with an orchestral score and all the other features of opera, except that the words would be spoken and not sung. It might have worked, with such voices. But Coquelin, though it was for him and his style of acting that the most operatic of melodramas, *Cyrano de Bergerac*, was written, did not think a spoken opera possible, so nothing came of it. You might say that *Pelléas and Mélisande* came of it, or from an idea very like it, but the point of the story in connection with Willa Cather is that at the time the speaking voice and the singing voice were nearly interchangeable, not quite, but so nearly as to be an open question. Willa Cather's remark that "singing is idealized speech" may not have a very definite meaning now, but it would have been perfectly clear and irritating to Sarah Bernhardt.

Then there was oratory, and not only the golden voice of Sarah but the silver-tongued orator of the Platte was heard in the land. It was a great age of oratory, and the astonishing thing is that you could go to hear Bryan or Ingersoll and pay no attention to what they had to say about free silver or the existence of God, you listened to the rhetorical style of their speeches as you would to the negotiation of notes by the voices of great singers. The content was there, if you were interested, but it was mainly a pretext for virtuosity or style of expression. Listening to revivalists must have been much the same: there could have been nothing very novel in the content, the expression of the voice could sweep the congregation into a paroxysm of interest. Like the orator, the revivalist was close to singing, at least to the hymnal, and both persons could be combined, as in Bryan.

In her story "Two Friends" (1932) Willa Cather describes the style of one of the friends thus: "Every sentence he uttered was alive, never languid, prefunctory, slovenly, unaccented." That could be a description of oratory, or of her own prose, but it happens to be of a conversational manner merely, even if the conversationalist is imbued with the manner of his idol, William Jennings Bryan. His manner has virtues in common with oratory—aliveness, energy, intention, precision, and accentuation—which are also virtues in the rendering of musical phrases, not only of sentences. Today, in listening to conversation, our attention is certainly not on the sentences and the way they are delivered, and insofar as we listen to oratory our attention is toward whatever information may or may not be forthcoming, not on the expression or execution. But in those days oratory was a major art and conversation was a concomitant minor one at least. Good pronunciation and intonation were accomplishments anybody at all ought to have, whatever he might be uttering. All the vocal arts were so closely related, all being utterance, that they could involve or imply each other. The simplest word of prose, spoken or written, not only of poetry, could at least approximate the emotional vibration of a word sung.

Here is a small example. In My Ántonia, Lena Lingard says to Jim Burden, who has to leave her and the University of Nebraska for higher things, as it were, at Harvard: " 'You are going, but you haven't gone yet, have you?' " That is excellent Ovid if you like or, if you do not, an excellent line for an actress to deliver in a play by someone like Musset. But you may hear it as more poignant. To my ear, which is not a good one and I may be straining it, the voice could be the voice of Manon or of Marguerite Gautier, though the speaker is a very Norwegian seamstress. Ultimately I suppose it might echo the divine voice of Calypso speaking to Odysseus: "You are going, but you haven't gone yet, have you?" Is one to hear a whole chorus of traditional temptresses backing up Lena's voice or is one to hear a single voice? And is it Lena's only, or is it also the essential expression of an archetype, the Delaying Temptress, which need not suggest any particular temptress of tradition, but is at least a universal in excess of the particular dalliance in Lincoln. Willa Cather did believe in universals, and she heard single voices, melodies or songs, more than accompaniments and orchestrations, and that much would be properly classical of her, but it hardly settles the sonority of Lena's voice, which may just possibly be Wagnerian, though I hate to think so. I shall come back to these uncertainties shortly, but just now let me call them the hazards of the vocal mode and note that they help to make Willa Cather what she is called—elusive.

Along with intoning Virgil to himself, Tom Outland wrote an account of his excavations among the Indian ruins. The style was appropriately dry and factual. "Yet," says Willa Cather, "through this austerity one felt the kindling imagination, the ardour and excitement of the boy, like the vibration in a voice when the speaker strives to conceal his emotion by using only conventional phrases."

That effect, of passion conveyed through a dry or plain style, as dry as archeological notes, was, in 1925, the time of The Professor's House, moving into fashion and was to make Ernest Hemingway's fortune, but it has another connection, more to my purpose, with the voice and vocabulary of Virgil himself, which seem to have got into Tom Outland. In his own time a rather harsh critic said Virgil was the inventor of a new kind of mannerism (*cacozelia*), neither inflated nor thin, but made of ordinary words—*communibus verbis*—and thus not apparent.

That style, mannered or not, was at least highly cultivated and would correspond, in English, to that of Dryden or Pope, which is neither inflated like Milton nor thin like Defoe, but made of ordinary words, about as ordinary as "You are going, but you haven't gone yet, have you?" The style is, I believe, known in the schools as the Augustan style, and the question about it is and has been, do you hear the vibration of any emotion in it? Sometimes you do and sometimes you do not. It is difficult now, for the general reader to make out anything stirring under the perfection of Pope except the quick intelligence, but once in a while a vibration of great violence will come through. The very clever portrait of Atticus can suddenly seem heartbroken, even hysterical; other satires seem to have a cold fury under the mere spitefulness; and it was Pope, not Byron or Heine, who said, "This long disease, my life." But most of the time one feels the classical restraint is not restraining anything hard to restrain.

In Virgil's case, some of the inner vibration was lost even in his own time. A contemporary critic said he would find fault with certain things in Virgil if he could only find fault also with Virgil's voice, and facial expression, and impersonation, because the same verses, when Virgil was reciting them, sounded well, but without him they were empty and mute. It is well to remember that Virgil composed his poetry less for the page than for the voice, and apparently too much for his own voice, which was a peculiar one. It was too weak for oratory, which, in Virgil's youth, the age of Cicero, certainly had to be loud, so he gave it up after pleading one case. He also had something like asthma, so the voice was probably wheezy or rich with overtones and its natural projection would have been *en sourdine*. But he could manipulate it very effectively in recitation; it is said to have been sweet or delightful (*suavitate*) and full of wonderful allurements (*lenociniis*). This may help to explain the trouble-some remark of Horace, that Virgil's work was soft and clever. Perhaps the expression of the voice, under the formal versification and plain wording, was soft and charming, suave and seductive, though it of course had to vary for the speeches of his characters, which are sometimes vehement, and with his subjects, from moonlight scenes to storms and battles. Well, the voice is gone and we cannot hope to know exactly how it went, how it enlivened passages that now seem empty and mute, but Willa Cather was right in taking the poetry as essentially vocal and if she recited much of it aloud herself she no doubt got closer to the original vibration of the utterance than more scholarship of the silent kind would have brought her. To a literary scholar it is an incredible fact, though probably a fact, that the *Eclogues* of Virgil were staged and sung or chanted, but with her addiction to opera and the approximations to it in her work Willa Cather would have had little trouble recognizing that the poetry of Virgil was not only vocal but for a kind of histrionic performance, by himself and others, and potentially even operatic. When he says "I sing of arms and the man" he may almost mean it.

In *My Ántonia* there is an odd instance of someone reading Virgil in silence—Jim Burden studying the *Georgics*. But even in silence the voice of his friend and teacher, Gaston Cleric, returns to him, and he says, "as I sat staring at my book, the fervour of his voice stirred through the quantities on the page before me." The quantities are of course the long and short syllables of Classical metrics, and it is typical of Willa Cather's vocal approach that it is not so much the words or their meanings that the fervor stirs through as it is their metrical value, syllable by syllable. Elsewhere Jim Burden does not *read* the *Aeneid* aloud, he *scans* it aloud. His mind is on the duration of syllables as a singer's would be on the duration of notes. What this can mean for readers of Willa Cather's prose is, I think, that not only every word counts, but every syllable counts, as in a poem. Though there is no metric to her prose, however rhythmical it may be, and cadenced, one should attend to the syllabification, to the cunning use of words of one syllable, or a few, or many, which has its effect. *My Ántonia* ends with these words: "the precious, the incommunicable past," where the word *precious*, of two syllables or almost three, is succeeded and as it were augmented by the six syllables of *incommunicable*, which in turn introduces the final monosyllable, *past*. So introduced, the monosyllable gains an enormous emphasis, and surely anyone can hear the fervor stirring in it. The device is Virgilian, perhaps too recognizably so, though it remains, I think, moving, and makes a fine close to the book.

There is something like it in a passage of the *Georgics*, where Virgil is apparently tiring of a topic and says he is wasting precious time on details. But this bit of Romantic irony turns into the line *"Sed fugit interea, fugit inreparabile tempus,"* which means "But it flies meanwhile, it flies, unrecoverable time" and has an eloquence far beyond the occasion. The line is clever, in the manipulation of long and short words and long and short syllables, but I think it is also irresistible. It is very simple, in thought, rhetoric, and diction, and that could be a mannerism, as the critic said, or it could be the appropriate vehicle for a quite basic and universal emotion. Is there any fervor stirring in it, or any ardor, as in Tom Outland's archeological notes? What is commonly heard in Virgil is melancholy, of no great energy compared to tragic passages in, say, Homer, and the fervor Jim Burden feels in reading the *Georgics* may be gratuitously supplies by Gaston Cleric's voice and wide of Virgil's original expression.

But probably not. Virgil was a very popular poet in his time, with a public of Romans, who liked their strong passions as well as their ceremonies, their gladiators as well as their financiers. Once, when he entered a theatre the whole audience rose to greet him, an honor usually reserved for the emperor himself. A merely sad, gentle, and clever poet would scarcely command so enthusiastic a response in that public at large. Fervor and ardor and the like there must have been, even combined with melancholy. The combination, a note of fervid melancholy or melancholy fervor, is more vividly expressed no doubt in such disciples of Virgil as Dante and Tasso, but very likely they got it from Virgil. At any rate, for Willa Cather he was a model, and as she had a virtual dogma that great art is based on strong passions and the strongest passions are mainly the savage and barbaric ones she must have found something of the kind in Virgil, and generally, not only when his subject is a nominal barbarian like Dido or Turnus or Megentius. And all that under a quiet or veiled voice. There are other sources for her own manner, naturally, but what she thought was the "perfect utterance" of the *Georgics* must have been a major one.

There is a magnificently exaggerated description of that kind of expression in a work which seems very remote but may easily have helped to determine her manner, Edgar Allan Poe's quite unclassical and Gothic story, "Ligeia." "Of all the women whom I have ever known," says the narrator, "she, the outwardly calm, the ever-placid Ligeia, was the most violently a prey to the tumultuous vultures of stern passion. And of such passion I could form no estimate, save by the miraculous expansion of those eyes which at once so delighted and appalled me,—by the almost magical melody, modulation, distinctness, and placidity of her very low voice,—and by the fierce energy (rendered doubly effective by contrast with her manner of utterance) of the wild words which she habitually uttered." Later, as things get worse, we find: "Yet not until the last instance, amid the most convulsive writhings of her fierce spirit, was shaken the external placidity of her demeanor. Her voice grew more gentle—grew more low—yet I would not wish to dwell upon the wild meaning of the quietly uttered words."

What Ligeia is going on about is of course universal death, as in what is supposed, in the story, to be her poem, "The Conqueror Worm," a very tortuous little poem in form and ghastly in content. In the event of tumultuous vultures or convulsive writhings of spirit there are naturally two manners of utterance but, to my knowledge, there are no dignified terms for them. The best I find come from popular singing, to belt it out and to cool it. That would hardly be Willa Cather's terminology. For her the alternatives were clear very early, not in words but in the styles of two great rival actresses, Sarah Bernhardt, who certainly belted it out, and Eleanora Duse, who certainly cooled it, if not to redoubled effect like Ligeia, at least with equal power. Willa Cather called Sarah's art one of color and the Duse's an art of marble. Though she could sometimes write with the overt vehemence, the full color, of Sarah, she ordinarily keeps to the more reserved or marmoreal style of the Duse, but in either manner the tumultuous vultures of stern passion are pretty constantly there.

The association of the Classics and classicism in general with white marble is fairly constant in the cultural world and not foolish, however gaudy and coloristic antiquity could in fact sometimes be. Willa Cather surely visualized what she calls "the drama of antique life" as she says Gaston Cleric did, as "white figures against blue backgrounds." That may be an impression of the Parthenon pediments against the blue sky, or of the Portland vase, which was once admired as the essence of antiquity, though now it is an atypical piece of rather decadent bric-à-brac. Be that as it may, white was important in Willa Cather's youth, and it was not altogether a sign of purity. It had an erotic content, as the complexions of women were most attractive if kept very white, not bronzed or tan. What makes Lena Lingard particularly dangerous is the fact that even out tending the cattle all day, "her legs and arms, curiously enough, in spite of constant exposure to the sun, kept a miraculous whiteness which somehow made her seem more undressed than other girls who went scantily clad." So white was a kind of nakedness, any way you looked at it.

With white went a passionate paleness, no doubt left over from the great Romantics, and the painting of the period was full of it, what with the Pre-Raphaelites, Whistler, Corot, Puvis de Chavannes. In 1903 Willa Cather could call her book of poems *April Twilights*, with full confidence that the incipient colors of April—as against the full colors of May or June—and twilights, as against the extreme chiaroscuro of noon or midnight, would have as much or more power. The pallor was not weakness at all, and could be stark, as she calls a painting by Burne-Jones, and in her own prose it is sometimes rendered in terms of hard materials, as in this passage from *Shadows on the Rock*: "A bright rain-grey light, silver and cut steel and pearl on the grey roofs and walls." We may not respond immediately to that tonality now, but it was real and forcible at the time and may be so again.

It was also a matter of good taste. Her own taste in dress was more an appetite than taste for loud colors, but she knew from her elegant mother and from fashion generally that loud colors should be used with great care, only in telling little touches or on special occasions. Her taste in jewels, as they appear in her work at least, is not for the saturated colors of rubies, emeralds, and sapphires, or the brilliance of diamonds, so much as for the paler and less aggressive colors of tiger-eyes, turquoises, and topazes. Whiteness and pallor were no doubt associated in her mind with classical austerity, and those qualities in her descriptive passages correspond to qualities in her vocabulary and rhetoric, colorless if you like, but hard, precise, and passionate.

Her prose, at least in her mature works, is also without brilliance, avoiding epigrams, witticisms, and paradox. It rarely so much as indulges in general ideas. William Dean Howells had worked out a similar prose, and she most probably learned much from him, though she had a revulsion of her own against the glittering manner of Wilde. But Howells, when he struck out all the witty things in his work, got a merely *mild* result—or so she thought—and mildness was the last thing Willa Cather wanted. The problem for her was how to be colorless, how to keep a dull finish as she liked it on silver, and still be thrilling. One of her solutions, the most conspicuous one, was a frequent use of atrocity, both physical and moral. She had rather a fancy for dismemberment, for people being eaten alive by wolves or something, and for cannibals, what another critic than myself might call the basic Dionysiac material, but she renders then in a matter-of-fact and nearly casual way.

Here is a description of the carp being fed by Louis XIV at Fontainebleau. " 'The carp there are monsters, really. They came grunting and snorting like a thousand pigs. They piled up on each other in hills as high as the rim of the basin, with all their muzzles out; they caught a loaf and devoured it before it could touch the water. No long before that, a care-taker's little girl fell into the pond, and the carp tore her to pieces while her father was running to the spot. Some of them are very old and have an individual renown. One old creature, red and rusty down to his belly, they call the Cardinal.' "

One could hardly make less of the caretaker and his little girl, but the essential horror of the story, or rather of the moment, is intact, the more vivid for the lack of elaboration. That is the classic way, a reluctance to develop a theme beyond the bare statement. Indeed Willa Cather does not even make the running father the end of the paragraph, which would be a kind of emphasis, but goes calmly on with information about the carp, ending the paragraph with something of a flourish, a red one, the Cardinal. Typically, the full color is muted, or graduated from red to rusty down to the belly. You are free to surmise what is in that belly, but Willa Cather does not prompt you to. Ligeia herself was not quieter than that.

From a passage in the *Georgics*, which Jim Burden is studying, she drew the epigraph for *My Ántonia*, "*Optima dies . . . prima fugit*," meaning approximately, "The best days are the first to flee," as she says. The four words extracted are much compressed, more peremptory and sculptural than the original text and making a better epigraph, but the text in full is even more expressive of Willa Cather's view of life, in *My Ántonia* and in most of her work. Three lines of it go like this:

> optima quaeque dies miseris mortalibus aevi
> prima fugit: subeunt morbi tristisque senectus
> et labor et durae rapit inclementia mortis,

which means

> And so, for each poor mortal creature the best time
> of life is first to go; diseases come along
> and sad old age, and things become laborious,
> and death, hard death, unsparingly takes us away.

That is a questionable translation, mine, but it presents plainly enough, several of Willa Cather's favorite themes, diseases and the increasing laboriousness of life, in addition to age and death. Other passages in the *Georgics* are as close to her sense of things. The poem is not about nature but about farming, quite a different matter. It is not idyllic, like the *Eclogues*, where you find the bland remark that love conquers all. In the *Georgics* it is brute labor which conquers all and does not by any means always conquer. It can only struggle against the fatal current of things toward the worse.

That view of poor mortals struggling in a desperate universe reckons of course with death as a governing fact, as steadily as a Lucretius did or indeed a Ligeia, but it also dwells on temporality, seeing the course of a lifetime, from youth to decrepitude, as a long and gradual decline, relieved by fugitive moments of happiness or of hard-won success. You may think that temporality and processiveness are not classical, and in very strict theory they are not, but in classical literature there is a kind of secondary tradition, beginning with the *Odyssey*, in which the basis of composition is not action, as in the *Iliad*, so much as the passage of time, or of a lifetime. Most of Willa Cather's work is composed on that basis and she may have derived from the *Odyssey* many of her techniques, especially that of long sad retrospect, the motif of absence or exile, and her very frequent device of having a person return home and find things changed—an excellent device for realizing the passage of time experientially, not as a concept. At any rate, a vision of the world which supports that kind of composition is plainly formulated in the *Georgics*. Not that she got that vision from Virgil alone, but his formulations had her full sympathy and are simpler to deal with than the whole tradition of pessimism she had behind her, Flaubert, Poe, *The City of Dreadful Night*, Carlyle, and so on. Those few lines from the *Georgics* can help to mark off a great deal of what her fiction is from what it is not.

Certain kinds of novels cannot well be written in the Virgilian perspective. The society novel, or civilized novel, which can treat the texture of the present in a drawing room as if it were definitive, and human associations as if they were substantial, cannot often afford to see it all in the open, as precarious and transitory, exposed to a largely destructive natural universe. Willa Cather did not write society novels, though a story like "Flavia and Her Artists" (1905) shows she might have done so and at least tried her hand at that genre, as at many others.

She wrote a powerful story about an industrial accident, "Behind the Singer Tower" (1912), but she did not write social novels. It is rather surprising that she did not, since she knew the muckrakers, but no doubt she felt that such subjects did not suit her voice. She might find herself vociferating instead of singing or speaking. Nor would social subjects do very well under the Virgilian perspective, where kings and shepherds, friends and enemies, empires and individuals, are equally doomed and leave little behind them but the land. With luck, a memory. Then social novels tend to be progressive, whatever horrors they may describe in the present state of things, but for Virgil and for Willa Cather the golden age is in the past. In Virgil there is some hope for its return, but his settled perspective is backward, like Willa Cather's. Marxist or even liberal criticism cannot do much with either of them, except perhaps to resign themselves to the existence of masterpieces somewhat to the right of center.

Nor did she write psychological novels, though here and there she finds a use for the stream-of-consciousness technique, in reveries and dreams, and so on, the passing thought. She had the notion, quite early, that "our psychologies" as she called them, are an excessive refinement, to be swept away by barbarian invasions, which would bring us back to hard and healthy work on the land. The notion is naturally not articulate in

Virgil, though the nostalgia for the land is certainly there, even in the *Aeneid*. In Willa Cather the nostalgia for the farm is persistent and also for the frontier and the wilderness, for savage conditions as well as laborious ones. There is, under such conditions, no time for anything very subtle in the way of psychology. Her characters are so to say practical, having endurance and competence or not having them. They are brutal or delicate, energetic or lasting by immobility, like the Ácoma Indians in *Death Comes for the Archbishop*, who are compared to rock-turtles. Her characters have rudimentary passions, often ugly ones, but they do not have intricate states of mind. Some of them are indeed pathological cases, but they simply go crazy and are sent to an asylum or, if relatively harmless, are humorously tolerated, like Crazy Mary in *My Ántonia*. Then there are monsters, like Ivy Peters in *A Lost Lady*, or the unspeakable murderer in *Death Comes for the Archbishop*, but they are not analyzed or explained. The murderer is simply called degenerate and is hanged, which is rather summary but, I think, a mercy for the reader.

Nor did she write experimental novels. Under the Virgilian perspective the motive in writing is less to make something new than to make something as lasting as possible, more perennial than bronze, as Horace has it, and anyone can feel that a work's chances of lasting are greater if it is based on what has already lasted, that is, on long tradition, than if it is based on novelty or contemporaneity. For a work to last, it had better have some force of originality in it, but the originality may well be in the spirit or in the content, as with Virgil, and not require any radical break with traditional form. Willa Cather loosened the conventions of, say, the *Woman's Home Companion* considerably but she did not by any means scrap them. I am of two minds or three about that, but I am told on good authority that modernism is falling apart all over the place, and if so, Willa Cather may already appear, not old-fashioned, which she only is in her early work and in superficial detail, but permanent and universal as she meant to be.

Another kind of novel she did not write was the dramaturgical, that is, a novel built like a play, with a unified plot or action to the casual continuity of which everything rigorously contributes. That Aristotelian convention is all very well, but under the Virgilian perspective, of the passage of lifetimes, single dramatic actions appear as episodes, especially when seen in retrospect, and are rarely rounded off with an exit march. Ordinarily we outlive our dramas, dozens of them, as Odysseus does his adventures and exploits, and we are not contained in any one of them. The novels of Willa Cather are made up of episodes, even of little anec-dotes, with characters who are often arbitrary apparitions of disappearances, dramaturgically useless enough, but like people who come to us and leave us in life, moving in something experientially more terrible than almost any action, the passage of time and the dissolution of things in it. The idea and the techniques for expressing it are to some extent in Virgil, but, as I say, more evident in the *Odyssey*. Just now, let me offer this essentially nondramaturgical tendency of Willa Cather as one among many reasons for her forbidding the conversion of her novels into plays or movies. The events in her novels are often dramatic, in a sense, even melodramatic, but they are not put together to make a single action or plot, as in a well-made play.

The kinds of novels she did not write, society, social, psychological, and so on, were immensely in vogue in her time. There were Proust, and Virginia Woolf, Joyce and Dos Passos, Upton Sinclair, Faulkner and Hemingway, there was still Edith Wharton, and against all that elaboration and innovation she looks very simple. Indeed she is simple, or simplified, but not in any way naive, not even politically. She was after the practical essentials of survival, of getting something done, and of dying in the given world, finally between the land and the stars. Those essentials are quite simple, available to anyone by the age of fifteen, as she said her material had been to her. To keep them simple and present, however, to stay at the radical center of human being, takes a good deal of discipline and even strategy. It was not just an idiosyncrasy that she liked to write in a tent or that she built a cottage in so remote and primitive a place as Grand Manan. That closeness to the rudimentary world is in the *Georgics* and in the *Aeneid*, but is clearest perhaps in the *Odyssey*, where shelter and survival are great issues, and a bed of leaves can be a luxury.

The *Georgics*, as I said, are not idyllic. They are not about landscape but about the land. They are a farmer's almanac or handbook, based on such grim old authors as Hesiod and Cato the Censor. Natural beauty, general ideas, and Virgil's note of lofty or fervent melancholy, have to get into the *Georgics*, superinduced, as best they can. That handsome passage on deterioration and mortality in general happens to be brought in, rather arbitrarily, when his immediate topic is cattle-breeding. He has had to say which years in the early life of a cow are the best for breeding, and this prompts him to rise to a generality about all poor mortals. I think there is irony in Virgil's tone here, but perhaps not. Cows are in the world with us. At any rate, Willa Cather seems to have felt nothing captious in the transition. She speaks of "the perfect utterance of the 'Georgics,' where the pen was fitted to the matter as the plough is to the furrow." That kind of exactitude in dealing with a hard and basic subject matter is her own kind of perfection. An austere exactitude can provide an intellectual exhilaration well enough, but does it amount to a passion, even a "stern" passion, and what has it to do with poetry? Her express view of poetry in the *Georgics* and in general is puzzling but worth working out if you can do it.

Jim Burden is interrupted in his study of the *Georgics* by a visit from Lena Lingard, and when she has gone, she and her laughter have reminded him of other girls back home in Black Hawk, who were beautiful and easygoing but not the "nice" girls of the town. He says, "It came over me, as it had never done before, the relation between girls like those and the poetry of Virgil. If there were no girls like them in the world, there would be no poetry. I understood that clearly, for the first time. This revelation seemed to me inestimably precious. I clung to it as if it might suddenly vanish." When he returns to his book the memory of an old dream he had about Lena coming toward him across a harvest field "floated," he says, "on the page like a picture, and underneath it stood the mournful line: '*Optima dies . . . prima fugit.*' "

The idea, or the fugitive revelation, is put with great emphasis and its importance to Willa Cather is evident, but its meaning is not. There are no pretty girls to speak of in Virgil, he is anything but a love poet, so the relation must be to poetry in general. She may mean that the sources of poetry are ultimately sexual, which is all right and would have been worth saying at the time of writing, 1918, but I think she means more. In the context of Black Hawk the pretty laughing girls would be defined against Puritanism, or the bleak respectability of the Protestant churches. They would embody a kind of paganism and, in spite of their race, a Latinity—the life of the flesh, the senses, and finally the arts, as against virtues and sins and a supernatural attitude toward the perceptible world. Virgil's poetry would stand for the highest or most essential utterance of that pagan world, of which the girls are part, and the image of Lena in the harvest field floating on the page like a picture would make an apt enough illustration of the *Georgics*. But here we are in difficulties with Lena again. Her image is rather portentous and mysterious, the memory of a dream in the midst of a reverie, and part of a "revelation." Willa Cather may mean her to represent Venus or Aphrodite, in a number of her aspects, beauty and the fertility of nature as well as love proper, and in that case the relation of Lena and girls like her to the poetry of Virgil would be clear. Venus Genetrix, or the Lucretian Venus, the goddess who makes things grow, would infuse even the hardest facts of farming with a numinousness, and the poetry of the *Georgics* would come out of those facts, like wheat from the ground.

I do not like this much. There are schools of criticism which like symbols and working out mythical structures behind anything at all. Today they would spot Lena Lingard as the White Goddess at once, and go on from there, but I think Lena is a great myth in her own right, and does not need Venus or Calypso or Camille behind her. Still, it does look as if Willa Cather is suggesting Venus, and the critical question is how the suggestion works, whether it implies a whole structure of thought and detailed lore, or is simply an allusion in passing, a sort of elaborated adjective modifying the noun Lena. I think the latter, and that there is, in the narrative, as much economy of depth as there is economy of explicit statement. That, I think, would be classic, if classicism likes things simple and mainly flat. It may have what is called a depth of passion, but I would call that rather strength of passion and locate it not far from the explicit surface.

Some of Willa Cather's classical allusions are easier to deal with. In *The Professor's House*, the Professor, in despair over his impossible daughters, asks himself, very funnily, "Was there no way but Medea's?" One had best laugh and go right on reading, without making more of Medea than the archetype of infanticide, because if you think it over nothing more works out: Medea did not kill her children because they were impossible, she killed them for revenge on Jason, and they were sons, not daughters, in the first place. In an early story, a sort of parable, "The Way of the World" (1898), children build little towns in play, one of them is destroyed and its builder, says Willa Cather, "sat down with his empty pails in his deserted town, as Caius Marius once sat among the ruins of Carthage." Except for the tone of antique grandeur, its vocal value, so to say, that will not do at all. Marius was not a Carthaginian and had nothing to do with either the building or the destruction of Carthage. He just happened to take refuge there when driven from Rome, and Marius sitting among the ruins of Carthage, a fugitive, is simply a proverbial case of desolation redoubled. The full story, in Plutarch, does nothing at all for "The Way of the World."

But the tone of antique grandeur, the solemnity of the very names, Medea, Caius Marius, and Carthage is, or was, quite genuine, in a culture which took the history of mankind as seriously as it did religion. Names from cultural history were almost exactly like names from the Bible, Jezebel, Abraham, or Absalom, which have a handsome sound and a lofty archetypical meaning, perhaps accompanied by an image, but without much connection with the detail of their stories in the Bible. Invoking them was enough. The best thing one can do with them in reading now is to listen, with all one's ears, catch the vibration in passing, but not to stop and look or do research.

The best example I know of what not to look into is in *O Pioneers!*, the title of Part IV, "The White Mulberry Tree." It seems to invite the reader to recall the story of Pyramus and Thisbe in Ovid, where the blood of a dying lover stains the white mulberry tree red. About eleven years ago the late L.V. Jacks tried to work out parallels between the Pyramus and Thisbe story and the story of Emil and Marie, as if there might be a thematic substructure or counterpoint. He did find a few correspondences of detail, but the differences are very great. In manner, the story in Ovid has the charm and lightness of a fairy tale, while the story of Emil and Marie and her husband is a fairly realistic tragedy, with strongly motivated characters. Pyramus and Thisbe are suicides; Emil and Marie are murdered by her jealous husband. They are adulterers, while the love of Pyramus and Thisbe is unconsummated. One difference is comic: Ovid, to solve the difficulty of getting blood up into the tree to stain its berries, compares the spurt of blood from Pyramus's wound to the long whistling jet of water from a small leak in a lead pipe, which does well enough for a fairy tale. Willa Cather has some white berries lying already on the ground where they can be stained by the final writhings of Marie, which is more like realism. The story was originally, no doubt, a Babylonian myth connected with the death of a vegetation god, and getting the blood into the tree was probably done by a miracle, requiring no such ingenuity as Ovid's to make it appear plausible. What is one to make of all this in the chapter title and story by Willa Cather? The image of a white mulberry tree is certainly decorative, and even poignant, if you take into account the force of white and pallor at the time. If you take the detail of Ovid's story into account also you introduce a strident sort of comedy into Willa Cather's story and make an amusing technical problem of the tree which dominates it. If you take the Babylonian vegetation myth into account, you turn the story of Emil and Marie into some sort of fertility rite. Since this was the time (1913) of *The Golden Bough*, and *The Waste Land* was to appear nine years later, Willa Cather, who was, in her way, a modern, until 1922 or "thereabouts," may well have wanted to suggest some kind of ritual out of anthropology. She certainly meant to poetize and enlarge her regional or even local story, and the white mulberry tree, taken as some vast vague symbol of immemorial tragedy, even a Wagnerian sort of love-death, would certainly increase the dimensions. But the text of Ovid certainly does not.

The great temptation of Willa Cather was her own virtuosity. She could and did write almost any kind of story, even what she calls a "manly battle yarn," in *One of Ours*. She could write fantasies and parables and, when symbols and mythologies were being used, indulge in them herself.

But her real strength lay, I think, in another direction, in a special kind of concentrated realism, in reduction rather than complication or augmentation. In *A Lost Lady* she uses an expression which may help define this. She says that for Niel Herbert the books in his uncle's library were "living creatures, caught in the very behaviour of living,—surprised behind their misleading severity of form and phrase." She had just spoken of the *Heroides* of Ovid, which Niel has read over and over, so we are still with the classic Latin style as she felt it, severe but betraying "the very behaviour of living" behind it. Apart from the books themselves as living creatures, I would apply that expression to what it is that Willa Cather eminently catches in the characters of her major works. The behavior of living, not life; that is, the quick of the process, much rather than life as an aggregate of factual detail or life in a summary philosophical sense. The behavior of living especially in the course of a lifetime, long or short. Its "very" behavior—the actuality of living—not its conditions of causes or mythic significances, is her prime subject, and it has no need of symbols or ideas to sustain or augment it, though it may indeed use them for embellishment. All it needs is to be uttered, in voice or gesture or event. In Willa Cather's work it is habitually remembered, rather than presented raw, but it is remembered vividly, and memory, or the device of retrospect, is a fine way of isolating the vital aspect of persons and events, and getting rid of the real but irrelevant facts around it.

You will surely remember the death of Count Frontenac in *Shadows on the Rock*. After the extreme unction she says,

> Then, very courteously, he made a gesture with his left hand, indicating that he wished every one to draw back from the bed.
> "This I will do alone," his steady glance seemed to say.
> All drew back.
> "Merci," he said distinctly. That was the last word he spoke.

The severity of that passage is obvious, and the strong emotion just under the irreducible wording, but there is a distinction worth making, that although the chivalric character of Count Frontenac is perfectly rendered by the gesture of the left hand, the less commanding hand, by the steady glance, and his last word, the virtue and energy of the passage is not in that rendition so much as in putting us into direct contact with the very behavior of living a few moments before dying, as anyone potentially might live them. This grasp of what a teacher of mine called "livingness" is, I believe, the greatest strength of Willa Cather, to which her many other talents are subsidiary, though they were indeed sometimes insubordinate.

Distinct from her characters, there is the writer herself as a living creature, a mind and a temperament and especially a voice, uttering its sense of the narrative events as they come along, inflecting them, selecting them, accenting them or muting them, as if they were in a song. The last sentence of *Death Comes for the Archbishop* will, I hope, be a clear example. The Archbishop has died, just after dark—a typical lighting—the cathedral bell has sounded the knell, with various effects on the people waiting at the cathedral in Santa Fé. Then comes this extraordinary sentence, which looks so casual: "Eusabio and the Tesuque boys"—I have to explain that these are Indians—"went quietly away to tell their people; and the next morning the old Archbishop lay before the high altar in the church he had built." I wish I had time to analyze the effects of that sentence, but a few will serve. First, the conjunction *and*, which looks as if it joined two events in a perfunctory way, actually joins two solemn and uncanny silences, the tread of the departing Indians and the body of the Archbishop. It is the joining of emotional qualities, as in a song, not the mere facts. Then he is called the old, not the dead, Archbishop, and there we have the Virgilian and Catherian interest not only in the fact of death but in the long process of living and aging before it. Most remarkable is the phrase "in the church he had built." Why not say cathedral, since in fact it is a cathedral? Well, I should say Miss Cather's voice is negotiating an awesome hush, and the word cathedral has too many syllables and too florid a meaning, so she uses the smaller word, church. But if it is small and commonplace, it is also the more universal word. It was not a cathedral that Christ founded, but a church, and indeed it was a church, a religious congregation, that the Archbishop had founded in New Mexico, by fair means or foul, depending on your politics, but not just a cathedral. All this, if you please, in the utterance of a single short word.

Let me give one more example, somewhat less funerary. In *My Ántonia*, the Widow Steavens is telling how Ántonia came to say goodbye to her before departing on her perilous adventure to marry Donovan in Denver. The Widow Steavens, you may remember, is now the tenant on the Burden homestead, living in the house that had "always been a refuge" to Ántonia. The Widow Steavens says, " 'She laughed kind of flighty like, and whispered, "Good-bye, dear house!" and then ran out to the wagon.' " One should attend to the voices in Willa Cather, and read "kind of flighty like" as a musical notation, like, say, *agitato ma non troppo*, and the whisper as *mezzo piano* or softer. Then the words, "Good-bye, dear house," in all their simplicity, have the force of any devastating aria on the subject of parting and farewell. And she says "good-bye," not "farewell." Virgil himself would have used words as ordinary as that—something like *vale, cara domus*—spoken them with a vibrant whisper like Ántonia's, and made all Rome tremble.

EUDORA WELTY

The House of Willa Cather

Your invitation to come to the International Seminar of writers, scholars, and critics in commemoration of the centennial of Willa Cather's birth, to speak as a writer of fiction on the fiction of Willa Cather, brings me the very highest honor. I am grateful and filled with humility and pride together in coming before you. The great prize couched in the invitation has come from the incentive it gave me to read all her work again, read it from the beginning. How she refreshes the spirit! The quality that struck me with the strongest force as I read is what I should like to speak about as we meet to celebrate her—the remarkable, and rewarding, physical quality of her work.

"More than anything else I felt motion in the landscape; in the fresh, easy-blowing morning wind, and in the earth itself, as if the shaggy grass were a sort of loose hide, and underneath it herds of wild buffalo were galloping, galloping . . . ." All Willa Cather's prose, like this passage in My Ántonia, speaks of the world in a way to show it's alive. There is a quality of animation that seems naturally come by, that seems a born part of every novel. Her own living world is around us as we read, present to us through our eyes and ears and touch.

Of course it doesn't escape us that this physical landscape is brought home to us in a way that is subjective. "Overhead the stars shone gloriously. It was impossible not to notice them." Thus she rivets our eyes. "The summer moon hung full in the sky. For the time being it was the great fact in the world." Willa Cather would like our minds to receive what she is showing us not as its description—however beautiful—but as

From *The Art of Willa Cather*, edited by Bernice Slote and Virginia Faulkner. Copyright © 1974 by Eudora Welty. The University of Nebraska Press, 1974.

the thing described, the living thing itself. To this end she may eliminate its picture, the better to make us see something really there. It was her observation that "whatever is felt upon the page without being specifically named there—that, one might say, is created." "There were none of the signs of spring for which I used to watch in Virginia," says the narrator. "There was only—spring itself; the throb of it . . . . If I had been tossed down blindfold on that red prairie, I should have known that it was spring."

And so the texture, that informs us of so much in her prose, owes more than a little to its function. "It was over flat lands like this . . . that the larks sang." Now we see the land. And hear the lark.

What she has given us is of course not the landscape as you and I would see it, but her vision of it; we are looking at a work of art.

There is something very special, too, about its composition. Look at the Nebraska of her novels as a landscape she might have addressed herself to as an artist with a pencil or a brush. There is the foreground, with the living present, its human figures in action; and there is the horizon of infinite distance, where the departed, now invisible ancients have left only their faint track, cliff dwellings all but disappeared into thin air, pure light. But there is no intervening ground. There is no generation preceding the people now here alive, to fill up the gap between, to populate the stretch of emptiness. Nobody we can see, except the very youngest child, has been born here. Fathers and mothers traveled here, a few hardy grandparents who kept up will survive the life a little while too, and the rest of the antecedents have been left in their graveyards the width of the continent behind.

In this landscape we are made as aware of what isn't as of what is. There is no recent past. There is no middle distance; the perspectives of time and space run unbroken, unmarked, unmeasured to the vanishing point. With nothing in between, the living foreground and that almost mythological, almost phantasmagorical background are all but made one, as in a Chinese painting—and exactly as in one of the mirages that Willa Cather's people often meet, quite casually, in the desert:

> . . . a shallow silver lake that spread for many miles, a little misty in the sunlight. Here and there one saw reflected the image of a heifer, turned loose to live upon the sparse sand grass. They were magnified to a prepos- terous height and looked like mammoths, prehistoric beasts standing solitary in the waters that for many thousands of years actually washed over that desert: the mirage itself may be the ghost of that long-vanished sea.

Or that ancient life may be discovered through profound personal experience, through one of her "opening windows." Willa Cather brought past and present into juxtaposition to the most powerful effect. And that landscape itself must have shown her this juxtaposition. It existed in the world where she lived, she had the eyes to see it, and she made it a truth of her art. When the sword of Coronado and the plow against the sun are fused into one in My Ántonia, we are seeing another vision of it.

The past can be seen—she lets us see it—in physical form. It can be touched—Thea can flake off with her thumb the carbon from the rock roof that came from the cooking stove of the Ancient People. Thea comes to have intuitions about their lives so close to heart that she could walk the trail like the women whose feet had worn it, "trying to walk as they must have walked, with a feeling in her feet and knees and loins which she had never known before. . . . She could feel the weight of an Indian baby hanging to her back as she climbed." And so Niel, of a later day, in A Lost Lady, feels in saying goodbye to it: "He had seen the end of an era, the sunset of the pioneer. He had come upon it when already its glory was nearly spent. So in the buffalo times a traveller used to come upon the embers of a hunter's fire on the prairie, after the hunter was up and gone; the coals would be trampled out, but the ground was warm, and the flattened grass where he had slept and where his pony had grazed, told the story."

She saw the landscape had mystery as well as reality. She was undaunted by both. And when she writes of the vast spaces of the world lying out in the extending night, mystery comes to her page, and has a presence; it seems to me a presence not too different from that called up by Turgenev in his magical "Behzin Meadow."

Willa Cather saw her broad land in a sweep, but she saw selectively too—the detail that made all the difference. She never lost sight of the particular in the panorama. Her eye was on the human being. In her continuous, acutely conscious and responsible act of bringing human value into focus, it was her accomplishment to bring her gaze from that wide horizon, across the stretches of both space and time, to the intimacy and immediacy of the lives of a handful of human beings.

People she saw slowly, with care, in their differences: her chosen characters. They stood up out of their soil and against their sky, making, each of them and one by one, a figure to reckon with.

"For the first time, perhaps, since that land emerged from waters of geologic ages," she says of Alexandra in that memorable passage of O Pioneers!, "a human face was set toward it with love and yearning. It seemed beautiful to her, rich and strong and glorious. Her eyes drank in the breadth of it, until her tears blinded her. Then the Genius of the Divide, the great, free spirit which breathes across it, must have bent lower than it ever bent to a human will before. The history of every country begins in the heart of a man or a woman."

And the farther and wider she could see when she started out, the closer it brought her, we feel, full circle—to the thing she wanted, the living, uncopyable *identity* of it that all her working life she wrote in order to meet, to face, to give us as well as she knew it in stories and novels.

The lack of middle distance may have something to do with the way the characters in the foreground cast such long, backreaching shadows. In that lonely stretch of empty and waiting space, they take on heroic stature. And so, Jim Burden tells us—and this has been earned; we have almost reached the end of her novel: "Ántonia had always been one to leave images in the mind that did not fade—that grew stronger with time. . . . She lent herself to immemorial human attitudes which we recognize by instinct as universal and true. She was a battered woman now, not a lovely girl; but she still had that something which fires the imagination, could still stop one's breath for a moment by a look or gesture that somehow revealed the meaning in common things. She had only to stand in the orchard, to put her hand on a little crab tree and look up at the apples, to make you feel the goodness of planting and tending and harvesting at last. All the strong things of her heart came out in her body . . . . She was a rich mine of life, like the founders of early races."

A writer uses what he's been given. The work of William Faulkner—another writer of Southern origin, who was destined himself to live in the thick of his background and who had his own abiding sense of place and time and history—is packed most densely of all at the middle distance. The generations clustered just behind where the present-day characters are in action are in fact the tallest—and the most heavily burdened with that past. Faulkner's ancient peoples, his Indians, whose land was taken away by unjust treaty, who were expelled from their own, their race dispersed and brought to nothing, have made the land inimical to the white man. The slave has cursed him again. History for Faulkner is directly inherited; it has come down to the present with the taint of blood and the shame of wrongdoing a part of it. Along with the qualities of nobility and courage and endurance, there were for him corresponding qualities of guilt; there is torment in history and in Faulkner's wrestling with it, in his interpretation of it. Willa Cather's history was not thus bonded to the present; it did not imprison the present, but instructed it, passed on a meaning. It was pure, remained pure, and in its purity could come and go in crystal air. It had the character and something of the import of a vision. The spirit, and not the blood, received it.

In the world of her novels, history lies in persistence in the memory, in lost hidden places that wait to be found and to be known for what they are. Such history is barely accessible, the shell of it is only frailly held together, it will be loseable again. But the continuity is *there*.

Where does the continuity lie, then? It is made possible, it is carried out, is lived through, by the pioneer. And it is perceived by the artist. And even more profoundly, it exists, for Willa Cather, as a potential in the artist himself; it is his life's best meaning, his own personal, and responsible, connection with the world.

"That stream"—Thea is meditating in Panther Canyon—"was the only living thing left of the drama that had been played out in the cañon centuries ago. In the rapid, restless heart of it, flowing swifter than the rest, there was a continuity of life that reached back into the old time. . . . The stream and the broken pottery: what was any art but an effort to make a sheath, a mould in which to imprison for a moment the shining, elusive element which is life itself—life hurrying past us and running away, too strong to stop, too sweet to lose? The Indian women had held it in their jars. . . . In singing, one made a vessel of one's throat and nostrils and held it on one's breath, caught the stream in a scale of natural intervals."

When Thea holds the ancients' pottery in her hands, her feeling for art is born. When Willa Cather makes her novel one about art, she chooses art not of the word, but of the voice. And not the song, but the voice. She has been able to say everything—it is a dazzling translation—in terms of the human being a physical world.

The whole work of Willa Cather is an embodiment. The great thing it embodies is, of course passion. That is its vital principle.

She did not come out of Virginia for nothing, any more than she grew up in Nebraska for nothing. History awed and stirred Willa Cather; and the absence of a history as far as she could see around her, in her growing up, only made her look farther, gave her the clues to discover a deeper past. The scarcity of people, a sense of absence and emptiness, set to work in her mind ideas not of despair but of aspiration, the urgency to make out of whatever was there *something*—a thing of her own. She opened her mind to the past as she would to a wise teacher. When she saw the connections, the natural channels opening, she let the past come flooding into the present.

"To people off alone, as we were, there is something stirring about finding evidences of human labour and care in the soil of an empty country. It comes to you as a sort of message, makes you feel differently about the ground you walk over every day," says Tom Outland, in *The Professor's House*.

Willa Cather's story conceptions have their physical bases, and their physical counterparts. The shift that took place in her own life when her family moved from its settled home in Virginia to the unbroken prairie of the Divide came about when she was nine years old, so likely to be the most sensitive, most vulnerable year of childhood. Its wrench to the spirit was translated over and over again into the situations in her novels and stories. The shift from one home to another, the shift of feeling, must have become in itself the source of a distinctive fictional pattern which was to fall into place for her; it is the kaleidoscopic wrench to the heart that exposes the deeper feeling there. Not impossibly, the origin of her technique of juxtaposition lay in the Virginia–Nebraska move, too. She worked out some of her most significant effects by bringing widely separated lives, times, experiences together—placing them side by side or one within the other, opening out of it almost like a vision—like Tom Outland's story from *The Professor's House*—or existing along with it, waiting in its path, like the mirage.

Personal history may turn into a fictional pattern without closely reproducing it, without needing to reproduce it at all. Essences are what make patterns. Fictional patterns may well bite deeper than the events of a life will ever of themselves, or by themselves, testify to. The pattern is one of interpretation. There, the connections are as significant as what they join together, or perhaps more so. The meaning comes through the joined and completed structure, out of the worthiness of its accomplishment.

In the novel, relationships, development of acts and their effects, and any number of oblique, *felt* connections, which are as important and as indispensable as the factual ones, in composing the plot, form a structure of revelation. The pattern is the plot opened out, disclosing—this was its purpose—some human truth.

Of course it is a pattern uniquely marked by its author's character; the nature of personal feeling has given it its grain. Willa Cather's revered Flaubert said in a letter, "the secret of masterpieces lies in the concordance between the subject and the temperament of the author." The events of a story may have much or little to do with the writer's own life; but the story *pattern* is the nearest thing to a mirror image of his mind and heart.

The artist needs and seeks distance—his own best distance—in order to learn about his subject. To open up the new, to look back on the old, may bring forth like discoveries in the practice of art. Whether the comprehension keeps to the short perimeter around the present, or runs far back into the past, is secondary to the force, impellment, of human feeling involved: *this* determines its reach.

We need to know only what the work of Willa Cather in its course has to tell us—for it's a great deal—about her independence and courage of mind to guess that Miss Jewett's well-known advice—"You must find a quiet place. . . . You must find your own quiet centre of life and write from that"—would not have been the sign to her it was, unless she had arrived at that fact for herself, deep in her own nature. How could she not have? It was central to her life, basic to her conception of character, of situation, in fiction: the writing of one novel had been able to teach her that. When she read that truth of Miss Jewett's, isn't it likely that she simply *recognized* it? As she recognized, in the Dutch masters when she saw them in Paris, her own intention in a book to come:

"Just before I began the book [*The Professor's House*]," runs a well-known letter she wrote, "I had seen, in Paris, an exhibition of old and modern Dutch paintings. In many of them the scene presented was a living-room warmly furnished, or a kitchen full of food and coppers. But in most of the interiors, whether drawing-room or kitchen, there was a square window, open, through which one saw the masts of ships, or a stretch of grey sea. The feeling of the sea that one got through those square windows was remarkable, and gave me a sense of fleets of Dutch ships that ply quietly on all the waters of the globe."

It is not surprising that the act of recognition is one of the touchstones of her fiction. We see her writing in *The Song of the Lark*: "The faculty of observation was never highly developed in Thea Kronborg. A great deal escaped her eye as she passed through the world. But the things which were for her, she saw; she experienced them physically and remembered them as if they had once been part of herself. The roses she used to see in the florists' shops in Chicago were merely roses. But when she thought of the moonflowers that grew over Mrs. Tellamantez's door, it was as if she had been that vine and had opened up in white flowers every night." And, "Here, in Panther Cañon, there were again things which seemed destined for her." And before that, "When the English horns gave out the theme of the Largo [this is Thea hearing Dvořák's *New World Symphony* for the first time], she knew that what she wanted was exactly that. Here were the sand hills, the grasshoppers and locusts, all the things that wakened and chirped in the early morning; the reaching and reaching of high plains, the immeasurable yearning of all flat lands. There was home in it, too; first memories, first mornings long ago; the amazement of a new soul in a new world; a soul new and yet old, that had dreamed something despairing, something glorious, in the dark before it was born;

a soul obsessed by what it did not know, under the cloud of a past it could not recall."

Recognition, we feel, was for Willa Cather a learning process that didn't stop; and Willa Cather was a born learner. The beautiful early story "The Enchanted Bluff" about the boys whose whole wish was to escape from home and who fail in their lives when they never make the break, turned into a chapter of My Ántonia that is more beautiful. Here, as in "The Enchanted Bluff," we have children listening and dreaming as a story is being told to them; Jim tells the children about the coming of Coronado and his search for the Seven Golden Cities in the early days, coming right here to Nebraska, where a sword with the name of its Spanish maker was turned up by a farmer breaking sod. And

> Presently we saw a curious thing: There were no clouds, the sun was going down in a limpid, gold-washed sky. Just as the lower edge of the red disk rested on the high fields against the horizon, a great black figure suddenly appeared on the face of the sun. We sprang to our feet, straining our eyes toward it. In a moment we realized what it was. On some upland farm, a plough had been left standing in the field. The sun was sinking just behind it. Magnified across the distance by the horizontal light, it stood out against the sun, was exactly contained within the circle of the disk; the handles, the tongue, the share—black against the molten red. There it was, heroic in size, a picture writing on the sun.
>
> Even while we whispered about it, our vision disappeared; the ball dropped and dropped until the red tip went beneath the earth. The fields below us were dark, the sky was growing pale, and that forgotten plough had sunk back to its own littleness somewhere on the prairie.

The author has come to her quiet center. Nebraska, when she left it, was "Siberia"; now, for her writer's eyes, it is a radiant force of life itself.

The birth of Willa Cather came, as it happens, in the year Mark Twain began writing Huckleberry Finn. The authors' worlds were different, their frontiers were different—the events in Huck went back of course, to the 1830s and '40s—but they worked, in a way that came naturally to them both, to something of the same scale. They stand together in bigness—their sense of it, their authority over it. The difference I want to mention is not in scale or in authority over it, but in the fictional uses to which the world is put.

Through each of their lands there flows a river. Mark Twain's Mississippi is the wider and muddier. It is the route and channel of adventure to Huck; around every bend as he takes it, the river is both what he's looking for and what he dreads, and it's got for him what he'd not dreamed of till he finds it. It's *experience* he's on raft-level with; it can wash him overboard, he can plunge for it too, and endanger himself and refresh himself and cleanse himself or hide himself, or defy it, or live off it, dream on it, or show off on it. It is his to live through, and he lives through it—comes out at the other end alive, and ready to take off for a new frontier if they try too hard again to civilize him.

Willa Cather's river is filled with grandeur and power too; it too is both danger and rescue, the demander of courage and daring, of sacrifice and reverence and awe; it stirs the heart to a sense of destiny. But the river that waters the plains for Willa Cather is the pure stream of art.

The works of these two are totally unalike except in their very greatest respects, except in being about something big, in the apprehension of the new, and in movement, tireless movement in its direction. And both great writers say: Who can move best but the inspired child of his times? Whose story should better be told than that of the youth who has contrived to cut loose from ties and go flinging himself might and main, in every bit of his daring, in joy of life not to be denied, to vaunt himself in the love of vaunting, in the marvelous curiosity to find out everything, over the preposterous length and breadth of an opening new world, and in so doing to be one with it? The Mississippi River and the unbroken Prairie; comedy and tragedy; and indeed all destinies and destinations, all come subordinate to the charge of life itself. The two novelists remain a world apart, and yet both, at their best, celebrate through the living presence of that world, an undeniable force—the pursuit of truth. They recognize and confront a common evil—the defiling of the proud human spirit.

It is in looking back on Willa Cather's work that we learn how the vast exterior world she shows us novel by novel, a world ever-present and full of weight and substance and stir, visible to us along differing perspectives and in various mutations of time, has been the deliberately fitted form for each novel's own special needs. This world is here to serve her purpose by taking a fictional role, allying itself more or less openly with human destiny. It appears, according to role, a world with the power to crush and suffocate, and the power to give back life; a world to promise everything, and to deny everything; a world to open a way for living, or to close in life's face. It is all her great, expanding on-moving world; she has made it hers to take at its own beginnings and follow to its slow eclipse; and, in the full circle of it, to bring home the significance of the solitary human spirit which has elected to bring itself there, in its will and its struggle to survive.

She sought for the wholeness of the form—the roundness of the world, the full circle of life. The vital principle, this passion, has of its own a life—a seed, a birth, a growth, a maturing, a decline and sinking into death, back into the earth; it carries within it the pattern of life on earth, and is a part of the same continuity. It is "the old story writing itself over. . . . It is we who write it, with the best we have," says Alexandra, at the conclusion of O Pioneers!.

The emotions of Willa Cather's characters, too, have deep roots in the physical world—in that actual physical land to which they were born. In such a land, how clear it is from the start that identity—self-identity—is hard to seize, hard to claim, and hard to hold onto.

Another of the touchstones of her work, I think, is her feeling for the young. "There is no work of art so big or so beautiful," she writes, "that it was not once all contained in some youthful body, like this one [it is Thea's] which lay on the floor in the moonlight, pulsing with ardour and anticipation." The burning drive of the young, the desire to live, to do, to make, to achieve, no matter what the sacrifice, is the feeling most surpassingly alive to the author, most moving to us. Life has made her terribly certain that being young in the world is not easy. "If youth did not matter so much to itself, it would never have the heart to go on," she says, as Thea starts from home. And Doctor Archie, old friend and traveling companion, "knew that the splendid things of life are few, after all, and so very easy to miss." In O Pioneers! we read that "there is often a good deal of the child left in people who have had to grow up too soon." Miss Cather has a number of ways to tell us that life is most passionate in the promise, not in the fulfillment.

A strenuous physical life is lived throughout every novel, whether it is the struggle for survival or the keen experience of joy in simple physical well-being; it may reach in some characters the point of total identification with the living world around. It is a form of the passion that is all through Willa Cather's work; her work is written out of it. We see it in many modulations: desire—often exalted as ambition; devotion; loyalty; fidelty; physical nearness and kindness and comfort when it lies at rest. Love? It is affection that warms the life in her stories and hate that chills it. There is reconcilement, and there is pity. There is obsession here too, and so is the hunger for something impossible: all of these are forms of love. And there is marriage, though the marriages that occur along the way of the novels are milestones, hardly destinations; as required in the careful building of her plots, they are inclined to be unavailing. Sexual love is not often present in the here and now; we more often learn of it after it is over, or see it in its results. My own feeling is that along with her other superior gifts Willa Cather had a rare sureness as to *her* subject, the knowledge of just what to touch and what not to touch in the best interests of her story.

What her characters are mostly meant for, it seems to me, is to rebel. For her heroines in particular, rebelling is much easier than not rebelling, and we may include love, too, in not rebelling. It is the strong, clear impulse in Willa Cather's stories. It is the real springwater. It is rebelling, we should always add, not for its own sake as much as for the sake of something a great deal bigger—for the sake of integrity, of truth, of art. It is the other face of aspiration. Willa Cather used her own terms; and she left nothing out. What other honorable way is there for an artist to have her say?

The novels have the qualities and the components of love in proportions all their own, then; and I believe this may point again to the thought that they are concerned not with *two* but with *one*, in the number of human beings—not, finally, with relationships but with the desire in one heart and soul to claim what is its own, to achieve its measure of greatness, to overcome any terrible hardship, any terrible odds; and this desire is served by love, rewarded by love (but its absence or failure never compensated for by love); and most of the time, and at its highest moments, the desire is its own drive, its own gratification. One of its forms is indeed pride; and pride is not punished in Willa Cather's novels, it can be deserved.

"Her voice . . . had to do with that confidence, that sense of wholeness and inner well-being that she had felt at moments ever since she could remember. . . . It was as if she had an appointment to meet the rest of herself sometime, somewhere. It was moving to meet her and she was moving to meet it. That meeting awaited her, just as surely as, for the poor girl in the [train] seat behind her, there awaited a hole in the earth, already dug." And then in the city, at the concert, hearing the music that is to change her life, Thea says, "As long as she lived that ecstasy was going to be hers. She would live for it, work for it, die for it; but she was going to have it, time after time, height after height. . . . She would have it, what the trumpets were singing! She would have it, have it—it!"

How does Willa Cather make this an emotion for which we have such entire sympathy? Its intensity, I think, is the answer—Thea's intensity partaking of Willa Cather's. Thea's music teacher says of her, " 'Her secret? It is every artist's secret—passion. That is all. It is an open secret, and perfectly safe. Like heroism, it is inimitable in cheap materials.' "

This high desire, when merged into other than itself, merges into the whole world. An individuality can be made willing to lose itself only in something as big as the world. It *was* the world, in O Pioneers! and My

Ántonia. It was not the world itself, except in magnitude and undeniability, in *The Song of the Lark* and, consummately, in *The Professor's House*: it was art.

For this novelist, art, as she saw it and perfected it, always kept the proportions of the great world and the undeniability of the world, and it lived for her as certainly as this world lived. And the strongest *felt* relationship, a reader may come to believe, might not be any of those between the characters but the one their creator feels for them, for their developing, passionate lives.

In a landscape this wide and pulsing, it seems not at all out of keeping that the greatest passions made real to us are those *for* greatness, and for something larger than life. Men and women do of course fall in love in Willa Cather's novels and their relationship is brought into clear enough focus for us to put good reliance on; but the desire to make a work of art is a stronger one, and more lasting. In the long run, love of art—which is love accomplished without help or need of help from another—is what is deepest and realest in her work.

There is not a trace of disparagement in her treatment of the least of her characters. The irony of her stories is grave, never belittling; it is a showing of sympathy. She *contended* for the life of the individual. Her attack was positive and vigorous and unflinching and proud of winning. This contending was the essence of her stories, formed her plots, gave her room for action. And she did it without preaching. She lacked self-righteousness, and she just as wholly lacked bitterness; what a lesson *A Lost Lady* gives us in doing without bitterness. It is impossible to think of diminishment in anything she thought or wrote. She conceived of character along heroic lines. For her, the heroic life is the artist's as it is the pioneer's. She equated the two.

Set within the land is the dwelling—made by human hands to hold human life. As we know, the intensity of desire for building the house to live in—or worship in—fills all the Cather novels. It fills the past for her, it gives the present meaning; it provides for a future: the house is the physical form, the *evidence* that we have lived, are alive now; it will be evidence some day that we were alive once, evidence against the arguments of time and the tricks of history.

In her landscape, we learn from both seeing what is there and realizing what is not there; there is always felt the *absence* of habitation. We come to know what degrees there are of the burrow and the roof. "The houses on the Divide were small and were usually tucked away in low places; you did not see them until you came directly upon them," we read of the Scandinavian settlement in *O Pioneers!*, "Most of them were built

of the sod itself, and were only the unescapable ground in another form."
Mrs. Archie, in *The Song of the Lark*, of whom we are told "such little,
mean natures are among the darkest and most baffling of created things,"
liked to "have her house clean, empty, dark, locked, and to be out of
it—anywhere." The Professor's house, shabby and outgrown as it is, is a
dated house; but the cliff house, almost older than time, is timeless.

"I wish I could tell you what I saw there, just *as* I saw it, on that
first morning, through a veil of lightly falling snow," Tom Outland tells
him, in his story within the story. "Far up above me, a thousand feet or
so, set in a great cavern in the face of the cliff, I saw a little city of stone,
asleep. . . . It all hung together, seemed to have a kind of composition. . . . The tower was the fine thing that held all the jumble of houses
together and made them mean something. . . . I felt that only a strong
and aspiring people would have built it, and a people with a feeling for
design." "The town hung like a bird's nest in the cliff, . . . facing an
ocean of clear air. A people who had the hardihood to build there, and
who lived day after day looking down upon such grandeur, who came and
went by those hazardous trails, must have been . . . a fine people." " 'I see
them here, isolated, cut off from other tribes, working out their destiny,' "
said Father Duchene, the scholar, " 'making their mesa more and more
worthy to be a home for man. . . . Like you,' " he tells Tom Outland, " 'I
feel a reverence for this place. Wherever humanity has made that hardest
of all starts and lifted itself out of mere brutality, is a sacred spot. . . .
They built themselves into this mesa and humanized it.' "

The Professor's House is a novel with a unique form, and to read it
is to see it built before our eyes: the making of two unlike parts into a
whole under a sheltering third part which defines it and is as final as that
verse that comes to recite itself to the Professor's mind. The construction
is simple, forthright, and daring. By bringing the Professor's old house and
the cliff dwellers' house in combination to the mind, Willa Cather gives
them simultaneous existence, and with the measure of time taken away we
may see, in the way of a mirage, or a vision, humanity's dwelling places all
brought into one. And it was there all the time:

> For thee a house was built
> Ere thou wast born;
> For thee a mould was made
> Ere thou of woman camest.

Tom Outland's story, set into *The Professor's House* like the view
from the casement of that Dutch interior, is the objectively told, factual-
seeming counterpart of Thea's experience in the Ancient People's cliff

houses in *The Song of the Lark*, which was published ten years earlier. Tom Outland's story has a further difference: the tragic view.

It is the objective chronicler for whom the story comes to a tragic end. For Thea, who has seen in her discovery of the Ancient People something totally and exclusively her own, and her own secret, it remained, undamaged as a dream. She apprehended it in her own mind, and her own body, as a message for her. Tom Outland's Cliff City was there in the world, and he wanted the world to discover it as he had, to study it, venerate it, share it; and it was taken away from him, broken and desecrated; it brought about not the self-discovery of Thea, but a crisis and a lasting sorrow in human relationship. In the end, it is more of an interior story than Thea's ever was.

"Tom Outland's Story" is written with a compression and strength that the author had already showed us in *A Lost Lady*, and achieves a simplicity that, as it seems to me, nothing else she wrote ever surpassed. Such simplicity is not what a writer starts with; it is what the writer is able to end with, or hopes to be able.

The Professor's House in whole might show us that the novel, in its excellence as a work of art, stands, itself, as a house finished. In so much as it has perfection, perfection has not sealed it, but opened it to us.

A work of art is a *work*: something made, which in the making follows an idea that comes out of human life and leads back into human life. A work of art is the house that is *not* the grave. An achievement of order, passionately conceived and passionately carried out, it is not a thing of darkness. When it is finished, if it is good and sound, somehow all opacity has left it. It stands as clear as candor itself. The fine physical thing has become a transparency through which the idea it was made to embody is thus made totally visible. It could not have been this visible before it was embodied. We see human thought and feeling best and clearest by seeing it through something solid that our hands have made.

"Artistic growth is, more than it is anything else, a refining of the sense of truthfulness." This is said at the end of *The Song of the Lark*. "The stupid believe that to be truthful is easy; only the artist, the great artist, knows how difficult it is." And, Thea's teacher has told her, " 'Every artist makes himself born. It is very much harder than the other time, and longer.' "

In the Cather novels, there is a setting apart of the artist in value, a setting apart of his life from that of other people. Artists, in her considered and lifelong view, are perhaps greater and more deserving to be made way for than other human beings. This could never have been a popular view, but in trying to understand it I think she extolled the artist not for what would seem vanity, or for anything less than a function he could perform—the great thing that only an artist would be able, in her eyes, to do. The artist has a role. Thea, meditating on this role, thought, of the people who cared about her singing, "Perhaps each of them concealed another person in himself, just as she did. . . . What if one's second self could somehow speak to all those second selves?" At base, I think this is an aspect of the Cather sense of obligation to give of oneself. "If he achieves anything noble, anything enduring, it must be by giving himself absolutely to his material. And this gift of sympathy is his great gift," Willa Cather said; "it is the fine thing in him that alone can make his work fine." The artist is set apart the more entirely, all but symbolically, to give himsef away, to fulfill the ultimate role of dedication.

Today, neither the artist nor the world holds this idea, and it has faded, along with some of her other strong beliefs (the hero and the heroine, the sanctity of the family), from our own view. Our ideas of history and art are different from hers, as tomorrow's will be different from today's. We have arrived at new places to stand to obtain our own viewpoint of history. Art, since it grows out of its times, is of itself, and by rights, a changing body. But truth?

Truth is the rock. Willa Cather saw it as unassailable. Today the question is asked if this is indeed so. Many of us align ourselves with Willa Cather—I do—in thinking the truth will hold out; but there are many who feel another way, and indeed, I believe, many who would not feel life was over if there were no truth there.

One of the strangest things about art, nevertheless, is that the rock it is built on is not its real test. Our greatest poem made a mistake about the construction of the universe, but this will never bring the poem down.

Yet plain enough is the structure Willa Cather built on these rocks she herself believed were eternal. Her work we, today, see entirely on its own, without need of that support. It holds itself independently, as that future church appears to be doing above the dreaming head of Saint Francis of Assisi in Giotto's fresco. Her work has its own firm reason for existence. And here it stands, a monument more unshakable than she might have dreamed, to the independent human spirit she most adored.

She made this work out of her life, her perishable life, which is so much safer a material to build with than convictions, however immutable they seem to the one who so passionately holds them. It is out of our own lives that we, in turn, reach out to it. Because the house of Willa Cather contained, embodied, a spirit, it will always seem to us inhabited. There is life in that house, the spirit she made it for, made it out of; it is all one substance: it is her might and her heart and soul, all together, and it abides.

JOHN J. MURPHY

Willa Cather's Archbishop: A Western and Classical Perspective

T he hero rather than setting or situa-
tion is the main thing in *Death Comes for the Archbishop*. Willa Cather
admitted that for a long time she had no intention of writing the novel:
"the story of the Church and the Spanish missionaries was always what
most interested me; but I hadn't the most remote idea of trying to write
about it." What changed her mind were stories she had heard about
Archbishop Lamy of Santa Fe and her discovery of Howlett's biography of
Bishop Machebeuf. She was intrigued by the reaction of the French priests
to the people and country of New Mexico, the Western experience as
filtered through the hero she would fabricate from these and other sources,
a hero at once "fearless and fine and very, very well-bred. . . . What I felt
curious about was the daily life of such a man in a crude frontier society."
In this way she revealed her interest in creating a Western hero, one
sharing the experiences of Leatherstocking, the Virginian, and even Huckleberry Finn, yet responding to these experiences with a more cultivated
sensibility. Beyond this local or national type are similarities to the heroes
of classical literature, particularly Aeneas, whose destiny was to shape a
new culture in Italy by transplanting the home gods of Troy. Thus
Archbishop Latour reflects Cather's cyclical view of history, in which the
American experience repeats the European, and our West the larger West.

From *Western American Literature* 13, no. 3 (Summer 1978). Copyright © 1978 by Western
Literature Association.

I

Jean Marie Latour is introduced wearing buckskin like Natty Bumppo, although the far western setting of the novel demands an equestrian hero like the Virginian. Cather opens with "a solitary horseman, followed by a pack-mule, . . . pushing through an arid stretch of country somewhere in central New Mexico." This horseman is atypical, however: "Under his buckskin riding coat he wore a black vest and the cravat and collar of a churchman." Even aside from his calling, he is unusual: "His bowed head was not that of an ordinary man, —it was built for the seat of a fine intelligence. . . . There was a singular elegance about the hands below the fringed cuffs of the buckskin jacket. Everything showed him to be a man of gentle birth—brave, sensitive, courteous. His manners . . . were distinguished." Cather presents us with the cultivated counterpart of the naturally attractive hero described by Wister's narrator at the beginning of *The Virginian*: "in his eye, in his face, in the whole man, there dominated a something potent to be felt . . . by man or woman." Wister's tall stranger and Cather's young priest are knights-errant in the wilderness, rescuing those in need, righting wrongs, bringing law to lawless regions.

The Virginian's exploits range from pranks to gun duels, but there is always decency about them. The rescue of Molly Wood from the river, while a humorous situation, is of a maiden in distress, the kind of affair Natty Bumppo specialized in in the New York forests. The Virginian's role in lynching the cattle thieves is of more serious dimension, a haunting episode leading to tears for his old friend Steve. This and the famous gun duel with Trampas jeopardize his relationship with Molly, but he is forced into them by the corrupt condition of Wyoming law. In trying to justify the hero's actions, Judge Henry explains to Molly, "We are in a very bad way, and we are trying to make that way a little better until civilization can reach us." Even the Wyoming bishop cannot really condemn the Virginian's actions under the circumstances.

New Mexico too is in a bad way, and Latour has to contend with similar lawlessness. "The Lonely Road to Mora" episode combines the hero's rescue of the female in distress and a situation of self-defense. After the terrified Magdalena warns the priests about the murderous Buck Scales, Latour draws his pistol on the outlaw. When Magdalena escapes, Latour watches over her until the buckskin-clad, conventional Western hero, Kit Carson, takes her home to his wife. In a more amusing vein, and more befitting a courtly type, is Latour's administering to Isabella Olivares during the difficulty she has admitting her age. Latour's confrontations with the wayward native clergy make him a kind of frontier lawman forced to compromise in imperfect situations until the appropriate time for action. Rather than "lose the parish of Taos in order to punish its priest," he allows the excesses of Father Martinez to continue until he can get a strong replacement. Martinez, Gallegos and Lucero, a trio of clergymen as lawless as any company of cattle rustlers, challenge the new bishop's authority by practices as varied as political intrigue, gambling, hoarding money and siring children. Patiently, but firmly, Latour replaces them, although Lucero and Martinez organize a rival church of their own.

Cather's hero shares with Natty Bumppo concern over the exploitation and destruction of the land by new settlers. Natty complains that white men's explorations "always foretell waste and destruction" and demonstrates less wasteful Indian methods of hunting and fishing. Latour is sensitive to the Indian respect for nature: "it was the Indian's way to pass through a country without disturbing anything. . . . It was the Indian manner to vanish into the landscape, not to stand out against it. . . . They seemed to have none of the European's desire to 'master' nature, to arrange and re-create. They spent their ingenuity in the other direction; in accommodating themselves to the scene in which they found themselves." Just as Natty laments the sacrificing of New York forests for the ugly, jerry-built structures of Templeton, Latour is disturbed by the proliferation in Santa Fe of "flimsy wooden buildings with double porches, scrollwork and jack-straw posts and banisters painted white," which destroy the setting of his golden Romanesque cathedral. He is forced to contend with the confusions of life brought about by the discovery of gold in Colorado, where wandering prospectors and their followers crowd into the mountains, pollute the water and succumb to fever. Latour assigns these Colorado problems as the special task of Father Vaillant, who eventually becomes the bishop of Denver.

Also, Latour's Indian companionships associate him with Cooper's hero. Natty's lifelong friendship with Chingachgook and his relationship with Uncas and Hist have their parallels in Latour's dealing with Jacinto and especially the Navajo leader Eusabio. Like Natty, Latour is able to communicate with Indians. At Laguna, he talks with Jacinto about Indian names and legends. The Navajo Eusabio becomes Latour's friend for life, and his desert home the place Latour visits during a period of spiritual aridity. The two men share Christianity, concern for the welfare of the Navajos, and a respect for each other reminiscent of Natty and Chingachgook. The nobility of both relationships and the silent intercourse characterizing them are suggested in a meeting between Eusabio and Latour after the death of Eusabio's son: "At first he did not open his lips, merely stood holding Father Latour's very fine white hand in his very fine dark one, and looked into his face with a message of sorrow and resignation in his deep-set, eagle eyes." The scene recalls Natty's attempt to comfort Chingachgook at the grave of Uncas, when he declares, "Sagamore, you are not alone," and Chingachgook grasps his hand with warmth of feeling.

Celibacy and perpetual boyhood also characterize the Western hero. Natty Bumppo's refusal to involve himself with Judith Hutter and his foolishness in the unequal affair with Mabel Dunham illustrate the bachelor aspect Wister ridicules in the story of the rooster fleeing Judge Henry's ranch because of a fear of petticoats. The Virginian himself decides to move on when the community begins to fill with young marrieds and a school is contemplated:

> ". . . Well if this hyeh Territory is goin' to get full o' fam'ly men and empty o' game, I believe I'll—"
> "Get married yourself," suggested Mr. Taylor.
> "Me! I ain't near reached the marriageable age. No, seh!"

This reminds us of Huck Finn's constant efforts to avoid the complexities of society by moving on, by lighting out for new territory to escape that "cramped up and smothery" feeling in conflict with the easy freedom of the raft, where one floated "wherever the current wanted," where one could throw off the restraints of civilization and go naked, "day and night." The threat marriage and domestic life represent to the perpetually boyish Western hero is most clearly dramatized in Crane's "The Bride Comes to Yellow Sky," when gun-happy Scratchy Wilson desists from his constant pistol dueling with Sheriff Jack Potter when confronted with the news of Potter's recent marriage. Wilson calls off the feud, muttering "Married!" Wilson "was not a student of chivalry; it was merely that in the presence of this foreign condition he was a simple child of the earlier plains."

Wilson seems an extreme case beside Latour, whose celibacy is a condition of his religious vocation; nevertheless, the churchman leads a bachelor life like typical Western heroes and most Cather heroes. Near the end of the novel, when the elderly Latour grows homesick for New Mexico while visiting Clermont, we are made aware of this boyhood existence, now a kind of reward for a life of service: "In New Mexico he always awoke a young man; not until he rose and began to shave did he realize that he was growing older. His first consciousness was a sense of the light dry wind blowing in through the windows, with the fragrance of hot sun and sage-brush and sweet clover; a wind that made one's body feel light and one's heart cry 'To-day, to-day,' like a child's." The Old World could not bestow this youth, but the wind of the "light-hearted mornings of the desert, . . . that wind . . . made one a boy again. He had noticed that this peculiar quality in the air of new countries vanished after they were tamed by men and made to bear harvests." This resembles the Virginian's hankering after an undomesticated territory without schools. The atmosphere of freedom becomes necessary for Latour: "he had come back to die in exile for the sake of it. Something soft and wild and free, something that whispered to the ear on the pillow, lightened the heart, softly, softly picked the lock, slid the bolts, and released the prisoned spirit of man into the wind, into the blue and gold, into the morning, into the morning!"

II

Latour is a variation of the typical Western hero, and his life spans the epoch of far-western expansion: "he had come with the buffalo, and he had lived to see railway trains running into Santa Fe." Yet, Cather takes us beyond the world of Leatherstocking and the American West. *Death Comes for the Archbishop* opens in the gardens of a villa in the Sabine hills, beneath which Rome spreads before a setting sun, the dome of St. Peter's the distinctive feature on the horizon. The discussion concerns bringing the order of the Roman Church to the vast New Mexican territory. Besides two references to the romances of Fenimore Cooper, one of the discussants, a New World missionary, is referred to as "an Odysseus of the Church," and he compares the job to be done in New Mexico to cleaning out an Augean stable. The American West is thus given classical perspective and Cather's priests the status of classical heroes. As a missionary of Roman law and order, Latour suggests Aeneas. There are surprising resemblances between them. Although Cather might have been aware of the Virgilian aspect of Latour's ship-wreck in Galveston harbor, the fated dimension of his tasks and his communication with the world beyond are unmistakable similarities.

Aeneas' destiny is to bring about the Roman peace, when, as Jupiter foretells, "the age of violence [shall] be mellowing into peace." Unlike the typical American Western hero, Aeneas is not confused about being on the side of civilization. Hector charges him in a dream to save the holy things and gods of Troy and plant them in an Italian home (II, 291–97). Despite the jealousy of Juno and the stumbling blocks she sends his way, Aeneas manages to fulfill Jupiter's prophecy. His mother Venus is always there to help him, of course, to maneuver a friendly reception in

Carthage, to direct him to the golden bough, to cure his wounds before the final contest with Turnus. As discussed over dinner by a few ecclesiastics, Latour's destiny seems hardly so awesome: "He will have to deal with savagery and ignorance, with dissolute priests and political intrigue. He must be a man to whom order is necessary—as dear as life." However, a mysterious world operates here too. In "The Lonely Road to Mora" incident, for example, the warning given the priests by Magdalena "seemed evidence that some protecting power was mindful of them." Cather's inclusion of the stories of miracles like Guadalupe, where the Virgin appeared to Brother Juan, requested a church to be built and imprinted her portrait on his coarse garment, suggests manipulation by the other world. Latour's experience with the peasant Sada before the Mary altar in "December Night," when "The beautiful concept of Mary pierced the priest's heart like a sword," is essentially a visitation from above: "He received the miracle in [Sada's] heart into his own, saw through her eyes. . . ." A few chapters later he takes Vaillant to the golden hillside from which his Romanesque cathedral will be built and explains how he discovered this singular hill by chance, when he had to divert his route due to a washout. "Oh, such things are never accidents, Jean," responds Vaillant. The rescue of Latour in the red-hilled desert through the discovery of the pastoral oasis of Aqua Secreta is given supernatural dimension by Cather's balancing this episode with the one in which Junipero Serra is entertained by the Holy Family in the desert.

Confrontation with the other world is not always beneficent, however. Aeneas is frequently tortured by Juno and her lackeys, especially during the war with the Rutulians, about which Venus complains to Jupiter:

> Now Juno is dredging up the Underworld—a province
> Hitherto unexplored—and has suddenly loosed Allecto
> On the earth, to spread delirium through the Italian towns.
> (X, 39–41)

Also, Aeneas himself suffers chilling experiences in the underworld during his search for his father Anchises. After entering a dark cave, he witnesses the shapes of Death, Agony, and War, and unfortunate souls occupying places of mourning and punishment, those experiences Dante would employ in his own great poem, which D. H. Stewart has applied to Cather's novel. The self indulgence of Gallegos, sensuality of Trinidad, avarice of Lucero, and lusts and seductions of Martinez, accompanied by the heresy and discord sown by the latter two, provide Latour with underworld experiences and enough opposition to require heroic effort.

The diabolical dimension of this crew is suggested in the death scene of Lucero, when, surrounded by candlelight, he perceives Martinez in torment and utters his last words, "Eat your tail, Martinez, eat your tail!" Even the vanity of Doña Isabella has otherworldly ramifications, since it jeopardizes the building of the cathedral, symbol of the success of Latour's mission. However, Latour feels most at a loss when confronted with the superstitions of the Indians. "Snake Root" includes material on the ceremonial fire and snake worship, practices confirmed by Jeb Orchard and by Latour himself when, in the foul-smelling cave, he witnesses Jacinto flattened against the rock and listening at the oval hole in the rear wall. "The Mass at Acoma" contains both aspects of Latour's difficulties. While the Indians cluster about him in their shawls and blankets, he feels threatened and ineffectual: "He felt as if he were celebrating Mass at the bottom of the sea, for antediluvian creatures; for types of life so old, so hardened, so shut within their shells, that the sacrifice of Calvary could hardly reach back so far." He begins to long for the comfort of his own tradition: "He was on a naked rock in the desert, in the stone age, a prey to homesickness for his own kind, his own epoch, for European man and his glorious history of desire and dreams." The Acoma legend of Fray Baltazar, the final part of this book, is a compendium of most of the excesses of the native clergy.

In addition to the missionary dimension and the influence of other-worldly supportive and opposing forces, there are specific qualities of character shared by Aeneas and Latour. Wendell Clausen has pointed out the piety of Virgil's hero, his awareness and acceptance of fate, even when the cost is loss of almost every human attachment. When compared to Odysseus or Achilles "Aeneas is almost devoid of passion or personality," "seems curiously inert," and "more burdened by memory than any other ancient hero." His "actions may be described as valiant, patriotic, devoted; but more and more he becomes the hero who acts in some other and higher interest, like a priest." All these qualities describe Latour, who, firmly, but knowing pain and terror, had decided to leave his native France for missionary work in the New World. Perhaps a greater sacrifice for Latour occurs when, beyond mid-life, he relinquishes Father Vaillant for the Colorado missions. He had recalled Vaillant from Tucson because he wanted his companionship, yet he suggests to his vicar the need for a priest at Camp Denver. Latour is disappointed at Vaillant's enthusiastic willingness to leave Santa Fe: "he was a little hurt that his old comrade should leave him without one regret. He seemed to know, as if it had been revealed to him, that this was a final break; that their lives would part here, and that they would never work together again." At this point he confesses his motives for recalling Vaillant: "I sent for you because I felt the need of your companionship. I used my authority as a Bishop to gratify my personal wish. That was selfish, if you will, but surely natural enough. We are countrymen, and are bound by early memories." These words suggest both the burden of memory and the sadness of what duty demands, and, as he returns home from his leave-taking from Vaillant, Latour reflects on these demands: "He was forty-seven years old, and he had been a missionary in the New World for twenty years—ten of them in New Mexico. If he were a parish priest at home, there would be nephews coming to him for help in their Latin or a bit of pocket-money; nieces to run into his garden and bring their sewing and keep an eye on his housekeeping." However, back in his study he successfully transforms his loneliness into something positive: "It was just this solitariness of love in which a priest's life could be like his Master's. It was not solitude of atrophy, of negation, but of perpetual flowering."

Latour's lack of passion, bordering on coldness for some readers, and the difficulty he has making friends are more than compensated for by the presence of supporting characters. In effect, Cather's method is to embody in others the qualities in which her hero seems deficient. Marintez rather than Latour is her passionate character; however, Marintez was "like something picturesque and impressive, but really impotent, left over from the past." Next to Latour, the buckskin-clad Kit Carson is the typical adventurer, the more legendary hero of the frontier, but Carson proves brutal in his treatment of the Navajos and is dismissed as "misguided." Vaillant is warmer, more popular and more active than Latour, who in his humility feels inferior to his vicar. This is obvious when he requests Vaillant's blessing before one of their separations: "Blanchet, . . . you are a better man than I. You have been a great harvester of souls without pride and without shame—and I am always a little cold—*un pédant*, as you used to say. If hereafter we have stars in our crowns, yours will be a constellation. Give me your blessing." Latour feels that his somewhat quieter work in Santa Fe pales beside the more aggressive and celebrated mission in Colorado. However, Vaillant's work depends upon Latour, for he was responsible for Vaillant coming to the New World, had "to forge a new will in that devout and exhausted priest," and directed his missionary work, including Colorado.

Clausen concludes his consideration of Aeneas by noting Virgil's "perception of Roman history as a long Pyrrhic victory of the human spirit" and his suggestion of a less than optimistic view of Rome's future by having Aeneas depart from the underworld through the gate of ivory, the gate of false dreams. Cather's comments about the failure of the twentieth-century priests of New Mexico to respect the old mission churches and their decorations and her generally pessimistic view of the outcome of Western pioneer endeavor cast Latour's accomplishments in similar light. Maybe this is why her novel is, from beginning to end, riddled with the light of the setting sun. Yet, there is something everlasting in those "fearless and fine and very, very well-bred" qualities of her hero. Her combining of the Western tradition and the classical tradition and the perspective of death from which the novel is written suggest Latour's timelessness. Facing death, when life reveals itself as "an experience of the Ego, in no sense the Ego itself," he acquires an insight outside of "calendared time": "He sat in the middle of his own consciousness; none of his former states of mind were lost or outgrown. They were all within reach of his hand, and all comprehensible."

JOHN HOLLANDER

"*A Lost Lady*"

A Lost Lady is not Willa Cather's most famous work, but it is an undoubted masterpiece. It is one of those strong, intense shorter novels which literary modernism prefers to great, sprawling ones, and whose careful and significant structure and control of indirection enlist the reader in filling and fitting it out. An "unfurnished" novel is what the author herself called such books, in an essay called "The Novel Démeublé" published the same year A Lost Lady was written. We think of such modern classics as *To the Lighthouse, The Good Soldier, Miss Lonelyhearts* or *Ethan Frome* as tales in which episodes are like realms, where a smaller canvas generates vast depths within it. A Lost Lady is this kind of book. Written in the year *The Waste Land* was published, it takes place in earlier times—starting in the eighteen-eighties and 'nineties—but its author was full of the same sense of dislocation and revisionary anxiety to which Eliot's poem was, at the time, heard to speak. Writing in the mid-nineteen-thirties, Willa Cather remarked that "the world broke in two in 1922 or thereabout"; and the notion that World War I had broken not only bodies and hearts, but continuities, paradigms, private and public worlds of expectation, underlies some of the contractions and obliqueness of this at once powerful and exquisite chronicle.

One thinks of My Ántonia, published five years earlier, and *Death Comes for the Archbishop*, which appeared five years later, as centers of Willa Cather's imaginative geography, the later of these southwestern, the earlier Nebraskan. It is My Ántonia to which A Lost Lady implicitly alludes in its use of a southern-born, male observer to register the power of a

From A Lost Lady by Willa Cather with an Introduction by John Hollander. Copyright ©
1983 by John Hollander. The Limited Editions Club, 1983.

remarkable female protagonist. But if the earlier, larger story uses a narrator's consciousness to mirror its heroine in her world, the later, shorter book, with its more elegantly problematic heroine, is more concerned to represent something of the nature of fictional mirroring itself.

When confronting important works of literature, we often find that the simplest of questions—those which are seldom asked lest the questioner appear naive—can be most revealing, can, by very virtue of having been raised, shed light on central issues. We take the titles of major works of art, for example, far too casually, as if something strange or ambiguous in them were only a fault of our comprehension. It is only a child who might—but seldom does—bring us a book, asking "Why '*Leaves* of Grass'? Why not '*Blades*' " and thereby cause us to brood about the biblical and secular allusions, and the ambiguous grammar of the word "of," in that profound and resonant phrase, and thereby help us to avoid being trapped on the deceptively easy surface of Whitman's great poetry. A *Lost Lady* has such a phrase for its title, and a naive question about that title points out a way into the book which touches on its complexities.

For Mrs. Forrester is far from "lost," if we take the title to denote a lady bewildered, a lady who has lost her way or her condition. It is Niel Herbert to whom she, and her state of ladyship, are lost, and he who is forlorn, while she ends her life in wealth and only faintly clouded dignity. And just as we must not mistake Marian Forrester for a Nebraska Emma Bovary, so—it has been pointed out more than once—we must not forget how central to the novel is Niel's sentimental education. (Willa Cather always admired Flaubert—her *Obscure Destinies* of 1932 is, like Gertrude Stein's *Three Lives*, more than formally related to the *Trois Contes*—and Frédéric Moreau is one of Niel Herbert's precursors, even as the latter seems to anticipate Hemingway's Nick Adams or John O'Hara's Jim Malloy as apprentices in the connoisseurship of experience.) Neither Niel nor Mrs. Forrester is the center of the work: they are more like the two foci of an ellipse, an elliptical world which they generate and within which their spatial and emotional relations become significant.

Indeed, the author had, at an early stage in the writing of it, revised several chapters of the book into Niel's first-person narrative, only to settle on the artfully disembodied narration in the summer of 1922, after which she apparently wrote the whole novel without—in the words of her companion Edith Lewis—"any break or hesitation." She herself wrote later on that "A *Lost Lady* was a beautiful ghost in my mind for twenty years before it came together as a possible subject for presentation," and she was undoubtedly thinking of Mrs. Forrester as a central figure whom she wanted to present free and clear of the strictures of fictional entanglement and novelistic device. The Forresters seem to have been based on a couple Willa Cather had known as a child in Red Cloud, Nebraska: Silas Garber had been a founder of the town and, later, Governor of the state, and he and his wife had been important presences in her youth. Niel Herbert, a southerner growing up in Sweet Water (Willa Cather had herself been born in Virginia, where she lived until the age of ten), is a figuration of the author in her early awe of the Garbers. Not for Niel alone, but for the whole town, Mrs. Forrester "glittered when she walked," like E. A. Robinson's Richard Cory, but with eyes "lively, laughing, intimate, nearly always a little mocking." Her freedom of spirit has great power for Niel ("She mocked outrageously at the proprieties she observed and inherited the magic of contradictions"), but that very magic of contradiction affects the way in which her contingency, her relation to Captain Forrester, "her comprehension of a man like the railroad-builder, her loyalty to him, stamped her more than anything else."

Her husband represents the force of American westward expansion—as does the Burlington Railroad itself—which is always being glorified in retrospect at the expense of a fallen, later form of enterprise, instanced in the life and works of Ivy Peters. Peters is no low or comic villain, no Snopes to Forrester's Sartoris; the moment of skillful cruelty at which we first encounter him is not merely that of a particular character, but of a declining phase of what it means to be entrepreneurial in America. Captain Forrester's accident is the event that brings his wife from the grand realm of Denver to permanent residence in Sweet Water, but it also marks a boundary in Willa Cather's chart of American history.

But these are questions which only a later, grown-up Niel, only a man having come to a knowledge like that of the narrator's, like that of a subsequent phase of self, could comprehend. Niel's attraction to Mrs. Forrester is from the first a matter of sensibility. At the opening of the book, the reader is shown the boy's experience of Mrs. Forrester's closeness in the good-humored tenderness of her ministrations. A bit further on, at the end of the third chapter, Niel walks home through a winter sunset entranced with the thought that she would be around now for the whole year. He thereupon remembers his first glimpse of her, being driven to church in a carriage,

> a lady, alone, in a black dress all puffs and ruffles, and a black hat, carrying a parasol with a carved ivory handle [a Flaubertian detail like, as one critic has observed, the antithetical bunch of roses flung into the mud in Chapter VII]. As the carriage stopped she lifted her dress to alight; out of a swirl of foamy white petticoats she thrust a shiny, black

slipper. She stepped lightly to the ground and with a nod to the driver went into the church. The little boy followed her through the open door, saw her enter a pew and kneel.

Rounding off this recollection is Niel's sense, on that later evening walk, that "he was proud now that at the first moment he had recognized her as belonging to a different world from any he had ever known." And then, in a master-stroke of closure, the chapter ends with an emblem of bright but illusory hope, of intimations of sexuality presented and withdrawn at once, of striving subject and elusive object, of contingent accessibility, that represents the boy's attachment, his possession of a sense of her ladyship, in a mode that modern literature made central to the way in which inner lives are glimpsed:

> Niel paused for a moment at the end of the lane to look up at the last skeleton poplar in the long row; just above its pointed tip hung the hollow, silver winter moon.

If such a moment seems Hemingwayan (or, in another way, Tennysonian, in fact), we must remember that Willa Cather's obvious lack of interest in formal "experiment" in narrative technique belies an attention to matters of construction which, although they do not puzzle us into deeper understanding like Conrad's or Faulkner's ambiguities of sequence, nevertheless help shape the significance of the way in which the reader learns of events. The unequivocal scene in Chapter VI between Mrs. Forrester and Frank Ellinger in the snow is observed at first only by the narrator, then at the end, as the lovers emerge from the cedars, by one of the boys of the town to whom she had always behaved so beautifully. Without Niel's sensibility, and without his possessive sense of her, young Adolph Blum would never betray her, nor feel betrayed by her, nor "lose" her in any way. The final paragraph of that chapter is, in its sense of the social moment (if not in any way in its style), like John O'Hara or even Scott Fitzgerald:

> But with Adolph Blum her secrets were safe. His mind was feudal; the rich and fortunate were also the privileged. These warm-blooded, quick-breathing people took chances,—followed impulses only dimly understandable to a boy who was wet and weather-chapped all the year . . . She treated him like a human being. His little chats with her, her nod and smile when she passed him on the street, were among the pleasantest things he had to remember. She bought game of him in the closed season, and didn't give him away.

But this is just such a privileged and acrid revelation which Willa Cather so elegantly withholds from Niel, for his sense of alienation from

Mrs. Forrester must develop gradually—must crystallize, as Stendhal proposed that love does—and the ineradicable moment of Niel comes later on, with what Wallace Stevens called "a later reason," in the scenes of her desperation in the law office, and her possessive caress by Ivy Peters. It is only in Part II, indeed, in which an Ivy Peters comes to supplant both a figure of work like Captain Forrester, and a figure of play like Frank Ellinger, that such a *rite de passage* could be enacted, and such a moment of direct erotic consequence could be grasped.

The relation of the two parts of this short novel is another instance of its telling structure, exhibiting not so much a reciprocal, as an unfolding, pattern of losses. In Part I, Marian Forrester loses her husband's vitality and energy, and her winter life in Denver society. Then there is a financial loss; and the first part ends with Niel's doubt about her and her "sense of tempered steel, a blade that could fence with anyone and never break." Then the book, and its world, break in two, and although Niel's loss of his lady accelerates in Part II, it is only there, at the dinner party scene almost at the end, that we learn of her earlier life. Marian Ormsby had lost her first fiancé, Ned Montgomery, shot by the husband of another woman. Sent away to the mountains by her family to escape ensuing publicity, Marian thereupon lost her guide on a climb, a young man killed in the same fall which lost her the use of her legs. Captain Forrester had rescued her, attended her in recovery, and subsequently married her. Then she loses Forrester, then even Ivy Peters (whose children, we imagine, will populate another place of fictional Nebraska in the wry, post-heroic novels of that other major Nebraskan, Wright Morris).

Then at last she finds a final husband who, though "stingy" and "cranky," has surely cared well enough for her to be capable of executing a final appropriate gesture in her behalf. Marian Forrester lived through her losses and gains. Niel loses her; what he can finally regain is a realization of how "she had had a hand in breaking him in to life," and a sense of how the very uncertainty of her nature may have been her glory. In what is almost a summary passage Willa Cather speaks not only of her lost lady, but of the fruitful indeterminacies of art itself:

> He would like to call up the shade of the young Mrs. Forrester, as the witch of Endor had called up Samuel's, and challenge it, demand the secret of that ardour; ask her whether she really had found some ever-blooming, ever-burning, ever-piercing joy, or whether it was all fine play-acting. Probably she had found no more than another; but she had always the power of suggesting things much lovelier than herself, as the perfume of a single flower may call up the whole sweetness of spring.

But knowledge of this kind can only come in response to loss, even as those fallings from us, those vanishings of early light, themselves provide the tallow of our later illumination. Of all this, A *Lost Lady* makes us acutely aware. It is one of the small triumphs of the American imagination.

MARILYN ARNOLD

Two of the Lost

Two of Cather's finest stories, "A Wagner Matinee" and "Paul's Case," [are found in] the *Troll Garden* collection. Both deal with sensitive characters whose environments shackle their artistic spirits. Although it portrays the East-West conflict that is prominent in Cather's work, especially in books like *The Song of the Lark* and *Lucy Gayheart* where the artist is particularly sensitive to the strictures of western family life and mentality, "A Wagner Matinee" is not so much about the contrasting world of Boston and Nebraska as it is about Aunt Georgiana and what those worlds have in turn made of her. As a young woman she had taught music in the Boston Conservatory, but she turned her back on that world when she fell inexplicably in love with a shiftless young New Englander and went west with him to stake out a homestead in the rugged prairie lands of Nebraska. After thirty years of unrelieved toil, she returns to Boston to settle the matter of a small legacy from a deceased relative. She is met there by a nephew who as a youngster had lived with her family and worked for her husband on the Nebraska farm. He has planned a surprise for her, a Wagner concert, the first real music she has heard in half a lifetime. She is moved immeasurably as the artist in her nature, so long asleep, trembles to consciousness. When the concert is over she cannot bear to leave, because "just outside the door of the concert hall" is the world she must take up again, "the tall, unpainted house, with weather-curled boards; naked as a tower, the crooked-backed ash seedlings where the dish-cloths hung to dry; the gaunt, moulting turkeys picking up refuse about the kitchen door."

From *Willa Cather's Short Fiction*. Copyright © 1984 by Marilyn Arnold. Ohio University Press, Athens, 1984.

This story may be, as some have suggested, chiefly an indictment of "the toll exacted by the land," but more than that it is a revelation of human love and appreciation. A nephew discovers a new depth of feeling for an aunt who, in spite of the narrow circumstances of her own life, taught him an appreciation for the fine and the beautiful, gave to him gifts she could not give to herself, opened doors for him that were forever closed to her. Out of this young man's memory a wonderful, almost heroic, portrait takes shape; this portrait is the woman, and this woman is the story. Georgiana arrives in Boston, black with soot and sick with travel, a "misshapen figure" in a "black stuff dress." Her nephew Clark, so terribly aware of her oddness, nevertheless regards her with unmistakable "awe and respect." Every detail, even down to her bent shoulders, "sunken chest," "ill-fitting false teeth," and "skin as yellow as a Mongolian's," is mellowed by his loving regard for her. Seen through another pair of eyes she would have been a country caricature, but seen through his eyes, she becomes a symbol of the pioneer spirit.

Through Clark's memory Cather reconstructs incidents that define Georgiana's character. His earliest recollections must have come to him secondhand, perhaps as an old family story. He remembers hearing that as "an angular, spectacled woman of thirty," she conceived an "extravagant passion" for "a handsome country boy of twenty-one" and eloped with him, "eluding the reproaches of her family" by going to the Nebraska frontier where, through incredible hardships, she and Howard Carpenter managed to establish themselves. Georgiana becomes for Clark something like what Ántonia was to become for Jim Burden, heroic and wonderful, if not mythic. In spite of coarse outward circumstances, she retained a fineness of spirit with which she unconsciously and continually blessed his life. He reflects gratefully, "I owed to this woman most of the good that ever came my way in my boyhood, and had a reverential affection for her." He remembers the countless times that she stood at her ironing board at midnight, after the day's chores were over and the six young children were in bed, drilling him on Latin verbs, or listening to him read Shakespeare. He recalls further, "She taught me my scales and exercises, too—on the little parlour organ, which her husband had bought her after fifteen years, during which she had not so much as seen any instrument, but an accordion that belonged to one of the Norwegian farmhands." It was she who gave Clark "her old text-book on mythology," the first book he ever owned. It was she who listened to him practice, counting out the time with him. Once as he struggled with an old piece of her music he had found, she came up behind him, put her hands over his eyes, and drew his head to her shoulder. With trembling voice she warned, "Don't love it so well, Clark, or it may be taken from you. Oh! dear boy, pray that whatever your sacrifice may be, it be not that."

Now, years later, he wonders if the concert will mean anything to her, wishing "for her own sake . . . her taste for such things quite dead, and the long struggle mercifully ended at last." Her chief concern as they travel the city she had once known so well is for "a certain weakling calf" at home, and "a freshly-opened kit of mackerel in the cellar" which could spoil in her absence. But when the music begins, she meets it in a rush of combined anguish and joy. By turns she clutches at Clark's coat sleeve, or moves her "bent and knotted" fingers across an imaginary keyboard on her old dress, or weeps silently. Clark knows then that the feeling "never really died," that "the soul that can suffer so excruciatingly and so interminably; it withers to the outward eye only; like that strange moss which can lie on a dusty shelf half a century and yet, if placed in water, grows green again."

However much this story discloses the irreclaimable loss suffered by a woman who exchanged her artistic loves and drives for the cruelties of frontier life, however painful the experience in the concert hall is for all of us who sit with Clark beside Aunt Georgiana, we are not back "on the Divide" with Canute Canuteson. Even in our grief we are in an atmosphere of human caring and appreciation; we are in the presence of genuine feelings unashamedly expressed. Cather evokes these feelings through the momentary collision between the world of music and culture which Georgiana had rejected so long ago and the stark, barren world she chose out of love. Her two worlds pause in equipoise as the concert ends and the musicians exit, "leaving the stage to the chairs and music stands, empty as a winter cornfield." And, as Clark observes, just outside that door in Boston is Nebraska waiting to claim its stepchild.

After thirty years, Aunt Georgiana has tasted again of the goblin fruit, the luscious nectar that never satisfies, but only increases the appetite. Again the lure is the world of art, quite different from the evil materialism of the fabled troll garden, but a lure nevertheless. Appropriately, Cather leaves the story at the door of the concert hall, with the return to Nebraska as inevitable as the winter prairie wind. The cold, harsh world of the Divide may yet again scar over the wound newly opened, and Georgiana may slip gratefully into the somnambulant routine of her life in Nebraska; but for the moment she is caught hopelessly between the two worlds that have shaped her life. Clark's mournful observation at the beginning of the Pilgrim's chorus (*Tannhauser* overture) seems to define the mood of the story in terms of opposition, change, and loss: "With the battle between the two motives, with the frenzy of the

Venusberg theme and its ripping of strings, there came to me an overwhelming sense of the waste and wear we are so powerless to combat; and
I saw again the tall, naked house on the prairie, black and trim as a
wooden fortress. . . "

"Paul's Case," the final story in *The Troll Garden*, is drawn from
Cather's experiences as a high school English teacher and lower-middle-
class neighborhood dweller in Pittsburgh. It was the only story for some
time that Cather allowed to be anthologized. Published seven years before
Cather's first novel would appear, it remains one of her most widely read
and acclaimed works.

Eccentric, maybe even half-crazy, Paul abhors the dull respectability of his neighborhood on Cordelia Street and his high school. He finds
his only pleasure as an usher at Carnegie Hall and as a hanger-on with the
stock theater company where he can bask in the artificial glow emanating
from stage lights which never play on him, from hotel lobbies he is
forbidden to enter, from music and paintings he does not understand, and
from the lives of performers he completely misinterprets. By comparison,
school and home are drab, unbearable; he cannot be bothered with them.
After a minor inquisition in which his teachers "fell upon him without
mercy," Paul still shows no inclination to study or to be agreeable. It is
decided finally that he must quit school and go to work, and that he must
forego Carnegie Hall and the stock company.

Thus imprisoned in Cordelia Street with all legitimate avenues of
escape effectually closed, Paul commits a desperate act. Entrusted to
deliver his company's weekend bank deposit, Paul makes his decision and
takes flight. Structurally, the story is as bold as Paul. Part 1 ends with the
adult collusion that separates Paul from the only thing he loves; part 2
begins in abrupt juxtaposition with Paul on a train bound for New York.
Once in New York he lives for several marvelous days the life he had
always believed he was suited to live, the life of a wealthy boy in a
luxurious room at the Waldorf, wearing fine clothes, eating elegant food,
and surrounding himself with flowers. But those self-indulgent days make
it impossible for him to return to Cordelia Street. When Paul learns from
the Pittsburgh newspapers that his father has repaid the stolen money and
is en route to New York to retrieve him, he takes a ferry to Newark and a
cab out of town. Then he dismisses the cab and struggles through deep
snow along the bank beside the Pennsylvania tracks. When the train
comes he leaps into its path. In the instant before he dies, however, he
suffers a heartbreaking realization: he had been too impatient in grabbing
his one moment of splendor; he should have gone to exotic lands across
the seas.

A fitting climax to the *Troll Garden* collection, "Paul's Case" is the most overt treatment of the troll garden/goblin market theme in the book. Paul is obviously the hungry forest child who is utterly helpless before the luscious appeal of the garden, represented for him in the trappings of wealth and in his adolescent perception of the artist's world. For Paul there is no reasoned choice, no weighing of alternatives and consequences, no will to resist; for him there is only ugliness and the garden, and he must have the garden. But Paul is also Cather's ultimate alien. He belongs nowhere, and can never belong. Expanding the theme she had introduced in her early stories on the Divide, Cather portrays in Paul a being who is alienated by more than environment and lack of human contact and understanding. Peter, Canute, Serge, and Lou could all have been saved by altered environmental circumstances and human caring, but not Paul. He thinks an environmental change is all he needs, but he is wrong. And he will admit no need for the love of mere mortals.

Paul knows that he is unsuited for Cordelia Street; what he does not know is that he is unsuited for the worlds of art and wealth as well. Paul is an alien because he has a warped perception of everything; he is unable to see anything in his world as it really is. His mind reconstructs the world in his image of it, and then he tries to inhabit the world he conceives. Since in truth one segment of Paul's world is better than he imagines it to be, and the other is worse than he imagines, he is always out of step no matter where he is. Cordelia Street is repulsive to him, utterly ugly with its "grimy zinc tub[s]" and "cracked mirror[s]" and its insufferable monotony. Cather indicates, however, that Paul's view is not necessarily correct. Cordelia Street is a respectable neighborhood where semisuccessful white collar workers and their wives rear great broods of children and attend ice cream socials at church. The fact that Paul's father can readily make good Paul's theft suggests that he is far from destitute.

Paul wants to believe that Cordelia Street and his high school represent the very antithesis of the world for which he was made, the world of wealth and glamour. What he fails to perceive is that the ideals of Cordelia Street are identical with his own. He only thinks his values are out of place there; in actuality they are not. Cordelia Street, like Paul, worships glamour and money and the things money can buy. Its gods are the wealthy business magnates for whom the men on Cordelia Street work. Up and down the street people like Paul's father sit on their front steps and exchange "legends of the iron kings," tales of their bosses who cruise the Mediterranean but still keep office hours on their yachts, "knocking off work enough to keep two stenographers busy." The street fairly buzzes with "stories of palaces in Venice, yachts on the Mediterranean, and high play at Monte Carlo," stories absorbed greedily by the underlings of the "various chiefs and overlords" whom Paul would like to emulate. Cordelia Street constructs a golden vision of the world Paul longs to enter.

The only thing within Paul's reach that approximates that fairy world is the world of art—music, drama, painting. It seems to offer what he seeks. But he is just as wrong in his perception of that world as he is in his perception of Cordelia Street. He mistakes its stagey glitter for its essence. Like Flavia, he knows nothing of true art. Since mere finery is what he craves, "symphonies, as such," do not mean "anything in particular to Paul"; but he loves them for their show just as he loves paintings and the theater. For him art is the soloist's "elaborate gown and a tiara, and above all . . . that indefinable air of achievement, that world-shine." He longs to enter what he perceives to be a tropical world of shiny, glistening surfaces and basking ease." But not being an artist himself he has no real place in that spangled world.

Cather makes it clear that not only is Paul not an artist, but his perception of the artist's life and the artist's glittering world is miles from the truth. The artists in this story have no delusions—and no wealth. Scarcely the "veritable queen of Romance" that Paul believes her to be, the German soloist is, in fact, "by no means in her first youth, and the mother of many children." Paul's notions about the stock company players are equally distorted, and they, "especially the women," are "vastly amused" when they learn of the romantic stories Paul has told about them. "They were hardworking women, most of them supporting indigent husbands or brothers, and they laughed rather bitterly at having stirred the boy to such fervid and florid inventions." It is a further irony that Paul's idols "agreed with the faculty and with his father that Paul's was a bad case." His alienation from the world of art is complete.

Paul's last desperate effort to find place, to be where "his surroundings explained him," is also destined to failure, again because he mistakes artificial sheen for reality—and because he can make no distinction between the radiance of art and the shimmer of the Waldorf. The latter is just another version of the opera house to him. Art equals shine; shine equals wealth. To him it is all one desire. In New York, with a thousand dollars at his disposal, he believes he is home at last, for "on every side of him towered the glaring affirmation of the omnipotence of wealth." Here, he thinks, is the center of life; ". . . the plot of all dramas, the text of all romances, the nerve-stuff of all sensations was whirling about him like the snow flakes." He glides easily about the Waldorf, at last with "his own people," feeling "as though he were exploring the chambers of an enchanted palace, built and peopled for him alone."

But Paul has merely purchased the sensation of home, played his only ace for a few days of belonging. With stolen money he buys an artificial environment in which to enclose himself—linens, suits, gorgeous people, a fine room, and the hotel itself. Even Central Park is not real, but is "a wonderful stage winterpiece." The Waldorf encasing Paul is the final symbol of his alienation because its artificial splendor isolates him from encroaching reality. Cather represents the Waldorf and its displaced occupant in repeated references to the alien hothouse flowers that bloom "under glass cases" on the streets of New York, all the "more lovely and alluring that they blossomed thus unnaturally in the snow." Like Paul, the flowers can survive for a time if they are protected by artificial light and heat. But even then, their days are limited, and if they are ever removed from their heated cases, they wither and die.

In the story's final scenes, Cather continues to equate Paul symbolically with flowers out of place in a harsh environment. Walking along the tracks, having made the decision never to return to Cordelia Street, Paul notices that "the carnations in his coat were drooping with the cold, . . . their red glory over. It occurred to him that all the flowers he had seen in the glass cases that first night must have gone the same way, long before this. It was only one splendid breath they had, in spite of their brave mockery at the winter outside the glass; and it was a losing game in the end, it seemed, this revolt against the homilies by which the world is run." As if prompted by this symbolic description of his own brief moment of splendor and its inevitable end. Paul buries a blossom in the snow, acknowledging his death in a cold world that holds no lasting home for him.

Paul misconceives the garden of art as a glittering world of wealth and ease, and he fails to perceive that the chief difference between Cordelia Street and the Waldorf is the difference between wanting and having—a difference not of kind but of degree. Understanding these worlds so little, he has no home in either of them. Only in his death, when he "drop[s] back into the immense design of things," does the alien child appear to find place.

Thus, the pursuit of art and the pursuit of wealth exact their tolls. One by one the stories in *The Troll Garden* show the consequences of such pursuits, whether misguided or true, whether understood by the seekers or not. And then, in the climactic story, "Paul's Case," the two are seen as one goal, a final impossible and intolerable irony in which Paul equates God and mammon.

Chronology

1873	Born December 7, near Winchester, Virginia, to Charles F. Cather and Mary Virginia Boak Cather. Willa was to be the oldest of seven children.
1884	Moves with her parents to a ranch in Webster County, Nebraska.
1885	Cather family moves to Red Cloud, Nebraska.
1890	Moves to Lincoln to complete preparation for entering the University of Nebraska.
1891–95	Attends University of Nebraska, paying her way by working as a newspaper columnist during her two final years.
1895–96	Stays at home in Red Cloud.
1896–97	Goes to Pittsburgh to work as a magazine editor.
1897–1901	Works as newspaper editor and drama reviewer for Pittsburgh's *Daily Leader*.
1901–02	Teaches English and Latin at Central High School in Pittsburgh.
1903	*April Twilights* (a book of poems).
1903–06	Teaches at Allegheny High in Pittsburgh.
1905	*The Troll Garden* (short stories).
1906–12	Moves to New York City to join editorial staff of *McLure's Magazine*.
1908	Moves into apartment with Edith Lewis, subsequently her lifelong companion.
1912	*Alexander's Bridge* (her first published novel).
1913	*O, Pioneers!*
1915	*The Song of the Lark*.
1918	*My Ántonia*.
1920	*Youth and the Bright Medusa* (stories).
1922	*One of Ours*.
1923	*A Lost Lady*.
1925	*The Professor's House*.
1926	*My Mortal Enemy*.
1927	*Death Comes for the Archbishop*.
1931	*Shadows on the Rock*.
1932	*Obscure Destinies* (stories).

1935   *Lucy Gayheart.*
1936   *Not Under Forty* (essays).
1940   *Sapphira and the Slave Girl.*
1947   Dies at her home in New York City on April 24.
1948   *The Old Beauty* (stories).
1949   *Willa Cather on Writing* (essays).

Contributors

HAROLD BLOOM, Sterling Professor of the Humanities at Yale University, is the author of *The Anxiety of Influence, Poetry and Repression,* and many other volumes of literary criticism. His forthcoming study, *Freud: Transference and Authority,* attempts a full-scale reading of all of Freud's major writings. A MacArthur Prize Fellow, he is general editor of five series of literary criticism published by Chelsea House. During 1987–88, he was appointed Charles Eliot Norton Professor of Poetry at Harvard University.

LIONEL TRILLING, University Professor at Columbia, was the foremost American literary critic of his era. His most influential books include *The Liberal Imagination, The Opposing Self,* and *Beyond Culture.*

ALFRED KAZIN is Distinguished Professor of English at the City University of New York. His books include *On Native Ground, Contemporaries* and *An American Procession.*

E. K. BROWN was Professor of English at the University of Chicago. His books include *Willa Cather: A Critical Biography* and *Rhythm in the Novel.*

DAVID DAICHES is Regius Professor of English Emeritus at the University of Edinburgh. He has published studies of Virginia Woolf and of Willa Cather, as well as *The Novel in the Modern World.*

MORTON D. ZABEL was Professor of English at the University of Chicago. He was best known for his critical writing on Henry James and on modern fiction.

JAMES E. MILLER, JR., is Professor of English at the University of Chicago. He has written widely upon American literature, and upon Walt Whitman in particular.

JOHN H. RANDALL III is Professor of English at Wellesley College and the author of *The Landscape and the Looking Glass,* a study of Willa Cather.

DOROTHY VAN GHENT, who taught at the Universities of Montana and Vermont, and also at Brandeis and Harvard, wrote *The English Novel: Form and Function.*

TERENCE MARTIN teaches English at Indiana University. His books include *Nathaniel Hawthorne* and *Instructed Vision,* a study of the influence of Scottish philosophy upon the origins of American fiction.

BLANCHE H. GELFANT is Professor of English at Dartmouth College. She is the author of *The American City Novel* and *American Women Writing.*

DONALD SUTHERLAND wrote *Gertrude Stein: A Biography of the Work* and *On Romanticism.*

EUDORA WELTY, one of our most distinguished novelists, recently published the widely read *One Writer's Beginnings.*

JOHN J. MURPHY, Professor of English at Merrimack College, edited *Critical Essays on Willa Cather.*

JOHN HOLLANDER is Professor of English at Yale. His recent books include *Spectral Emanations: New and Selected Poems, Rhyme's Reason* and *The Figure of Echo.*

MARILYN ARNOLD is Professor of English at Brigham Young University, and the author of *Willa Cather's Short Fiction.*

Bibliography

Arnold, Marilyn. "*One of Ours*: Willa Cather's Losing Battle." *Western American Literature* 3, vol. 13 (Fall 1978): 259–66.

Bennett, Mildred. *The World of Willa Cather*. Lincoln: University of Nebraska Press, 1961.

Bloom, Edward Allen, and Lillian D. Bloom. *Willa Cather's Gift of Sympathy*. Carbondale: Southern Illinois University Press, 1962.

———. "Willa Cather's Novels of the Frontier: A Study in Thematic Symbolism." *American Literature* 1, vol. 13 (March 1949): 71–93

Brown, E. K. "Homage to Willa Cather." *The Yale Review* 1, vol. 36 (September 1946): 77–92.

———. "Willa Cather and the West." *The University of Toronto Quarterly* 4, vol. 5 (July 1936): 544–66

———. *Willa Cather, A Critical Biography*. Completed by Leon Edel. New York: Knopf, 1953.

Comeau, Paul. "Willa Cather's *Lucy Gayheart*: A Long Perspective." *Prairie Schooner* 1–2, vol. 55 (Spring–Summer 1981): 199–209.

Cooperman, Stanley. "Willa Cather and the Bright Face of Death." *Literature and Psychology* 1, vol. 12 (Winter 1963): 81–87.

Daiches, David. *Willa Cather, A Critical Introduction*. Ithaca: Cornell University Press, 1951.

Edel, Leon. "Willa Cather's *The Professor's House*: An Inquiry into the Use of Psychology in Literary Criticism." *Literature and Psychology* 5, vol. 4 (November 1954): 69–79.

Fryer, Judith. "Cather's Felicitous Space." *Prairie Schooner* 1–2, vol. 55 (Spring–Summer 1981): 185–97.

Gerber, Philip L. *Willa Cather*. Boston: Twayne Publishers, 1975.

Greene, George. "Willa Cather's Grand Manan." *Prairie Schooner* 1–2, vol. 55 (Spring–Summer 1981): 233–40.

Jessup, Josephine Luire. *The Faith of our Feminists: A Study in the Novels of Edith Wharton, Ellen Glasgow and Willa Cather*. New York: R. R. Smith, 1950.

Lewis, Edith. *Willa Cather Living: A Personal Record*. New York: Knopf, 1953.

McFarland, Dorothy Tuck. *Willa Cather*. New York: Frederick Ungar, 1972.

Miller, Bruce E. "The Testing of Willa Cather's Humanism: *A Lost Lady* and Other Cather Novels." *Kansas Quarterly* 4, vol. 5 (Fall 1973): 43–49.

Miller, James E. Jr. "*My Ántonia* and the American Dream." *Prairie Schooner* 2, vol. 47 (Summer 1973): 112–23.

Moseley, Ann. "The Dual Nature of Art in *The Song of the Lark.*" *Western American Literature* 4, vol. 14 (Winter 1980): 19–32.

Murphy, John J. "*One of Ours* as American Naturalism." *Great Plains Quarterly* 4, vol. 2 (Fall 1982): 232–38.

Murphy, John J., ed. *Five Essays on Willa Cather, the Merrimack Symposium.* Andover, Mass.: Merrimack College, 1974.

Randall, John Herman. *The Landscape and the Looking Glass.* Boston: Houghton Mifflin Co., 1960.

Rosowski, Susan J. "Willa Cather—A Pioneer in Art." *Prairie Schooner* 1–2, vol. 55 (Spring–Summer 1981): 141–54.

———. "Willa Cather's *A Lost Lady*: Art Versus the Closing Frontier." *Great Plains Quarterly* 4, vol. 2 (Fall 1982): 239–48.

Schroeter, James. *Willa Cather and Her Critics.* Ithaca: Cornell University Press, 1967.

Sergeant, Elizabeth Shepley. *Willa Cather, A Memoir.* Philadelphia: Lippincott, 1953.

Slote, Bernice. "An Exploration of Cather's Early Writing." *Great Plains Quarterly* 4, vol. 2 (Fall 1982): 210–17.

———. "Willa Cather's Sense of History." *Women, Women Writers and the West.* Edited by L. L. Lee and Merrill Lewis. Troy, N. Y.: Whitston Publishing Co., 1979.

Stouck, David. "Marriage and Friendship in My Ántonia." *Great Plains Quarterly* 4, vol. 2 (Fall 1982): 224–31.

———. *Willa Cather's Imagination.* Lincoln: University of Nebraska Press, 1975.

———. "Willa Cather's Unfurnished Novel: Narrative in Perspectives." *Wascana Review* 4, vol. 6 (1972): 41–51.

Van Doren, Carl. "Willa Cather." In *The American Novel*, pp. 281–93. New York: MacMillan, 1921.

Van Ghent, Dorothy. *Willa Cather.* Minneapolis: University of Minnesota Press, 1964.

Wasserman, Loretta. "The Lovely Storm: Sexual Initiation in Two Early Willa Cather Novels." *Studies in the Novel* 4, vol. 14 (Winter 1982): 348–58.

West, Rebecca. "Uncle Bennett." *The Strange Necessity.* New York: Doubleday, 1928.

Whaley, Elizabeth Gates. "Cather's 'My Mortal Enemy'." *Prairie Schooner* 2, vol. 47 (Summer 1973): 124–33.

Woodress, James. *Willa Cather, Her Life and Art.* New York: Pegasus, 1970.

Acknowledgments

"Willa Cather" by Lionel Trilling from *Speaking of Literature and Society*, copyright © 1980 by Diana Trilling and James Trilling. Reprinted by permission of Harcourt Brace Jovanovich, Inc.

"Elegy: Willa Cather" by Alfred Kazin from *On Native Grounds* by Alfred Kazin, copyright © 1942, 1970 by Alfred Kazin. Reprinted by permission of Harcourt Brace Jovanovich, Inc.

"*The Professor's House*" by E. K. Brown from *Rhythm in the Novel* by E. K. Brown, copyright © Canada, 1950 by University of Toronto Press. Reprinted by permission of the University of Toronto Press.

"The Claims of History" by David Daiches from *Willa Cather: A Critical Introduction* by David Daiches, copyright © 1951 by Cornell University. Reprinted by permission of Cornell University Press.

"Willa Cather: The Tone of Time" by Morton D. Zabel from *Craft and Character in Modern Fiction* by Morton D. Zabel, copyright © 1940, 1947 by Morton D. Zabel. Reprinted by permission of Viking Penguin, Inc.

"My Ántonia: A Frontier Drama of Time" by James E. Miller, Jr., from *American Quarterly* 4, vol. 10 (1958), copyright © 1958 by the Trustees of the University of Pennsylvania. Reprinted by permission.

"The Protestant Past: *Sapphira and the Slave Girl*" by John H. Randall III from *The Landscape and the Looking Glass* by John H. Randall III, copyright © 1960 by John H. Randall III. Reprinted by permission of Houghton Mifflin Company.

"Willa Cather" by Dorothy Van Ghent from *Willa Cather* (Pamphlets on American Writers) no. 36 (1964), copyright © 1964 by University of Minnesota. Reprinted by permission of the University of Minnesota Press.

"The Drama of Memory in My Ántonia" by Terence Martin from *PMLA* 84, no. 2 (March 1969), copyright © 1969 by Modern Language Association of America. Reprinted by permission of the Modern Language Association of America.

"The Forgotten Reaping-Hook: Sex in My Ántonia" by Blanche H. Gelfant from *American Literature* 43, no. 1 (March 1971), copyright © 1971 by Duke University Press. Reprinted by permission.

"Willa Cather: The Classic Voice" by Donald Sutherland from *The Art of Willa Cather*, edited by Bernice Slote and Virginia Faulkner, copyright © 1974 by University of Nebraska Press. Reprinted by permission of the University of Nebraska Press.

"The House of Willa Cather" by Eudora Welty from *The Art of Willa Cather*, edited by Bernice Slote and Virginia Faulkner, copyright © 1974 by Eudora Welty. Reprinted by permission of Russell & Volkening, Inc., as agents of the author.

"Willa Cather's Archbishop: A Western and Classical Perspective" by John J. Murphy from *Western American Literature* 13, no. 3 (Summer 1978), copyright © 1978 by Western Literature Association. Reprinted by permission.

"A Lost Lady" by John Hollander from *A Lost Lady* by Willa Cather with an Introduction by John Hollander, copyright © 1983 by John Hollander. Reprinted by permission.

"Two of the Lost" by Marilyn Arnold from *Willa Cather's Short Fiction* by Marilyn Arnold, copyright © 1984 by Marilyn Arnold. Reprinted by permission of the Ohio University Press, Athens.

Index